SOMETHING HIDDEN BEHIND THE RANGES

SOMETHING HIDDEN BEHIND THE RANGES

A HIMALAYAN QUEST

by

Daniel Taylor-Ide

MERCURY HOUSE ✒ SAN FRANCISCO

Mercury House and colophon are registered trademarks of Mercury House, Inc.
Printed on recycled, acid-free paper
Manufactured in the United States of America

All photographs by the author unless otherwise indicated.
Map and cross-section on pp. 45 and 202 by Bill Nelson.

Library of Congress Cataloging-in-Publication Data
Taylor-Ide, Daniel.
Something hidden behind the ranges: a Himalayan quest /
by Daniel Taylor-Ide.
p.   cm.
ISBN 1-56279-073-0
1. Nepal—Description and travel. 2. Natural History—Nepal. 3. Ethnology—
Nepal. 4. Yeti. 5. Taylor-Ide—Journeys—Nepal. I. Title.
DS493.53.T39   1995
954.96—dc20   94-38624
CIP
5   4   3   2   1
FIRST EDITION

To all mothers, but especially J & M,
who nurture their children to feel good about themselves

Something hidden. Go and find it. Go and look behind the Ranges –
Something lost behind the Ranges. Lost and waiting for you. Go!
 – Rudyard Kipling, from "The Explorer" (1898)

Acknowledgments

Greatest appreciation goes to the families of Taylors and Ides, a few of whom are named in these stories, but all of whom walked important trails with me during the writing. From a wife who pressed me toward honesty in the telling of tales, to parents and siblings who did not scoff when others would have, to in-laws who reminded me to accept others, to my three children who through their interruptions made the writing fun; to this strong and kind family, I record my deepest thanks.

The actual writing of the manuscript began when I was director of the West Virginia Scholars Academy. During those years I prodded some of West Virginia's finest youths to delve into themselves and write autobiographical theses. One day while walking across the Spruce Knob meadows, I realized that for integrity I too had to delve and write. Many in the Academy were helpful, but two deserve naming, Elizabeth Wehner and Dave Cockley.

My friend Mohan Sainju tells of Hanuman, king of the monkeys in Hindu mythology. Time and again, with an impending crisis (such as Lord Rama needing a special medicinal plant) Hanuman was called upon. "I cannot do the job. I don't know what to do," he answered. But when told, "You can do it – yes, Hanuman, give it a try," Hanuman would attempt the task, and with the confidence he was given, he got the job done. The following are those who, in their individual ways, told me I could write an integrated tale of Himalayan ecology, its people, places, and myths, as well as the changes that the region is currently experiencing as threatening mount from its growing population and accelerating aspirations.

During much of this writing I was chief executive officer of the Woodlands Mountain Institute. Many at Woodlands were patient as I took leave to explore yet another valley or to write these pages. Those who were particularly involved in this process included Dan Terry, Charlotte Feagans, Chun-Wuei Su Chien, Brenda Simmons, Tashi Lama, Carol Mick, Bob Davis, the Eastman family, and Gabriel Campbell.

It is wonderful to count one's father as teacher and friend, and Dad's endless rewriting of his own work set an important example, while his joyous love of the Himalaya both introduced me to these mountains and brought me closer to him. But there were also other friends who became my teachers: Bob Fleming; Tirtha Shresatha; John, Margaret, and Derek Craighead; Mr. Nick and his "aboggable snowman"; Narayan Shrestha; Bishou Shah; Pasang; Lendoop; Harlan Judy; Sohan Singh; Kazi Nepali; Denner Denckle; and Bette Rothman. On two expeditions into the Kama Valley a collection of what had been choppy chapters came together in a new perspective, and so the thanks of shared trails go to Tom, Claudia, Sal, Nancy, and Lawry.

Then there are those who helped by asking questions: H.M. King Birendra, H.R.H. Prince Gyanendra, Scott McVay, Charles Merrill, Mike Stranahan; my proposition was, after all, rather outrageous. A special word of appreciation must be raised to the bold folks at the International Fund for Animal Welfare, a creative group the likes of which the nonprofit world could use more of, and also to Richard Greenwell of the International Society of Cryptozoology.

Finally the time comes when a manuscript becomes a book. Bob Silverstein gave me hope when the text was really rough. Wade Davis reintroduced me to Howard Boyer, and I must pause for more than a moment to thank Howard, who is both kind and artistically demanding. He saw strength in this manuscript early on, and he saw how to bring out its strength later on. That strength, though, was really brought out by the most amazing and capable of editors, Ann Hawthorne. I know I am not the first author to say that Ann is the best. And at the end of this writing adventure I had the good fortune to find Tom Christensen and the folks at Mercury House. The fabulous artistic job you can see in their production of the book is also reflected in the warm interpersonal ways that they relate to each other and to the authors whom they publish.

Writing the manuscript was fun. Draft after draft allowed me to return to times and places otherwise lost in memory, to relive their adventures. The stories told here were wonderful to experience and sometimes even better to re-experience in the warmth of memory. For a half a lifetime of these unique experiences I am grateful – as I now look forward to the second half. Some kids grow up with teddy bears and fears of boogymen when they step into the woods; I was lucky enough as I grew up to have the yeti, and to have him as a friend.

SOMETHING HIDDEN BEHIND THE RANGES

Introduction

In the course of my life in the Himalaya I ran a river, Nepal's Sun Kosi. Our expedition was the first, succeeding in currents where others had died trying to be the first. That expedition opened up for me the breadth of wildness in the Himalaya and changed a childhood quest for the Abominable Snowman into a deeper exploration.

The Sun Kosi (Golden River) starts high in Tibet on the glaciers of Shisha Pagma. As it runs through Nepal it picks up other rivers, the Tamba Kosi (Copper River), Bhote and Dudh Kosis (Tibetan and Milky Rivers), the Arun and Tamur. The combined rivers together carve through the last of the Himalaya, the Chotra Gorge, and then spread onto the Indian Plain, into the Ganges.

The Sun Kosi valleys are the watershed out of which have come virtually all of the reports of the yeti, and the glaciers that spawn these rivers are the snows in which most of the yeti footprints have been seen.

Our expedition lasted four days and nights. Thirty-three hours, two hundred miles, were lived on the river. We began just south of the Tibetan border and ended at the Indian border. The first day we lost altitude very fast, averaging a rapids every eight minutes. The most difficult day was the second, with two bad rapids that we ran just right. On the third day there came a long half hour of consistent froth. The trip took place at the end of the monsoon when the currents ran full and smothered the boulders with their foam.

Confronting the unknown deepened the waters of my understanding. The Himalaya of my youth became the background for comprehending the yeti story that had so fascinated me – and would for years to come. It also first made me think about biological resilience, in species and even ecosystems, and especially the resilience of the human species.

At first, on this river trip as with my quest for the yeti, we were free, free from the engagement of the quest. Then, gripped by the idea, we gave up that freedom. We were harnessed because the idea presumed us capable. Were we to admit incapability? To assay our youthful selves we went to the river for testing.

Arriving at its banks, standing apart from the river, our lives stood free, a circular whole. Our attention was free to roam and to choose through 360 perceptions. But when we entered the river and became directed by its rushing waters, we cascaded down vibrant points of its path. We knew only upstream and down. Here, there, we could stop where we willed. But such stops were only pauses. The circle of earlier awareness was traded for the straight line of our quest: hearing rapids, sensing danger; then, oars straining, a brief moment of freedom to choose the chute through the rapids. Finally, sweeping into the chute, the current driving us on, precluding choice.

Mountain rivers run narrow and fast. In Himalayan rivers boulders, like us, run with the current, but they move along the bottom, pushed by the power of descending water. They create the rapids. Sometimes house-sized, they shift the rapids in the churning current. Eddies, rocks, fields, jungles, spirits, and people passed by – but the rapids defined our lives.

Forward, downward, we pounded within the river. We chose not our direction. We chose not our speed. Driven by the rain and the melted snow that had filled those mountains, our destiny was to flow. Ours was not freedom of direction but freedom to pause, to live, to glorify, and to enjoy.

The future loomed with questions. The present cascaded with answers, answers that floated into memories, answers that slipped through our fingers and could not be held. Each splash challenged our venture. After two days we knew we were the first to have gone so far. The challenge of the present in each rapids was very real. The challenge of the future, like the Chotra Gorge ahead, was an unknown haunting us with apparitions. Would we make it? Would we return to sleep in beds at night?

Onward, downward we went. Rapids reared. Water roiled over boulders, beckoning us. With an everlasting certainty the current that swept forward tried to capture us on each boulder.

We floated amid beauty that defined our lives: a strong blue sky, hard, hot tropical sun on ripening rice, farmers at harvest. As the days passed and the sun scorched our skin, sizzled bodies slipped overboard, skin tingling, burn turning to chill.

Waterfalls called to us before we could see them: at first a flat line across the river; then jaws opening and the call becoming a roar. Over the crests we'd go, fighting, struggling to save the raft from backwashing into the hungry chomp of the waterfall's tumbling teeth.

We drifted through Nepal's central hills into her sparsely settled foothills. We came to a valley pocket with no people, an unusual place cut off from the world by cliffs, where people had not yet labored to subtract nature from life. We pulled the raft onto that sylvan bank. Wild jungles still stood beside the river where it seemed human feet had not trod. But people had been there. In one clump of trees, sometime, somehow planted, ripened bananas fell unpicked to the ground. Bamboo forests stood uncut. Moss, wet and cool and thick, summoned us into the shade.

Around a bend in the river, standing in the water up to its knees, pumping its tail, a white-capped river chat dipped its beak into a puddle, and trilled out SHREEE. A spider's single strand spanned a rapids' narrows. We came closer and saw two strands and a lattice web in between. Droplets splashed up, danced like spherical prisms on the strands, sparkling with joy. The unappreciating current, though, crashed us through and carried us downward.

Traditional river navigation in the Himalaya consists of crossings by dugout canoes at the spots between rapids. Usually neither the crew nor passengers can swim. The dugout is towed upstream to the foot of the rapids above. Passengers, perhaps a goat, maybe some chickens, all snuggle in. With gunnels inches above water, one person in the bow and one in the stern, the crew of two pushes off and immediately starts to paddle furiously for the opposite bank before the current sucks them into the rapids below.

We met a lone Nepali who once tried more than such a crossing. He tried using the river for transportation. Broke, his daughter's wedding coming, he harvested a clump of bamboo, lashed it into a bundle twenty feet across, and rode that bundle downstream, and even through the Chotra Gorge, fifty miles to the bazaar. "Never," he vowed, "will I be so stupid again." So, we smiled, we are not the first over this section. We are not so great.

Waves, waterfalls, rocks. Our souls crowded with personal thoughts, with plans remembered and private hopes renewed. We tried, at first, to protect ourselves from each other, to maintain a distance as we worked out accommodations. The raft, though, held our lives. A wrong move by one could sink the rest. So, we kept distance, but in doing so, we built closeness. In entering the expedition we entrusted our lives to each other. Once, when I was thrown out of the raft, a friend's hand reached out, fingers gripped my wrist, tendons bulged, and up over the black tubes I was pulled, back into the raft. Such gifts form friends.

The raft held just four, four very separate people. Rubber sides prevented escape. For four days we were forced to live with each other. Souls met other souls. Full friendships formed: Terry, Cherie, Carl, Daniel.

And then, as the river flowed, it was over. The Indian border lay ahead and we pulled out. No longer would we run with the river that had become part of us. The river would now run in us. But from this running we came to know that hidden behind the ranges there was a new Himalayan quest. It was time to go and find it.

Chapter One

As important as learning good table manners in our family was learning to walk quietly. Mother taught the table manners. Dad taught the quiet walking. Stealth brought adventures closer in our jungles of postcolonial India. We made sure to wear soft rubber soles. Down would come the outside of the foot; then down rolled the rest of the sole, ready to lift in a moment if stick or leaf started to snap. But, like table manners, quiet walking was a skill we were always supposed to practice.

It was not good manners, but I was quietly walking toward the kitchen where Grandma kept her special cakes for tea in a screened-in cabinet that kept out the flies. My prey was a fold of icing, something an eleven-year-old finger could remove. Passing the dining room table, I was stopped by a photograph on the front page of *The Statesman,* July 4, 1956. A strange footprint, like that of a barefooted man, looked up at me. Picking up the paper, at age eleven I met the Abominable Snowman for the first time.

Rain and wind shook the windows of our old bungalow at 6,000 feet in the Himalaya. Grandpa bought this cluster of houses just after the First World War. Ever since, our family – uncles, aunts, and cousins – had come to the hill station of Mussoorie to escape the summer heat of India. Ever since, mementos and trophies had accumulated on the walls and floors of the main rooms, a large family's legacy in once colonial, now independent, India. To me, the interesting parts of that legacy had to do with wild animals.

All day I prowled the house. Today was Saturday, a day supposedly free from school walls, free from obedience to others. But the monsoon had pummeled Mussoorie for three weeks, its heavy drops clattering on the tin roof. The pervasive monsoon smell of mildew would last another two months. Outside those walls the jungles were alive with exotic creatures. I was trapped inside by the rain. Taking the newspaper to the living room with its comforting yellow walls, its big black bear skin on the floor, I settled into Grandma's old armchair to read about this mysterious footprint.

The captivating front-page picture was taken on the 1951 Everest reconnaissance expedition. Eric Shipton and Michael Ward found this track high on the Menlung Glacier on the Nepal/China border. The article speculated about what kind of animal made the print. The shape looked hominoid. Was it the signature in the snow of a barefooted man? But its size was superhuman, more than a foot long. Did it belong to a yeti?

Neither Shipton nor Ward had made a yeti claim. They simply photographed what they found and showed it to the world. Until that day I had never heard of the yeti. What captured my interest was the suggestion by the author of the article, a museum curator in England, that the track was that of a langur monkey. Langurs frequented our bungalow in Mussoorie, jumping on the tin roof, making thundering sounds as they ran across it, and leaving their small, round tracks in the mud around the building. I had chased langurs away from my toys for years. No museum curator could convince me that the track in this picture was made by a langur, even if it had been changed by melting snow.

Unlike other Himalayan animals, langurs do not mind human observers. So I often sat on the western side of the ridge below the bungalow, watching a particular troop feeding on leaves in the tops of chestnut trees. Langurs are social animals. Each troop is a community that cares for its members. Adults take turns grooming each other for hours at a time. A baby spends time with females besides its mother. Little langurs snuggle against bigger ones on cold evenings and show respect for their elders and play with them. A juvenile sometimes jumps onto an older langur's back, pretends to bite it, jumps off, runs to its head and, squealing and grimacing, gives the other animal a big hug, then scampers off.

Cows eating grass I could accept, and langurs making leaves their primary

The famous footprint photograph taken by Eric Shipton in 1951.

(Royal Geographic Society)

diet, but could a snowman be a leaf-eater? The food just did not fit with the animal. It is easy to know a lot about langurs – and museum curators should know such things. But if they didn't, maybe I had enough knowledge to start to work on this mystery. In the school library, I read everything I could find about the yeti. The next Saturday morning, I asked Mother whether I could walk downhill to the British Library, above where the car traffic stopped and where those who come to Mussoorie must start to walk. It's a long walk down there and back. Not even Mother, a reading teacher, was sure that I'd walk all day for books, but she let me go.

I found nothing helpful at the library, but on the way back I stopped at the bookstore on Mullingar Hill. I couldn't believe it. There was Shipton's book. I took it home with a promise that I would bring the money later. Normally an hour's walk from the bookstore up the hillside, this time the hike took the rest of the afternoon. I read the whole book, intrigued by Shipton's account of their discovery:

It was on one of the glaciers of the Menlung basin, at a height of 19,000 feet, that late one afternoon, we came across those curious footprints in the snow the report of which has caused a certain amount of public interest in this country. We did not follow them further than was convenient, a mile or so, for we were carrying heavy loads at the time, and besides we had reached a particularly interesting stage in the exploration of the basin. I have in the past found many sets of these curious footprints and have tried to follow them, but have always lost them on the moraine or rocks at the side of the glacier. These particular ones seemed to be very fresh, probably not more than twenty-four hours old.[1]

The next Saturday I went back to the bookstore. Over several visits the Indian owner began to develop a yeti interest too. The old man remembered my father as a boy thirty years before, coming into his store to read hunting books. He started to look out for books about the yeti, ordering titles I suspect he otherwise wouldn't have carried. "Don't worry, Danny, I can always sell these books by calling them mountain climbing," he chuckled. "English and American men like to read of higher exploits when they vacation here in the hills." Indeed, after I returned each book, I would usually next see it out in the store window under the sign, LATEST EXPEDITION.

Like Shipton's, the 1952 Swiss Everest expedition (which narrowly missed making the first ascent) reported finding yeti prints crossing a glacier. That same year the Belgian zoologist Bernard Heuvelmans published a scientific paper theorizing that the yeti represented a relic population of early hominoid, *Gigantopithecus*. Heuvelmans suggested that a remnant of these prehistoric people had survived in pristine high Himalayan valleys, retreating in response to increasing pressure by the more aggressive and resilient *Homo sapiens*. Around the world, as public awareness of the snowman grew, many accepted Heuvelmans's hypothesis. It gave a pedigree. An otherwise myth became more scientific. Now, attached to a taxonomic branch on the evolutionary tree, the yeti no longer floated dangerously loose in the high altitudes of unknown origins.

The summer of 1955 exploded with yeti interest with expeditions and reports of discoveries from throughout the Himalaya: Abbe Bordet found tracks at 12,350 feet, A. J. M. Smyth at 12,375, L. W. Davies at 12,000. The mountaineer Charles Evans found tracks that his Sherpas claimed belonged to a yeti at 10,000 feet, but Evans, seeing nail marks in the snow instead of rounded toes, concluded they were made by a bear. All these 1955 tracks were smaller than Shipton's, ranging from seven to nine inches long.

In November 1955, an expedition dispatched by the London *Daily Mail* specifically to hunt the yeti, consisting of a dozen Western scientists and three hundred Nepali porters, reported finding six sets of yeti tracks, most of them eight inches long and four inches wide, as well as yeti excrement containing mouse hair, fur from an unknown animal, a feather, an insect claw, and various plant products. The yeti, it was now decided, must be omnivorous.

I started to be afraid at night. I was reading a lot of claims about wild people, descriptions of humanoid monsters. Were there ape men outside my room? Could a stray yeti wander over from some other area? Langurs and rhesus monkeys came to our bungalow. Both are primates like the yeti. Other wild animals also came. When she was fourteen, Aunt Margaret shot a leopard from the front porch of our bungalow. I wanted to talk to Grandpa but was embarrassed to.

I pressed Mother to let me go out into the jungle. A month had passed since Dad was last there and took me camping. He continued his medical teaching down on the plains while we spent the summer in the cooler hills. He wouldn't rejoin us for another three weeks. So Mother gave me permission to spend a night on the ridge below Childers with a villager whom she trusted and who sometimes went with Dad when he hunted Himalayan chamois or *ghoral*.

The village hunter and I set off late on Saturday morning. It poured nonstop, and we arrived at the cave soaked. The leeches were out. The villager did not seem to mind. I did. Of all jungle animals, I disliked leeches the most. While the villager started a fire to make tea, I slipped to the back of the cave, stripped off my shorts and my undershorts, and found two blood-swollen leeches, thick around as my thumb, on the inside of my left thigh. A third had hooked itself inside the hollow behind my right knee. I leaned against the cave wall and sprinkled a pinch of salt on each. In the beam of my flashlight, the bloated beasts writhed and shriveled as salt grains wreaked havoc inside their engorged, sensitive skin. With eleven-year-old vengeance, I gleefully watched each leech fight a force it did not recognize, a couple of grains of the most basic of all chemicals, then collapse and drop off. I stamped on the dying creatures, grinding them into the dirt wth my heel. Only after pulling on dry clothes did I see that my vengeful glee had obliterated any tracks that might have been in the soft cave dust. I played my flashlight along the back wall anyway, looking for droppings.

Leeches fascinated Dad, too. Each of those worms, *Hirudinea*, Dad told me, is both male and female, containing one pair of ovaries and ten sets of testes. However, it takes two leeches to produce more. One mounts the other – it does not matter which – and a tiny penis comes out. Then eggs are laid and wrapped in a cocoon. When their babies come out, they immediately seek blood too. Each stands on its sucker tail, waving, twisting, a tiny mouth trying to grow up. I have looked at leech mouths under Dad's microscope. Each mouth has three jaws, not two. When leeches bite, these jaws come in and open the flesh with a Y cut. It really bleeds, and then the giant gut that is the leech sups.

Once bloated, leeches let go from their prey and grotesquely squirm to secluded shade. There, their blood starts to thicken. Water seeps out. A leech resting, digesting, soon lies in a puddle of clean fluid. During the first ten days, half of the water that was once blood seeps out. No digestive enzymes exist in the belly. Uniquely to the leech, bacteria multiply inside the gut and break down the blood.

Little worms. They live for months on that bellyful of blood, enduring any heat short of fire, any cold short of freezing. Light? Dark? They prefer dark. The one thing they cannot live with is a dry mouth. But they don't just take blood. These little moisture-loving worms can strangle you. Unsuspecting people or animals can be drinking water from a stream and ingest a tiny wisp of a leech. Uncomfortable in the acid of the stomach, it crawls up your throat, crosses to your windpipe, and in that moist air finds a habitat it enjoys. It attaches to the inside of your trachea and starts to suck. As it swells bigger with blood the air passage fills with the chubby leech. When it is as fat as your thumb, even a big cow can be strangled to death by an animal a million times smaller. When Dad told me this story I never again questioned whether I could drink straight from streams.

I SQUATTED FOR A WHILE BY THE MOUTH OF THE CAVE WITH MY HUNTER friend, talking about leeches, about the jungle, feeding sticks into our cookfire, boiling water to make tea. Finally, the rain stopped, and the evening sun shone long golden rays under billowing gray monsoon clouds. Leaving my friend to watch the rice and lentils cooking, I headed out to walk the trails. There was not much chance to find footprints after a rain, but I was always hopeful – and maybe I would meet something else that would be out walking too.

A fire-breasted flowerpecker dashed overhead, sparkling with moisture from the rain, iridescent in the slanting shafts of the sun. A red dot, compact like a Christmas tree light, blazed on its blue-green breast. The bird settled into a clump of mistletoe on the oak down the hill. If the mistletoe berries are ripe, the flowerpecker will eat them and perpetuate the special life cycle it shares with its host. Botanists have named the plant *Loranthus viscum* because the berry seeds come out sticky after passing through an animal's body. To get those sticky seeds off, the flowerpecker rubs its bottom against tree bark. Seeds that fall to the ground do not grow, for the parasitic mistletoe needs the bark of a broad-leafed tree to germinate, preferably bark with moisture-laden moss. Once rooted, the mistletoe grows to feed another fire-breasted flowerpecker, or the rarer scarlet-backed flowerpecker.

This monsoon trip to the cave became the first of countless yeti searches.

Chapter Two

A couple of weeks later, while sharing tea and talking of jungle cabbages and kings, my bookseller friend said, "Danny, your quest is in your blood. I have watched the Taylors over many years. I think your family has a passion for jungle mysteries." He knew that Grandpa, an ex-cowboy from Kansas turned medical missionary, arrived on a mailboat in Bombay in 1914 with his wife and one-year-old baby, Uncle John.

Grandpa and Grandma spent two years learning the language and getting advice about how things were done in colonial India. About the time Dad was born in 1916, they picked their spot on the edge of the jungle in the Himalayan foothills. For the next twenty-five years – for six months each year – Grandpa and Grandma loaded children and possessions into oxcarts and bounced them over rutted jungle tracks, running medical clinics for the sick by day and magic-lantern shows for Jesus by night. I wondered how the bookseller knew so much about Grandpa's history. Was it because they both played in the Mussoorie Chess League? But Grandpa never talked when he played chess.

Climbing the hill afterward, I stopped at an overlook. The British built this town as a retreat from summer heat, a generation before my grandparents came. White cottages and larger white bungalows were scattered across these

Himalayan ridges, perched like a flock of birds on branches. In the valleys below, dark monsoon clouds swirled fast and strong. It must be raining hard on the Indian plains. On evenings such as these, standing above the clouds and the monsoon rains, the Himalayan forests wrapped in mist seemed like a world apart.

Off beside the rising cloud from Dehra Dun Valley white stripes flashed on the underside of a big bird's wings. An adult Himalayan griffon rode the upward wind coming off the ridge to my left. With wings eight feet across, griffons are the big trucks of the Himalayan skies. Stolidly they circle back and forth, climbing higher, searching for dead meat. Like the condor, such big vultures are found only in the mountains, where they catch the strong updrafts they need in order to fly.

This one flew round and round over one spot. It might have seen a carcass in the valley, but it was too wise a bird to descend. In a narrow valley it leaves the food for smaller birds like crows. A young griffon (one that has not yet earned its white wing stripes) might descend to the valley floor, but it soon learns that without a strong wind it cannot take off, especially with a bellyful of meat. Hopping and flapping laboriously, it can be overtaken by almost any predator until it gains a hundred feet or so up the hill slope; then it can plunge off into the air, searching once again for an updraft to carry it back up above the ridges. Like the griffon, I too circled the forests looking.

We were studying colonial Indian history at school. As I watched the griffon soar over the ridges, I pondered the bookseller's stories of my grandparents' early years here. What was it like for Grandpa and Grandma forty years ago? In the India of King George V, most missionaries found their calling transplanting life-changing Western institutions – colleges, hospitals, churches – to that Hindu and Muslim land. Life for those Westerners was lonely, especially in stations away from the big cities. It took four months for a letter from India to make its way to Kansas and a reply to come back. In 1956 it still felt lonely, even though now we could send a telegram to my other grandparents in Pennsylvania and get an answer the next day.

I always enjoyed listening to Grandpa talk. It was clear that beyond his missionary work the jungle had been the major attraction for him. Throughout the years, whenever a slack hour or two opened in the clinic schedule, the jungle is where he headed. Uncle John, Dad, and their younger brother, Gordon, did the same, carrying first slingshots and then, as they got older, guns.

Trophies soon covered the walls, the floors, even the piano of the family bungalow. Pet pythons, pangolins, and leopard cubs roamed through the tent that served as their home for half the year. When the family returned to town for the other half of the year, these animals moved to pens at the zoo in Lucknow. Jungle lore became family lore. For three generations our family has sought the jungle as a refuge.

So most of the time I saw school as a waste of my childhood; there was so much to do outside its walls. One day, though, we were assigned a paper on anything that interested us. At first I thought I'd do tigers, but as I walked home, I decided to write about yetis instead. I organized the notes I already had and tracked down more information. The bookseller helped. There turned out to be even more than I thought.

In 1889, returning to the hot plains of India from a high-altitude hunt on windswept Himalayan glaciers, an energetic British Army physician, Major L. A. Waddell, brought a trophy more sensational than the mountain sheep or bear he had sought. Out of the snows Waddell brought reports of large, mysterious hominoidlike footprints that ascended a glacier, then disappeared. In 1889, the yeti walked across the snows and into Western consciousness.

That was the beginning of the reign of science. It was also the era of Queen Victoria, when the British were uncovering, and explaining, mysteries throughout the world. Darwin's *Origin of Species* had revolutionized the understanding of human genealogy. A search was under way for Darwin's "missing link" to explain, in the oversimplified perception of the time, how monkeys evolved into humans.

With the caution befitting a Victorian man of science and a physician in the British army, Waddell did not categorize the footprints. Instead, at a scientific loss as to their maker, he relayed the legend "of hairy wild men who are believed to live amongst the eternal snows, along with the mythical white lions, whose roar is reputed to be heard during storms. The belief in these creatures is universal. . . ."[2]

Since then, year after year, unexplained fact after unexplained fact, more evidence mounted suggesting that out there somewhere roamed some apelike kin to humans. Some yeti reports must have been fabrication. Others must have been mistaken identity. But could all the reports be wrong? Were local villagers in valley after valley lying when they told of seeing the animal, of having their livestock attacked? Just one sighting, just one set of positive footprints would change the yeti from myth to reality. A thousand yetis wouldn't have to be found. All we needed was one.

In 1915, confirmation of Waddell's report came in a letter to the Royal Zoological Society from the forestry officer J. R. P. Gent. It described

> another animal but cannot make out what it is, a big monkey or ape perhaps. . . . It is a beast of very high elevations and only comes down to Phalut in the cold weather. It is covered with longish hair, face also hairy, the ordinary yellowish-brown color of the Bengal monkey. Stands about 4 feet high and goes about on the ground chiefly. . . .[3]

In 1921 the Royal Geographical Society sent a well-equipped expedition led by Lt. Col. C. K. Howard-Bury to reconnoiter an ascent route for Mount Everest. The group first approached Everest from the east, over the Cho La and into the spectacular Kama Valley. From a distance they saw dark figures crossing another snowfield. While traversing a very high pass, they came across a line of elongated, humanlike tracks in the snow. Expedition porters claimed both figures and tracks were *metoh kangmi,* a name the expedition translated as "Abominable Snowman." Thereafter, until the 1950s, all but three yeti discoveries were reported by nonscientists (usually mountaineers) exploring high-altitude, snow-covered terrain.

Author's father (r), age three, and author's uncle, age five, with pet pangolin in 1919

(photo by John C. Taylor, Sr.)

In 1925 the yeti was seen by a naturalist who was also a fellow of Britain's Royal Geographical Society. On the Zemu Glacier of Sikkim, N. A. Tombazi noticed that his porters were excited by an animal

> two to three hundred yards away down the valley to the East of our camp. Unquestionably, the figure in outline was exactly like a human being, walking upright and stopping occasionally to uproot or pull at some dwarf rhododendron bushes. It showed up dark against the snow and, so far as I could make out wore no clothes.[4]

Tombazi was establishing his reputation as a biologist by applying the newly developing tool of photography to his scientific work. While he was attaching his telephoto lens, in the way that plagues so many "almost" discoveries, the animal walked out of the camera's view and into the dwarf rhododendron. Disappointed in having missed his capture on film, Tombazi rushed to the spot, where he

> examined the footprints which were clearly visible on the surface of the snow. They were similar in shape to those of man, but only six to seven inches long and four inches wide at the broadest part of the foot. The marks of five distinct toes were perfectly clear. . . . The prints were undoubtedly of a biped, the order of the spoor having no characteristics whatever of any imaginable quadruped.[5] [Over the years these dimensions would be repeatedly confirmed in other footprint sightings.]

These reports from the southern rim of Tibet confirmed reports from Tibet's eastern side, reports of wild, humanlike animals living deep in the bamboo jungles of China. Were these Chinese "wild men," the source of mysterious pieces of skin, soft, mostly white but with peculiar black spots, that had been showing up in China since 1869? Something wearing a white-and-black robe roamed the eastern edge of the Tibetan plateau. The identity of this animal was revealed when Teddy and Kermit Roosevelt shot it on one of their epic postpresidential expeditions. It became known as the giant panda. But local people said that the panda was not the wild man. The wild man, they asserted, was still living in the forest – a man with skin, not an animal with fur. The question remained unanswered: What makes the mysterious, humanlike footprints in the snow? Through the 1920s, on both the eastern and western sides of Tibet, the search went on for this animal.

In the early 1930s still more yeti tracks were found. Wing Commander E. B. Beauman found hominoid-looking tracks on a glacial snowfield at 14,000 feet. Ronald Kaulback came across tracks at 16,000 feet. On a third glacier in the eastern Himalaya, Eric Shipton came upon his first set of mysterious tracks. By the end of the 1936 climbing season, two expeditions had claimed actually to have seen the yeti, five more had found its footprints, and many more reported hearing confirmation of the yeti's existence from Himalayan hunters and guides.

Local people claimed that hard evidence, yeti hands and scalps preserved as sacred relics, was locked away in Tibetan monasteries. And Sherpas who climbed with Westerners told of yeti relics in monasteries in Nepal's eastern valleys. In the 1930s no Westerner was permitted to reach any of these secluded mountain places. Tibet was a land forbidden to outsiders, and Nepal was even more tightly closed than Tibet. So this hard evidence was only more stories.

Science during this era was removing barriers to human understanding with one breakthrough after another. New truths were articulated about relationships in nature. The existence of new peoples was brought forward to the "civilized" world. One after another, fantastic postulates were proven by science and shown to have substance. Science fiction was gaining respectability as a new literary form. Anything seemed possible. Anything might not be fiction. The cornerstone of this bursting mind-set was Darwin's thesis of orderly evolution. But the missing link between humans and other living things remained undiscovered. Who would find the answer?

In 1934, in a back alley of Hong Kong, a young Dutch paleontologist, Ralph von Koenigswald, walked into a Chinese chemist's shop looking for fossils sold there as "dragon's teeth." He opened a jar and poured its contents out on the counter. Fossils of all sorts fell out. Among them he saw a human tooth, a third lower molar that was like no human tooth science had yet recorded – a tooth five or six times too large for prehistoric man. Here in his hand was the tooth of an extinct race of giants. For five years, month after month, von Koenigswald searched other chemists' shops up and down the China coast. In 1936, he found another molar, and in 1939, a third. *Gigantopithecus,* a race of human giants eleven to thirteen feet tall, fantastic omnivores who stood their ground in an ecosystem of saber-toothed tigers and wooly mammoths: Von Koenigswald's teeth were the fossil basis of Heuvelmans's hypothesis.

19,000-foot Himalayan peaks, too low to be named

Throughout 1937 yeti discoveries continued. H. W. Tilman encountered mysterious tracks on the Zemu Glacier. On a snowfield at 19,000 feet, again on the Zemu Glacier, John Hunt (who would lead the first successful ascent of Everest in 1953) discovered his first set of tracks, tracks similar in size to Tombazi's. And a discovery that same year by the mountaineer Frank Smythe became central to the mystery. Finding typical yeti prints in a snowfield at 20,000 feet, Smythe determinedly pursued them for some distance, and although film was then very expensive, the prize justified his photographing them extensively. "On the level the foot marks averaged 12 to 13 inches in length and 6 inches in breadth, but uphill they averaged only 8 inches in length. The stride was some 1½ to 2 feet on the level, but considerably less uphill, and the foot marks were turned outward at about the same angle as a man's. There were well-defined imprints of five toes."[6]

Smythe concluded that the tracks were made by a yeti, but subsequent analysis, made after his recovery from the fatigue and oxygen deprivation of high-altitude climbing, showed that his tracks were those of the Asiatic black bear, *Selanarctos thibetanus*.

Smythe's discovery showed that quadrupedal bears could overprint hind paws into forepaw tracks and create bipedal-appearing tracks that varied in size: larger tracks when the hind foot fell back as the bear went uphill and shorter tracks when the foot came forward for an overprint when the bear was going downhill. Were all yetis simply black bears making overprints? The Sherpas who had been with Evans in 1955 had also mistaken bear tracks for yeti prints. There was now a known animal that could make such prints.

I pondered all these things each day as I walked the mile back and forth to school. In traveling jungle trails, I had seen the prints of both langurs and black bears. Bears seemed the more likely to have made the prints. But I had never seen bear tracks in snow. Was the yeti in fact a bear? For a bear, Tombazi's prints were the right length. But Shipton's were almost double the size. It could be that something big was out there.

Chapter Three

In 1949, Dad had been the physician accompanying the first Western expedition to enter western Nepal – the first outsiders to visit the mountains Annapurna and Dhaulagiri. When he returned after several months in the high, unexplored Himalaya, he developed a mysterious sickness in his lungs. Month after month he got weaker, until Mother took him on the long train trip to southern India for diagnosis. My sister and I stayed with Grandma and Grandpa.

Over the years Grandpa had become larger than life to me. Drawing strength from his daily dialogues with God, he paid little attention to the Western missionary community. Focusing on family, he wrapped us all in his spiritual beliefs. Sometimes, when he relaxed and did not feel the need to be actively teaching, he talked about mysteries not understood by the Western spiritual dogma, which even the people who experience them don't try to explain. India is a place that accepts happenings and ideas that as a Westerner, as the son and grandson of scientific-thinking physicians, I might otherwise feel the need to explain. Spiritual mysteries – as opposed to spiritual answers – are one foundation of Indian religious faith.

One of Grandpa's Hindu friends, a *sadhu* or holy man, often spoke of times and people encountered during meditations, especially of times yet to come.

Sometimes he and Grandpa talked about Grandpa's friends back in the States, people the sadhu had never met. Then when Grandpa opened his mail from the States, he learned that the things the sadhu predicted had happened. Somehow they both accepted that such understanding was possible for people like the sadhu. Grandpa and the sadhu forged their friendship from shared mysteries. Grandpa talked about this to me, about living a life filled with faith that allows us to probe the unknown, about how we still see through a glass darkly, about skills and insights known only in the East. "There are senses beyond science, Danny, beyond the five the West acknowledges. These sixth senses are senses we can develop. Prayer is one, but there are others. The most skilled among all wildlife observers of India, Jim Corbett, talks of a sense of impending danger."

One morning Grandpa took me hunting. Awakening me in the predawn cold, he led me to a bush blind along a bank above a dried-up riverbed. Sprigs stuck out of Grandpa's hat, making it look like the top of the bush we sat behind. His eyes swept the dry riverbed. Through the early dawn hours, I sat very still looking through the peephole Grandpa had made for me in the middle of the bush, snuggling in the rough wool of his jacket. My job was to watch. That was the morning I learned how a leopard walks, how it stalks along the forested edge of a riverbed.

While we surveyed the dry riverbed, the sun pushed on up. No leopards were likely to come now. We moved to the edge of the riverbank and let our legs hang over the ledge. Sitting beside me, Grandpa opened a thermos of hot sweet milk and filled two cups. It washed into me with warmth, and I relaxed. Leopards were now under cover until evening. With the twigs bobbing on his cap, Grandpa told me about his adventure with a man-eating tigress two years before. I had heard this story from my father and uncle but never from Grandpa, for he seldom talked about himself.

It seemed this certain tigress attempted a meal of porcupine but was driven off by a swat of quills. Three of them stuck, then festered, making the tigress so lame she supplemented her diet with humans. Sportsmen who came to shoot her left birdshot in her rump and a slug in her shoulder. Crippled further, she became cagey.

Then one afternoon two girls, one a new bride everyone said was rather boisterous, were cutting fodder for their water buffalo. The bride,

Author's grandfather with 130-pound leopard, wounded on the first shot and then killed after being deflected in mid-leap by the family's Labrador.

mocking her friend's fear of the man-eater, was climbing down the tree. Suddenly the tigress stood out from a bush, seized her and disappeared into the jungle, teeth piercing the thrashing, screaming girl's chest and holding her sideways in her mouth like a dog might carry a bone.

On hands and knees we tracked the tigress through tunnels of thorns and undergrowth. The trail was easy to follow, fragments of torn clothes, drag marks, and lots of blood. Your father and uncle worked as though possessed, searching each day for fresher sign of the tigress and returning each night to watch at the spot where we had found the bride's hair and bones. I told them: 'Don't search where it has been. Decide where it will come. Be there, wait.'

I decided that sooner or later the tigress would walk a certain trail. I tied my cot high in a tree there and waited. On the fourth morning I awoke sensing her impending arrival. There were the usual morning sounds all around, but all was not normal – that sixth sense awakened me. It's more than a gut feeling; it's a developed sense that leads to knowledge. I waited twenty minutes. No birds gave alarm calls. In that cold light that grows out of the night, before the sun rises over the horizon, morning was coming to the jungle, light like this morning when those wild boar crossed this dry riverbed. Then the tigress limped down the trail into the sunlight. I killed her with my .405 magnum – Teddy Roosevelt's favorite caliber. That tigress died for that bride.

Over the years, other interests came and went – basketball, beetles, and horse chestnuts – but my yeti interest persisted. How will villagers here in Mussoorie identify the Shipton print? Taking my book with the Shipton picture from the shelf one day, I walked down the hill to the Sisters' Bazaar coolie stand, where a dozen hopefuls sat on the stone wall waiting for work. They were from villages throughout these hills, some more than a week's walk away, villagers who traveled the mountain trails all year. Like travelers throughout the ages who have moved without maps and guidebooks, these residents of the mountains share stories of the road when they meet at the resting places. They tell of trails, changes in them, and dangers on them. With each rest stop, with each shared smoke, their mental maps are updated.

I showed the Shipton photograph to a tall coolie, his jute cloak stained with black streaks from carrying charcoal in 150-pound loads. "Yes, little sahib, of course, I know that footprint. You know it, we all know it. That is a man's footprint. Don't be confused by round toe marks. In the snow, a man's toes look round and short, not long like they look in dirt or mud."

"But this couldn't be a man's footprint," I said. "This picture was taken high in the mountains, on a field of snow no person had traveled for many months."

"Sahib, you are still a boy. You do not know that in these mountains, even up very high, people travel. Never even in the most remote mountains can you think no one has passed. Maybe it is a holy man on pilgrimage – always there are pilgrims. Sometimes, too, people travel in secret. Sometimes they carry things they do not want others to find them with. Maybe valuable medicines?

Maybe something stolen? Maybe someone working for another government? In these mountains unknown tracks are sometimes found – and unknown tracks are never surprising."

"But coolieji, look at how big the footprint is. That axhead shows the footprint is thirteen inches long."

"Ah, I did not know the footprint to be so big. Of course maybe it is an unusual man. Unusual men walk in unusual places. And maybe too this is not a man's print but a print of a ghost. Ghosts make large prints."

"Coolieji, have you ever seen a yeti's footprint? Is this the track of a yeti?"

"What is a yeti?"

"The yeti is a wild man that lives in high mountains. It has long hair and a pointed head."

"Such wild men are never here in the mountains, little sahib." The other coolies crowded in closer, and they too examined the picture. They listened and nodded in agreement.

No yetis here? Don't all villagers know of the yeti? For years, in all mountaineers' accounts I had read reports about how the people of the Himalaya believe in the yeti. Yet today, here at the Sisters' Bazaar, was the first time, I suddenly realized, that I had ever actually asked Himalayan villagers about it. If the yeti existed, it seemed villagers would certainly talk about it and be careful of such an animal. Why did these coolies not admit it? Were they afraid? Was this another superstition (like some diseases and evil spirits) that villagers knew of but did not talk about? I wanted to ask my father, my friends, but I decided to keep quiet. There is something about the yeti that makes people laugh. I kept looking in private. Maybe I would see something no one else had seen. But neither my searches of the jungles around Mussoorie nor my discussions with villagers turned up anything.

THE NEXT SUMMER DAD RECEIVED A GRANT FROM THE UPJOHN PHARmaceutical Company to search the valleys east of Kulu for a plant, *nusha bhoota*, "the hair of the ghost." They wanted to make the plant into a new anesthetic drug. During the summer monsoon, when the flower is in bloom, villagers and shepherds walk carefully in the high pastures of those valleys, for when the sun shines, the blossoms emit vapors that allegedly anesthetize passing travelers, who then collapse in the high meadows. They awaken only when the sun is covered again by monsoon clouds and the vapors fade. Uncle Gordon said over dinner one night that maybe the travelers fall asleep because with heavy packs on a sunny day, lying for a while in a warm meadow is pleasant. Then when the clouds come and monsoon rains hit their faces, of course they awaken.

A month and a half before my birthday, Mother told me that she and Dad had decided I could join the expedition. That would be my birthday present. My job was to take care of the white mice and guinea pigs. Neither Mother nor Dad knew the reason I had pressed so hard to go. Three months before, Dad and Uncle Gordon were talking after dinner when I heard Gordon say, "You'd better keep your eyes open up there, Carl. In the monsoon those lush high pastures are perfect yeti habitat. You might have more luck finding the yeti than *nusha bhoota.*" If Dad was going into yeti land, I had to go too.

Once we got into the high mountains above treeline the weather was the same every day – cold, thin rain. We moved from valley to valley. The rain stayed with us. The higher we climbed, the thinner the rain – but always rain, nevertheless. At 10,000 feet, we stood around camp in clammy clothes trying to dry off, or we lay, wet and miserable, in soggy sleeping bags inside our tents. Warm moisture from our breath striking the cold fabric of our single-layer nylon tents condensed, and caused it to rain inside – just as it did outside when warm wet clouds from the South met cold clouds from the North. Dad

In search of the "Hair of the Ghost" – the author, age ten, on his first expedition

(*photo by Carl E. Taylor*)

explained that the higher one climbs, the less dense air gets. Because high-altitude air supports less moisture, drops of rain are smaller up higher. The drops inside the tent didn't seem any smaller to me.

Each morning before the scientists left, we shared hot tasteless oatmeal and sweet tea by the fire. After I fed the guinea pigs and white mice and cleaned the cages, there was not much to do. One morning, sitting on a stool under an umbrella by the cookfire, I waited out the day and the rain. Monsoon rains actually come and go, but they feel continual. Smoke swirled up from the cookfire in a chaotic dance, mimicking the wispy rainclouds that burst up the ridge. The little puffs rose up in a chain, then let go, caught by the wind and headed out into the spaces and clouds beyond. The clouds themselves puffed up over the ridges, wisped around us, then also blew on.

There was something hypnotic about looking out from this height. Clouds were above and below us. The separation between land and sky, the separation of horizontal layers taken for granted on the plains, did not exist here. Land and sky were one system, with moisture, air, life moving into, and changing into, each other. During the monsoon the clouds, the mountains, which normally seemed so big and far away in the Himalaya, seemed to come in beside you like a dancing partner.

A Tibetan shepherd stopped by camp that morning, his two sacks covered by an oiled canvas. He said he was carrying supplies into the Lahoul Valley — but he was very quiet about exactly what those supplies were. Our cook gave him a mug of the hot sweet tea, and we started to talk in Hindi. I pointed to my mice and guinea pigs.

"See over there, my work is to take care of those animals in those cages. Are there animals near here in these mountains that I should worry about, big animals that might attack my little animals?"

"Yes, sahib. Leopards come at night, bears also. After the monsoon the bears like to dig for wild mice."

"Are there any other animals that might attack them?"

The man stopped talking. He really wasn't interested in possible predators for my mice. But the cook refilled his mug, and that reminded him that the events of our camp were more interesting than life out on the trail. The shepherd started again. "There are martens and weasels, maybe even an eagle that you should be careful of. An eagle could see your animals through the wire of their cages. I think you should cover their cages with cloth."

"Are there wild jungle men? In these valleys are there manlike animals in the high snows?"

"Sahib, I do not understand. What do you mean, wild men in the high snows? What would such men eat?"

"I don't know. Maybe they would feed in meadows such as this one. Maybe they could eat plants. Maybe they could eat small animals like my mice."

"I have never heard of any such wild men. We do not have them around here. You do not need to be afraid of such men. But watch for bears."

And so in a second region of the Himalaya I found local people who claimed not to know the yeti. I had not thought before of the food problem. For at least half of the year the high slopes are covered with snow, so there would be no regular food source for the yeti. The chief foods here are grasses. Yetis have been assumed to be primates. Primates do not eat grasses.

Dad returned that evening, excited by a discovery. "Today I came into a valley covered with rose-pink primulas. Yesterday I was in the valley just east of it. The primulas there are dark purple. They are not just different colors. They are different species. The dark purple primulas have that white powder, farina, on their blossoms, and the rose-pink flowers lack farina. Why do two different species exist as monocultures in adjacent valleys? How do they keep themselves separated? I thought that except in gardens where people domesticate plants for uniformity, wildflowers are mixed. But both of these valleys are at 13,000 feet. Both look identical in soil type, both face north and have moist soil. Why would one valley have rose-pink and the other dark purple flowers, and each valley have none of the other type?"

Possible explanations were well along as we started eating our curried carrot and cabbage stew on hot rice. Each evening the last to join us for dinner was Vaid, one of our botanists, who had to interrupt his day's pressing of plants to eat with us. "Carl, the rose-pink is *Primula rosea,* and the dark purple is *Primula macrophylla.* One explanation for why you found monocultures of each is a theory advanced years ago by Kingdom-Ward. He asked the same question after walking through one valley in the eastern Himalaya and finding flowers of one color and, like you, walking the next day in another valley and finding flowers of a second color.

"After careful study, Kingdom-Ward discounted natural environmental factors, soil type, slope exposure, noticing that there are two remarkable features that are different. One is the color difference you noticed, the other is that the flowers are so abundant in the first place. Did you know that in pristine alpine meadows there are relatively few flowers? In pristine meadows grass is so thick and tall that it chokes out most flowers. Valleys lush with flowers are valleys that have been grazed, usually with domestic animals; the grazing creates enough room for the flowers to bloom in abundance. And I am sure you have noticed that all the meadows around here have their grasses well chewed down.

"So, first of all, when you enter an alpine valley and see a carpet of flowers, you know that you are not the first to come there this season. Since flower stems grow more quickly than grass, those meadows of flowers were prepared for you by a shepherd, maybe just a couple of weeks go. Recognizing that grazing brought the wealth of flowers, Kingdom-Ward linked this specifically to the difference in flower color. He suggested that maybe the colors differ because the valleys are grazed at different times. Could one flower dominate when the grass around it is cut earlier, another when it is cut later? It remains just a hypothesis, but it is a wonderful solution."

I was stunned. I had never understood that people could make nature more beautiful than it naturally was.

The next day I walked with Vaid toward the Kulu Valley from the alpine meadows. I was embarrassed to ask about the yeti; the two times I had brought up the subject, the scientists laughed. But I did ask him about how local people use Himalayan plants.

"Vaidji, some of these plants are pretty valuable? Which ones are they? Are they hard to find?"

"Danny, the people here have experimented with local plants for millennia. Some discoveries certainly work and those plants have become hunted. Some pharmaceutical companies right now are seeking a plant that looks like a coffee plant; you've probably seen it in the valleys below Mussoorie, *Rauwolfia sepentia*. It grows in dry, sandy gravel where there is forest cover, has dark glossy green leaves, red flowers. Its medicinal power is said to be in its roots, long tubers that local people grind into paste."

"What do they use the paste to cure?"

"Generally as a remedy for 'madness' but also for snakebite, birthing pain, grief after a death in the family, such things. Scientific tests of the plant have shown a positive effect on hypertension. In fact it works so well that the drug companies are buying as much wild *Rauwolfia* as they can. In many valleys, in slack parts of the agricultural season whole groups from the village search the jungle, digging up roots of the bushes. This, of course, is killing the plants. Commercial harvesting may well exterminate wild *Rauwolfia.*"

"Why don't the companies just grow the plants in special fields?"

"A bush takes years to grow. Then it must be killed for just one harvest. Why go to such expense? It is cheaper to pay villagers to harvest freely growing *Rauwolfia* in the jungle than to grow it in greenhouses."

"But this way the villagers make money off their plant."

"Maybe. But how much money are they really making? Maybe on a good day they double or triple their income over a day in the fields. But how long can they keep taking plants? When the bushes are gone, the villagers who developed the original knowledge over generations will not be better off, their income will be gone, and they will no longer be able to use the plant for themselves."

Our expedition left the Himalaya with a plant whose vapors killed one of my guinea pigs and three white mice, a plant the Upjohn Company could never get to grow in Michigan greenhouses. We also left with a young adolescent who now knew that yetis were not to be easily found. My optimism had dimmed. I would not readily discover what half a century of major expeditions led by the greatest Himalayan explorers had failed to discover. I began to wonder whether the animal existed at all. I placed a lot of trust in villagers; they knew their jungles, and none of the locals had spoken of encounters with the yeti.

Chapter Four

Our family returned to the United States as I entered the teenage years. I kept track of the yeti expeditions through the American press, which in general seemed to find the subject uninspiring. Mother, knowing my interest, kept her eyes open for news as well. I could see that even for the pros yeti exploration was no longer a romantic matter of one person pushing a limit. The expeditions were now major, and monied, scientific campaigns.

In 1957, 1958, and 1959 the Texas millionaire Tom Slick mounted three separate, progressively more sophisticated expeditions. They penetrated the long-closed valleys of eastern Nepal, particularly the area south of Everest, the Khumbu Valley; and east of Everest, the Arun Valley and its western drainages, including the sacred Barun where the jungles were exceedingly dense. The first expedition found three sets of footprints, yeti hair, and excrement. The second took along purebred bluetick bloodhounds, trained in Arizona on mountain lions and bears. These premier canines required jackets to protect them from the cold, lanolin to be rubbed daily into their paws to prevent cracking, and medicines to be taken regularly to ward off exotic diseases. During four months in the field, this second expedition found another set of yeti tracks and visited four remote monasteries to study two alleged yeti scalps and one mummified yeti hand. Slick suggested that he was on the verge of a major discovery but he did not let out much more.

His third expedition was a truly massive undertaking. Spending nine months in the field, trekking over a thousand miles through eastern Nepal, the members trapped two black bears and a leopard and found numerous yeti tracks, droppings, and repeated confirmation from local villagers of the animal's existence. Upon the return of the expedition, Slick suggested there may exist three yetis: a supernatural beast and two biologically real animals. Of the two real animals, one was smaller, like the Tombazi report, and the other was larger, with footprints like those seen by Shipton and Ward. Slick, not being accountable to an outside donor and not part of any academic or museum system, would not release his wealth of accumulated evidence until he had the relationship among these three worked out. But before that happened, he perished in an airplane crash. His data never came forward.

In 1961 the most publicized yeti expedition ever assembled left for the field, and the American newspapers gave that one coverage. *World Book Encyclopedia* funded Sir Edmund Hillary and a multidisciplinary team to spend a full year doing high-altitude research. Although their quest involved more than the yeti and they downplayed that aspect in all their public statements, it was the possibility of the yeti's discovery that fired news stories – and seemed to have motivated *World Book* to pay the bill. The seriousness of their yeti interest was proven by the fact that Shipton's former partner, Michael Ward, was a member of the team. Their discoveries were disheartening. The much-revered yeti scalp from Kumjung Monastery was borrowed for rigorous analysis at centers such as the Field Museum of Natural History in Chicago. Precise comparisons of hair proved that the scalp was a piece of serow (goat antelope) skin stretched and dried into a pointed scalplike cap.

The expedition's cultural investigation of Sherpa beliefs concluded that Westerners had not properly understood how Sherpas view the yeti. Skeptics responded that anthropologists were not part of Hillary's team; in fact, none of the researchers spoke the Sherpa language even passably. But the conclusions Hillary published were explicit: "To a Sherpa, the ability of a yeti to make himself invisible at will is just as important a part of his (the yeti's) description as his probable shape and size. . . . Pleasant though we felt it would be to believe in the existence . . . the members of my expedition – doctors, scientists, zoologists, and mountaineers alike – could not in all conscience view it as more than a fascinating fairy tale . . . molded by superstition, and enthusiastically nurtured by Western expeditions."[7]

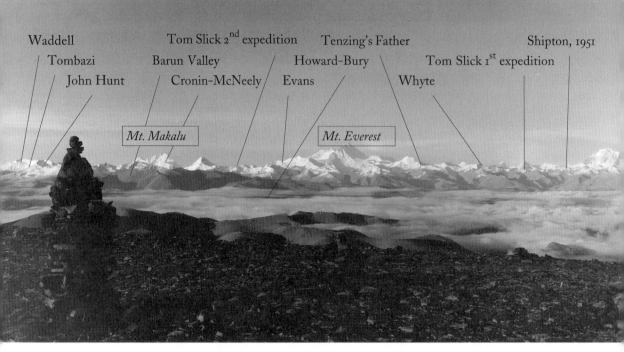

Waddell Tom Slick 2ⁿᵈ expedition Tenzing's Father Shipton, 1951
Tombazi Barun Valley Howard-Bury Tom Slick 1ˢᵗ expedition
John Hunt Cronin-McNeely Evans Whyte

Mt. Makalu

Mt. Everest

Approximate locations of major yeti discoveries

The English primatologist William C. Osman Hill, who was then issuing an authoritative multivolume series on the comparative anatomy and taxonomy of primates, termed Hillary's published conclusions "rather hasty." Hill concluded that the yeti was a "plantigrade mammal capable of bipedal progression." He refocused the hunt out of the high snows: "Searchers for the snowman have been looking in the wrong places. . . . [The yetis'] permanent home is undoubtedly the dense rhododendron thickets of the lower parts of the valley and it is here that future search should be directed."[8]

At last, in 1962, I returned to the Himalaya – to Nepal, the country of the yeti legends. Mother was making a movie on Nepali women; my job was to record the sound track. The site for filming, western Nepal, was the first place I had been in the Himalaya where I couldn't speak the language. Finally, I found a schoolteacher who spoke Hindi, and in the course of a long afternoon talk, he said, "Sahib, I first learned of yetis from a book on Nepal written for tourists. What does the writer mean, this animal yeti? Here in our Himalaya we do not have that animal. Then, sahib, I think some and I understand. Our word for this is not *yeti*. The Nepali word is *bun manchi*." Here was my first Himalayan villager who knew of the yeti. And now I knew what name to use.

One evening the following week a group of Hindi-speaking traders entered a tea stall where I was drinking tea. They had come from a valley high above the Marsyandi River on the north side of Annapurna, and were heading home from India, where they learned to speak Hindi. There is a growing practice in India of hiring people from Nepal as watchmen.

"Do you have wild men in your villages, *bun manchi?*" I asked one of them.

"Yes. *Bun manchi* are lower in the valley, below our villages. Sometimes they come into our villages, but usually they stay back in the jungles."

"What do they look like?"

"Adult *bun manchi* are shorter than I am, with much hair, sahib. *Bun manchi* travel at night, never in the day. Especially they like to come into cornfields. When they come, often you hear them screaming, a high, long scream like a very big eagle."

"Have you gone out to look at them? Do you scare them away from your fields?"

"No, sahib, it is best to let *bun manchi* alone. If you bother them they steal your children."

His traveling companions also told stories about *bun manchi*. At last I had found Himalayan villagers who themselves knew of the yeti and its habits. How I wanted to go up the Marsyandi valley and look for myself!

But Westerners were not allowed into the Marsyandi valley – neither I nor formal expeditions. For the next ten years, spinoffs from the Cold War game-playing kept closed that valley and other remote Himalayan valleys. The high mountain jungles of India, Nepal, Sikkim, Bhutan, and China, where Hill suggested the search should concentrate, remained, as before, forbidden territory. Serious scientists gave up the yeti search. Sir Edmund Hillary's expedition pretty well answered the questions. But yeti sightings continued by nonscientists. In the late 1960s the mountaineer Don Whillans looked out of his tent high on Annapurna and saw "an ape-like creature bounding away on all fours."

My interest in the yeti persisted. The hard facts had hidden, someplace, hard answers. Something had made not one but several series of documented footprints in the snow. Those photographs were real and were not folk legends. From 1969 through 1971 I returned to Nepal as a member of the U.S. State Department foreign aid program. I spent as many vacations as I could in the high valleys, searching. The valleys west of Everest, explored by Shipton and Ward in 1951, were still off limits. But many of the lower valleys were open, and a number of the lesser known higher valleys could be entered.

As I explored the kingdom, I talked with hundreds of Nepalis from all parts. Whenever conversations turned casual, I asked about the yeti. As my language skills in Nepali improved, I found I could steer responses by the way I asked questions. The innuendo of wording was critical. When I mentioned yeti, people responded positively. When I asked only about the mysteries of the jungle, local Nepalis virtually never mentioned it. Most respondents, though, were convinced of *bun manchi*. Villagers swore something was eating real crops in their real fields. They swore the beast was not bear, monkey, or other known animal. Was *bun manchi* therefore the yeti?

Close to my base in Kathmandu, I discovered the wildness of the Gosain-Kund Ridge, only a twenty-minute helicopter ride away, but a four-day trek, each way, on foot. An extravagance my salary allowed, the short flight meant I could slip off to look in otherwise ignored wildness whenever one of the periodic two- or three-day Nepali holidays piggybacked with a Western weekend.

It was ideal. I left work early, say on a Thursday afternoon. The chopper dropped me in one valley with a forty-pound pack. For four days and five nights, I walked solo to an adjoining valley for early morning pickup, usually on a Tuesday. After a quick shower I showed up at my desk at the U.S. Agency for International Development, fresh from having watched a high-altitude sunrise, ready to get back to work designing Nepal's family-planning program.

One fall trip, during the Nepali Festival of Lights, I bivouacked at 16,000 feet. Because a tent weighed too much, my practice was to replace it with a nylon bivvy bag into which I stuffed sleeping bag, insulated pad, boots, water bottle, flashlight, and a snack for the night. The bivouac site was under a low but dramatically overhanging rock in case snow fell during the night, and my backpack lay on the slope ten feet away, slightly downhill. I stuffed my down parka into a cotton pillowcase to simulate the feeling of home under my head. Soon I was asleep.

Early during the night the snow started, thick heavy flakes. I burrowed down into my sleeping bag. It never really snows in early October in that part of the Himalaya. The monsoon was over. Maybe an inch or so would dust the valley, providing ideal conditions for tracking animals. I thought about getting up early and combing the slopes. With the hood of the sleeping bag pulled tight over my head, I kept track of what was going on outside. After maybe an hour the slight wind that had been blowing stopped. The snow kept coming all night, through dawn. I wiggled head and shoulders out of the bivvy bag and looked. Rock rose about eight inches above my head and a wall of snow loomed about a foot away, extending from the ground to the ceiling. Through the soft snow, fresh oxygen somehow seeped through. Outside, I was pretty sure that the snow was still coming down. This was not just a dusting.

Better make breakfast at least. The snow would stop soon, and I needed to be ready to go. In the slot under the rock, with eight inches clearance, I fished my boots from inside the bivvy bag and pulled my parka out of the pillowcase. Snow filled my sleeping bag, bivvy bag, and most of my clothes and was starting to melt. The more I worked under the rock, the lower it seemed to settle. Fears flooded over me of being locked in, being trapped under a rock weighing tons, or most realistically, of being smothered by a barrier of snow, using up the oxygen and suffocating. Ridiculous, but I must get out.

It would have been too hard to get the stove set up under the rock – like trying to set up camp under a bed. I'd have to do everything outside. Whatever the weather was like up above, being there would be better than being under the rock. My water bottle was empty, and I needed to melt snow and get something to drink if I was to keep up the fluids I would need for moving at that altitude. I burrowed up and out from under the rock. I was standing in a blizzard, snow up well above my knees. I looked at my watch. Ten o'clock. It had been snowing for more than twelve hours.

I walked through the snow to my pack. Reaching down, I groped around my feet. Nothing. Stretching out before me, the surface of the snow was smooth. Back and forth, I tramped through the snow, groping for my pack. Could a yeti have carried it away? The pack must be there someplace. Snow sifted inside my clothes. Expecting a pleasant fall weekend, I was wearing cotton blue jeans, now soaked from melting snow. Back and forth I walked, feeling beneath the snow with my feet. Five hundred dollars worth of cameras were in that backpack.

The snow kept coming down. I looked back to the overhanging rock, and at first I couldn't see it. More snow had fallen, and I hadn't realized that a slight wind was filling in my tracks. My glasses were wet and caked with snow. I peered through them. Where was the overhanging rock? After a hot rush of panic and the cleaning of my glasses, I could see the indentation of the cave. I plowed up to my former campsite.

Reaching down under the rock, I grasped my bivvy bag, pulled it open, and fished out a candy bar. Standing there chewing, I thought about the helicopter. It was due to arrive an hour and a half after dawn tomorrow. My watch now read noon. In good weather it would be a five-hour walk to the pickup point, which was on the other side of the pass rising before me. With Cadbury's sugar now rushing through my veins, I knew I was in trouble.

It might take me two days in that snow to walk those five hours. Could I find my pack? Not knowing how much more time it would take, it was probably not worth trying. The most important thing was not to spend another night in that snow. With luck I would be able to descend to an altitude where the snow changed to rain. Would that be at 14,000 feet? Maybe. Almost certainly it would change at 13,000. Getting below the snow before nightfall was my best hope to prevent real trouble. Another night in that stuff, and wet as I was, the stakes would rise dramatically. I stuffed the bivvy bag, sleeping bag, and empty water bottle into the cotton pillowcase, tied it shut with the length of parachute cord I always carry in my pockets, slung it over my shoulder, and started off. I abandoned my planned route of following the ridge – just get up and over the pass and then down low on the other side. About ten feet from the overhanging rock, I stumbled over an obstacle. As I fell forward, my knee caught against my pack frame. My instincts about which way to head were more precise than my rational brain.

With spirits greatly improved after eating sardines soaked in mustard sauce from the American Embassy commissary, I pressed on. About two o'clock I crossed the pass, and as I headed into the other drainage the snow stopped. By three, descending rapidly through the snow, the visibility improved to at least a mile. I picked up speed. Downward I went through the snow, now only a foot deep. But I was tired. Spying a large, high, flat-topped boulder, I cleared off a big area, spread out my bivvy bag, and got the stove going. The change into dry pants was wonderful, and even better was to take off my sweat-soaked shirt and undershirt and pull a soft wool sweater over my tired skin. The fatigue had exhausted my extremities – they felt disassociated from me. It was four o'clock and teatime.

Sitting on the rock swirling the hot tea in my mug, I knew that underneath, other animals had their homes, homes under rocks, homes under the snow.

They are little animals, and I suspected that they live rather fine lives. The snow makes a fantastic blanket. The sun, especially at these low latitudes, sends warmth down through it. It is easy to burrow out tunnels. Thermometers placed in such subnivean cavities beneath the snow and above the earth register a pleasant sixty degrees Fahrenheit when temperatures above are well below freezing.

This alpine world under the snow is full of life: insects, especially spiders; voles chasing the insects; pikas and other small mammals rounding out this mini-ecosystem. During winter months these animals sleep long and deep in homes under rock and earth; but often they also poke around and eat. The snow gives them wonderful cover from the eyes of searching hawks.

Do the yetis know of these denizens of the lower snows? Might William C. Osman Hill be wrong in asserting that yetis have to live in the jungle because that is the only food supply? Might yetis be able to live up high, at least for part of the year, having found special ways of harvesting such small snow-bound animal larders? Who are these underground animals, representatives of the little life that is around us and hiding?

Running under the earth is a world of even smaller dimensions than the subnivean. Worms twist and burrow. Beetles chew. Ants scurry. In their daily quests, none of these species knows of the animals running above. Their reality is what is before their noses. Inside each of these – the beetles, the worms, the ants – is a still smaller eco-world of life. Bacteria burrow through tissue. Microbes thrive in a world that seems so small to us as to be without dimension. We deny it consciousness. They certainly know not of the insects around them, the animals above, or myself on the rock.

What is the reality in which we, any of us who is living, live? Or what is the reality beyond us? We know our burrows, the foot trails, the highways, the airways tunneling through the surface dirt and the cumuli of our skies, providing bearings by which we take our direction. Something is beyond. Many sense a greater spirit, but it is so vast we cannot agree on its name. We see part of its face and it gives us faith to live. But different people see different parts and give different names. The voice of this little-known part is not small or quiet – but that voice can be made small by neglect or it can be made quiet by fear. Our traditions pass to us visions from those who have seen, but the work is not done. Each of us must burrow and chew. Each of us must ultimately focus on our own reality, looking through that glass, dark as it is.

The great peak Makalu hiding behind lesser summits

Suddenly I looked at my watch. Five o'clock. I swallowed the last of my second cup of tea. There was an hour and a half of sunlight left, and I had a good set of flashlight batteries, but I also had miles to go before I should sleep. I stamped my boots clean and continued on down to the chopper site.

The following morning, in the meadow at 10,000 feet where I was to meet my pickup, I finished my first cup of tea and contemplated a thick carpet of primulas nearby: *Primula denticulata,* small purple-mauve flowers, common and widespread at that altitude. As I heated milk for my cereal, the sound of French-made helicopter blades approached. An hour later I was sitting at my desk, reading the weekend cable traffic from Washington.

IN 1972, THE YEAR AFTER I LEFT NEPAL, THE BEST-ORGANIZED, MOST serious yeti expedition ever departed from Kathmandu to the Arun Valley. Jeff McNeely and Ted Cronin, zoologists working in Thailand, while seeking funding and political permission were at first open about their intention to look for yetis. When such interest brought skeptical responses and little support, they broadened the focus of their research to a comprehensive ecological description of eastern Nepal, the first ever attempted.

For two years they operated out of a base camp in the heart of prime yeti country, isolated, dense jungle, near where Slick's second expedition made its finds fifteen years before. Working year round, they hoped that while they were learning about the habitat the yeti would find them. Letters from friends in Nepal kept me posted about their progress. In January 1973, Mother sent me an Associated Press report from Kathmandu announcing that the Arun Valley Expedition had found yeti tracks high on a ridge in the snow outside their tents. Plaster casts were made of the footprints. From a mere three column inches in the *Baltimore Sun* and no more than that in the *New York Times* I inferred that those tracks fit the Tombazi pattern.

Grandpa now lived with my parents in Baltimore, having left the Indian jungles after sixty years. When I passed through from West Virginia where I lived for most of the year, he and I talked of many things. Sometimes he talked about his great hunts and told again the story of killing the man-eating tigress.

One day, somewhat shyly, as though afraid he might shock me by showing an interest, he asked, "Danny, have you ever wondered about the yeti? There are things in the jungle, you know, we do not understand. Cronin and McNeely may really have found something." Grandpa and I talked into the night about how the Cronin/McNeely strategy might be improved there in the Arun Valley. What tactics were they overlooking? Grandpa wanted to see the plaster casts. "They're doing the basic part right," he said. "They're sitting in the tree, sitting in the best place they know, letting the yeti come to them. You know, it takes only one animal to prove that the yeti exists."

"I wonder what the tracks are like," I replied. "What have they really found? Someday I want to go to that Arun Valley and look for myself." On December 13, 1973, Grandpa died, before he and I had seen the plaster casts or the photographs.

In 1979, forty-two years after his first yeti discovery, Lord Hunt, the conqueror of Mount Everest, found tracks fourteen inches long, one inch longer than Shipton's. Returning to London, Lord Hunt proclaimed to a world that had more or less lost interest: "The real question is not whether yetis exist. It is how long they will continue to evade our attempts to locate them." In the same year, John Whyte led a mountaineering expedition and returned to London with photographs of more yeti tracks. Much smaller than Lord Hunt's, these tracks fit Tombazi's measurements, roughly eight inches by four, with four toes and a thumblike inside digit. Was Slick right? Were there two types of yetis? Or did Whyte's prints belong to a juvenile? Whyte's report added a new dimension to the yeti lore: sound. From a cliff above, while they were photographing the tracks, Whyte and other expedition members heard a piercing scream that lasted about ten seconds, a scream their Sherpas identified as the yeti's.

Shown on British television, Whyte's tracks and Lord Hunt's assertion rekindled interest in the yeti. More discoveries ensued. A Polish Everest expedition in 1980 found more yeti tracks – the large fourteen-inch variety. Then, in 1986, at 13,000 feet, near my old home valleys of the Indian Himalaya, the British traveler Anthony B. Wooldridge came upon a solitary yeti standing upright in a snow gully. He watched it for forty-five minutes and took many photographs. After eighty-seven years, at last we knew what the yeti looked like. Wooldridge obligingly sent me copies of his pictures. The best laboratories and the most conservative zoologists double-checked his photography for a hoax. Nothing suggested that the pictures were a trick.

But several years before Wooldridge took his photographs, I had resumed my own yeti search in the field. Here is that search as I recorded it in the field notes I kept at the time.

Chapter Five

Early May 1976. After two years of marriage, Jennifer and I have returned to Nepal to the Gokyo Valley west of Everest. When she agreed to marry me, I doubt that Jennifer ever imagined she was getting into a long-term relationship with the Abominable Snowman.

We met in 1969 during one of those long Nepali holidays, one of the times I did not head for the hills. It was the Indra Jatra festival. That afternoon several thousand people packed the streets of Kathmandu during the height of the ceremony. Standing in the crowd, I looked up and saw Jennifer for the first time. She was on a balcony, blonde hair blowing across her face in the light wind. "You should not let her slip away," Barry Bishop said to me that day as he and I snapped pictures for his employer, the *National Geographic*. "She has spirit – and sense. She grew up all over the world and can share your dreams."

Later, as the day turned to bacchanalian night, Jennifer and two pretty teenage girlfriends sat high on a temple platform above the same street, watching a traditional play. Below was a crowd of several hundred Nepali men, usually very decorous, their inhibitions now loosened by drink and the romantic epic of the play. As the three girls descended the temple stairs, first one man's hand, then a dozen others grabbed their legs and reached under their dresses. Jennifer's two companions shrieked. In the fervor of heroic rescue, I led them to my big black BMW motorcycle and with engine roaring and horn blaring, I tried to open an exit path only to have my wheel become stuck in a pothole. Jennifer sank from sight, slipping away under the men's feet to the edge of the square. There she crawled behind the skirts of women vendors selling beer and peered out at the antics of the rest of us.

During the next year Jennifer and I met on many evenings and weekends while I worked for the State Department and she studied Nepali folk music. On that motorcycle we explored the kingdom's hidden valleys and each other's secret dreams. After we left Nepal, we continued to meet in various parts of the world for four more years. In 1974 we were married on a mountaintop in West Virginia.

Now we have returned for a delayed honeymoon, with permission to come to the once-closed valleys of eastern Nepal. Two ridges separate the Gokyo Valley from Menlung, as close as the geopolitics of 1976 allow us to the site of the greatest yeti discovery. Twenty-five years and twenty miles from where Jennifer and I now walk, Eric Shipton and Michael Ward found those footprints made by an animal that is still a mystery.

The Home Ministry in Kathmandu has issued no other trekking permits for foreigners to this area this season, and no Nepalis will be this high this early. So, I suspect, Jennifer and I are the only humans within three days' walk. Here so close to the Menlung, we should also find signs, tracks, and perhaps the yeti. In the past twenty-five years, most expeditions to the Himalaya have consisted of from twenty to thirty-five people, including the porters. They would have been noisy. In this wide, treeless canyon with a twenty-mile-long glacier down its middle, the flanking rock cliffs would have reverberated with the sounds of their approach hours before the trekkers got close. The many crevices in the cliffs would have given animals places to hide.

Around three o'clock we arrive at our campsite at 16,500 feet. Fifteen minutes later, without even waiting to make tea, our four Sherpa porters head back down-valley to their families, leaving Jennifer and me alone at the foot of Cho Oyu, the world's sixth-highest peak, towering another 10,000 feet above. On the way up, the Sherpas recounted one yeti story after another: big male yetis carrying off young yaks; yetis that can't be followed because their feet are on backward and confuse the trackers; yetis with pointed heads and big bushy eyebrows; yetis whose hair grows upward above the waist and downward below it. Yetis who attack young women in the high meadows.

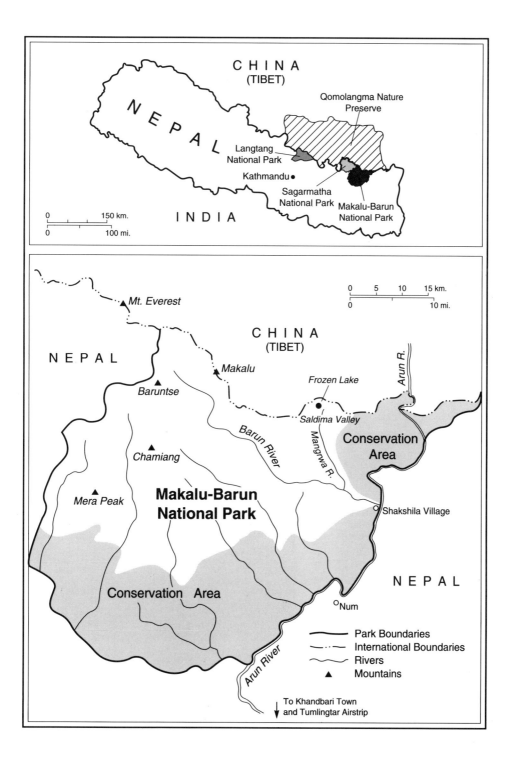

Yak and sheep herders will come to these high pastures in two months to escape the force of the monsoon. Spring is advancing. The grass here is already green and four inches tall. Under the soil, tubers thicken in the warming earth. Pikas feed everywhere, especially when the sun is out, and play near their holes. Whether the yeti's tastes are for tender, brown-furred animals or succulent plants, food here is abundant.

Two thousand feet above us, however, snow still covers the slopes. Yetis that have retreated up there from us will have to move about to find something to eat – and if they do, they'll leave tracks in the snow. If they descend, seeking the protection of the birch and rhododendron forests down below, they will have to make their way past our camp at night. But descending isn't likely; yetis wouldn't know that other people were headed up-valley behind us. And almost all yeti prints indicate that they travel away several hours ahead of their would-be discoverers. The animals must therefore be shy; their natural response, to flee. We have them trapped – unless the yetis driven up-valley by our presence move out through the high passes, still deep in snow.

We are quiet in camp for two days, letting the valley regain its peace. Our narrow two-person tent is pitched on soft grass. A stream splashing along its course six yards away camouflages our camp sounds as it drains the slopes west of the Upper Ngozumpa Glacier. Morning light hits this site early as the sun rises through a pass north of Everest, melting the frost on our tent, warming us before we unzip our sleeping bags and step out into the new day. Clouds are few in early May, so the sun shines strongly all day and washes the south face of Cho Oyu red at sunset.

Jennifer isn't well. She's suffered from altitude sickness, nausea, headache, lethargy, ever since we landed two weeks ago at Shangboche airstrip at 11,500 feet. We stayed at Shangboche for three nights, giving her time to acclimate, then went off with the porters we'd hired. The next night, at 13,000 feet, she was sick again. With finances tight, staying in camp and resting while paying porters seemed too expensive. So each day we climbed higher. The vertical gain wasn't great, but the days are long. Finally we arrived at 16,500.

Now while Jennifer rests, I am determined to make the most of our time here in the heart of yeti country. Is the creature here? I'm hyper-alert to the sights and sounds of the slopes around. Was that a bird or a whistle on the wind? Is something watching us from that summit above camp?

This early in the year water is in only three places. The most important is the stream that cuts sharply through the grassy meadow where we're camped. At every turn it forms something of a shore, leaving sand exposed. A yeti footprint made in sand rather than snow would give useful information; sand can't change shape by melting. Each morning I start searching where the stream flows from the glacier, walking, checking each little beach, looking for places where the overhanging grassy bank might have been broken.

A mile downstream, the Gokyo Valley widens. Rocks and earth have slid from a side valley, impounding a small lake. A shrunken shoreline shows that it was bigger last month, swollen by spring snowmelt. The belt of mud is perfect for taking footprints. Each morning I circle the lake, Cho Oyu's white precipitous face reflected in its mirrorlike surface. Picking up the stream again at the outflow, I follow it down to a second small lake and walk that shoreline too, looking.

Coming back to camp, I climb the eight-foot wall of the Ngozumpa Glacier and walk its icy length, looking. Small, dark gravel peppers the surface. Each day the sun warms the stones, and each night the stones radiate back their heat, settling a little lower into a growing cuplike depression in the ice; the darkest stones melt cups more than three times their diameter. From the size of the ice cups I guess it has been a month since a fresh snow. There are few

Jennifer ascending the upper Ngozumpa Glacier

other marks on that hard surface. Yesterday afternoon, when the snow was soft enough to take the impression of a footprint, did a yeti walk upon the glacier?

During my morning searches, Jennifer remains in the tent, deep in a novel that takes her to a different time and place. When I return, we sit on rocks by the stream and talk while she scrubs last night's chocolate pudding out of a pan and I start up the stove, balancing a coffeepot on the wire struts. Cooking on spongy meadow grass is tricky. We talk about the larger meaning of why we are here. "Civilized" people's need for wildness, their romantic view that wildness is innately innocent, pure, good. But I am beginning to suspect that my urge to find a yeti in the wilderness comes more from the wild man inside me than from any wild man out there.

Our days in camp slip by. We have been here a week. I dare not broach the idea of moving further up-valley. Jennifer seems to be accommodating, even enjoying, remaining in camp. The site is spectacular, with Cho Oyu just above. Without a climbing partner, it is dangerous to cross very severe terrain. Our two acres of meadow are protected on the east and north by the glacier's wall, on the south by a bend in the valley, and on the west by the valley side. But at the top of the western valley a rock summit perches above our camp like an umpire's chair above a tennis court. From up there an observer could see every action in the glade. I have an overwhelming sense that something is watching us from that summit.

My morning circuit of stream, lakes, and glacier is yielding nothing. One morning, I climb the valley wall to that summit. Footholds are flimsy, and the dense shingle of loose slate slides beneath my weight, but the angle is not so steep to risk setting off a slide, so I climb on. Although the rock is hot, and the ascent takes two and a half hours, as always, I save enough water in my bottle to mix with the plaster of paris that also rides in my pack, enough plaster to make one footprint cast. Near the top I climb slowly and pick up each loose slab. This hike is really dumb – but it is called for by something down inside me.

I continue my quest. Any animal of fifty pounds or more stepping on these rocks would make the top slab wobble and grind slightly against the one below. The gray lichen crust that forms where the two rocks join would then be broken, and the gray oxidized outer layer of rock would be ground off and show fresh slate beneath. I circle the summit three times, studying the underside of each loose rock. The lichen bonds are strong between all slabs. It has been a long, long time since any good-sized creature passed over them.

At last I reach the top. Below, the Ngozumpa Glacier, grandaddy of Himalayan snowfields, stretches southward. If ever yetis walked anywhere, they must have walked here. This is the valley where the father of Tenzing Norgay, who climbed Everest with Hillary, claimed to have seen a yeti while he was tending yaks. By Sherpa accounts, the Gokyo Valley has the finest grass of all Sherpa valleys. Two passes lead from here into Tibet. This place is the heart of yeti country.

Or is the yeti just a creature of the soul? There seems to be something very strong in Western culture that calls from within for a wild man: Caliban in Shakespeare's *Tempest;* Chingachgook in James Fenimore Cooper; Mozart's birdman/animalman in *The Magic Flute;* even "Tarzan of the Apes." (The romancing of wildness really took off with Rousseau's Noble Savage. As a result, French explorers spent two hundred years scouring the earth for "wild" good cultures.)

Sitting alone on the 19,000-foot rock pinnacle over camp 2,500 feet below, I scan the glacier with my twelve-power binoculars. Nothing moves on the ice. Early in the morning and late in the evening, over the last week, I've watched from other lookouts lower down. Nothing has moved on the glacier any of those times. Once I saw several large, golden, shaggy mountain *thar* on a rock ledge; and once I thought I'd spotted a musk deer in some bushes alongside a grassy meadow – but maybe not. The habitat is wrong; musk deer need more forest. What was that animal then?

With my thoughts far from settled I start the scramble back down to camp. My yeti-herding strategy, devised in West Virginia, seems full of misconceptions. Jennifer, waiting alone below, has been patient. It is time for us to leave.

Chapter Six

June 1979, Kathmandu. Three years later, with another medical research expedition over, I hurry with Dan Terry, the childhood companion with whom I shared my boldest adventures, through a gate and down a brick walkway toward Bob and Linda Fleming's small bungalow. As we walk over the bricks I look up to their second-floor balcony to see if the flying squirrel cage is still part of their home. We are here for lunch, but in the colonial British tradition we know that lunch at Bob and Linda's will start with a long, late-morning tea. Tomorrow I fly back to the United States and among all that must be done before I leave nothing is more important than a visit with these old friends.

"EEAL!"

"What's that?" Terry asks, turning toward the sound.

There against the brick wall on the north side, half hidden amid rain-drenched ferns, is a gray Nepali rat snake, genus *Ptyas*, six feet long. Disappearing into its mouth, its body pierced by the gray snake's razor-sharp teeth, is an ordinary frog, genus *Rana*, from the rice paddy on the other side of the brick wall. We can see its legs kicking, the last reflexes of life. The squeal lingers in our memory.

For Kathmandu, the day is hot and muggy. Leaving the monsoon steam outside, Terry and I enter the bungalow, its thick walls keeping the room cool. After we settle into our chairs, Nuche, the cook, brings hot tea and sets it on a low table. Already there is a tray containing the cups, strainer, milk, sugar, and glucose biscuits. Teatime, that ageless tradition, is much more relaxing than any coffeebreak. Dr. Robert L. Fleming, Jr., the old friend now preparing my teacup by adding a dollop of Nepali buffalo milk and a spoonful of coarse Indian sugar, knows the 1,800 miles of the Himalaya from Pakistan to Bhutan better than anyone else I know of. When he, Terry, and I were together at the Woodstock School in India, Bob's bird collection always won grand prize at the hobby show. Even then, he was the expert we looked to. Now, he's added a doctorate in zoology and thirty more years of Himalayan fieldwork. From two hundred expeditions, he's built a comprehensive understanding of Himalayan natural history as well as of the region's social, linguistic, and geophysical interrelationships. For forty-five years he's watched one of the least-known, most romantic corners of the earth lose wildlife and woods, triple its human population, and become another tourist stop.

I tell him about the villagers we talked to last month on our way to our research site. "There, where the Marsyandi Gorge narrows between Annapurna and Manaslu, they passed along more *bun manchi* stories, Bob. The villagers are building substantial fences around their fields. They believe real jungle men come into those fields at night. I've never seen people so convinced."

"I know the place, Dan'l. The trail is on the right side of the gorge, a thin black cliff runs above it on the right and the jungle comes down to the trail and abuts the fields. There's nothing to their *bun manchi*. The animal is probably a monkey or a bear."

"But poor people don't build fences like that because of imagination. Fences cost money – and lots of hard work."

"Well, they're worried about something that invades their fields. The jungle there is isolated, low, and wet enough to hold a good population of any number of species."

Leaning forward, elbows on his knees, teacup in one hand, saucer in the other, Terry breaks in. "Bob, you can't dismiss this as imagination or as just monkeys and bears. Villagers know their jungle. You grew up here. You know villagers know bears and monkeys. Why would they make up *bun manchi* for this crop eater when they can recognize the signs of bears and monkeys feeding better than you or I? Those villagers must have evidence. Maybe it's not yeti, but it's something."

"You two have looked for yetis for years – even built cars to look for them." Bob drops his head and peers over the top of his glasses, his eyes laughing. He remembers 1968 and the vw bus, YETI KA BHAI – "yeti's brother" – Terry and I owned. Eleven summers ago, after my first year in graduate school, we drove that bus from Germany to India where I was to do research with the Tibetan refugee community. Terry telephoned a message to my Harvard mail slot the week before: "You buy vw van. I pay gas to India. Rendezvous June 1st Switzerland." But he didn't say which airport in Switzerland, so on June 1, having a $400 van bought from a U.S. serviceman in Frankfurt, I met all flights from the States arriving in Zurich and, via long-distance phone calls, paged flights arriving at the Geneva airport. Terry paid the phone bill as well as the gas bill.

That summer of 1968, the youth of the West roamed the earth passing out flowers, and to some of them we sold seats to raise spending money. While under YETI KA BHAI, adjusting the clutch in Ankara, Turkey, we learned that Bobby Kennedy had been shot. South of Mount Ararat, we dodged bandits. One afternoon in Afghanistan's Baluchistan Desert, with the temperature a blistering 121 degrees Fahrenheit in the shade, the vw crankshaft bearings burned out. After five days, we rolled again, driving on bearings laminated up from a Spam can and Harvard bond stationery. Then they blew again, and this time the engine entrails flew through the crankcase. When we finally got to India, Bob laughed when he saw the blue and white YETI KA BHAI. Many folks would have called it an abominable bus.

Bob knows how far back our yeti fascination goes, and I half expect him to make another of his jokes. But putting down his teacup, he leans forward and drops his voice. "I am not putting you guys off. I agree something is out there. I really doubt that it's *bun manchi* but six years ago McNeely and Cronin showed me a plaster cast of the footprint they found, and that print was not made by any Himalayan animal I know. It looked similar to a gorilla's, with some sort of primatelike thumb. McNeely and Cronin's other discoveries have held, so I doubt this is a hoax."

Does this mean Bob believes in the yeti? Caught off balance by this news, I don't know what to say. Terry and Linda seem surprised too. Bob shifts in his chair. "Let's move to the table for lunch," he suggests. As we resettle in the dining room, no one says anything. Bob is going to have to make the next statement. He clearly finds it hard to expose himself as a believer, even

Dan Terry (left) and passenger with "Yeti's Brother"

among friends who already are. "Something is there . . . at least, I think something is out there."

None of us responds. Let Bob work himself in deeper. We all sit before piles of Nepali noodles and sauce, Bob at the head of the table, Linda at the other end. Linda smiles. She always knows more than she says. Terry twirls noodles randomly with his fork, head down, waiting.

"I don't think *bun manchi* has anything to do with the yeti," Bob says. "*Bun manchi* reports are probably all monkey or bear – both can appear very hominoid. But there are other stories. The McNeely/Cronin report is the most reliable. Something visited their 13,000-foot ridge camp that night. In the morning outside the tent were tracks they couldn't explain. I saw both the plaster cast and photographs made of tracks shielded from the sun. No animal in the Himalaya that I know could have made imprints like those casts and photographs."

Like a spy who has held his secret too long, Bob needs to talk. Terry and I remain silent, bent over the meal. The Cronin/McNeely evidence is not the news. What is news is that Bob Fleming, our authority since schooldays, accepts their data as unexplainable. He is careful not to say that there is a yeti, but his confession keeps coming.

"George Schaller also looked at their material. He and I talked about it here in our house. George is the one who said the prints were similar to those of the mountain gorilla, and George knows the mountain gorilla."

This is impressive. George publishes, knocking off study after biological study: the mountain gorilla, the lion, the tiger, the snow leopard, the giant panda. George is better known but lacks Bob's natural history depth across disciplines and specific Himalayan experience. If George does not dismiss the Arun Valley data, then . . .

Nuche brings dessert: chilled litchis, the insider's fruit of the tropics. Beneath a thin, gnarled, brown skin a soft, dewlike tropical flesh wraps around a hard, marble-sized seed. Squeezing gently on the skin to eject the fruit inside, I pop one litchi after another into my mouth. Moist, cold, delicate, melting on my tongue, litchis taste like early morning mist as it disappears at dawn.

We move back to the living room, and another pot of tea. Bob starts again. "The something doesn't live where its evidence has been found, in the snows. Vegetation is inadequate there, for this animal has to be an herbivore. Carnivores have larger home ranges and are easier to find since they signal their presence with identifiable kills. Schaller agrees that the yeti, if it exists, is an herbivore, not moving around much, living near its food in dense jungle, in behavior similar to the panda or gorilla.

"Where would you look for 'the something,' Terry?" Bob asks, his voice relaxed now.

"I'd think that bamboo must be its food," Terry replies. "But, if it's a primate, or even some sort of bear, the animal will use caves. It might eat bamboo or hide in it. But bamboo is wet when it rains and cold in winter. If 'the something' is out there and smart enough to have remained hidden for so long, it will have learned about the dryness and warmth of caves. Quietly check every cave, and you'll find 'the something' – at least you'll find some further evidence."

"I think the timing of the search is pretty important," Bob says. "Summer is out. The monsoon rains and leeches will overwhelm you."

"Spring should be good," Terry suggests. "The jungle is open. We can see farther. We could find caves."

I break in. "Sight may be important if we're trying to find caves. But how about fall, when food supply is the greatest? Also, animals are sexually active and vocal then. Forget caves – you're making an assumption that 'the something' uses caves. It must eat. It must have sex. Without either of these it couldn't survive. For these, fall is best."

"You've forgotten winter," Bob says.

"Winter's rough going," Terry replies. "Low snow in the jungle, slipping on undergrowth, getting your leg stuck in wet vines, that's tough."

"Yes, the winter rains bring low snow, but this snow also will drive animals low," Bob answers. "Whatever 'the something' is, there aren't many of them and since there isn't much low habitat in the Himalaya anymore, these animals will really be concentrated in winter, maybe easier to find. And in snow, tracking is easy, like having animals all sign their names with their paw prints on census forms."

As we leave the bungalow, Terry and I look over toward the brick wall to see what's become of the rat snake. In the corner, to our surprise, not one but two male rat snakes, each as thick as my arm, struggle, standing about two feet up out of the ferns, swaying, twisted around each other like two vines. They are fighting for territory.

In Nepali folklore the snake is lord of the underworld, the force controlling evil. Two rat snakes swaying back and forth upright like this are often mistaken for a cobra, the specific incarnation of the lord of the underworld. Despite the centrality of this religious symbolism, Nepalis usually kill snakes upon sight, especially in towns. And killing the lord of the underworld affects a Hindu's karma. Is karma, therefore, a reality, or is it, too, only folklore? In the doorway, we watch. Finally the hungry smaller snake wins, and the other slips away under the wall to digest his frog.

The following evening, leaving Kathmandu for the United States, I sit on the right side of the jet, as its shadow skips along the tops of billowing clouds. The jet climbs through 20,000 feet and outside my window, still above us, rise the Himalaya. The white snow and ice are at home with the clouds. Then as our plane levels off at the height of the mountains, the colors start to change. The setting sun, as it drops low on the left, reddens like a fireball, shining across the clouds and in across the aisle to where I sit. It fires up the clouds on the left into glorious reds. The snows of the Himalaya on the right turn deep red, then, as the sun settles into the fluff of clouds, lavender. As we soar toward Delhi, the summits drop behind. The high snows flash electric red when the sun finds a crack in the clouds, then turn again to cold lavender ice. Soon they will briefly glow pastel pink as the sun drops farther around the earth, its rays reflecting back onto the lofty summits from the outer atmosphere, as a mirror. After this glow, night settles in. When Royal Nepal Airlines leaves on time, the evening flight from Kathmandu to Delhi is one of the great airplane rides over Earth.

I look down on India below.

Chapter Seven

October 1, 1979: three years since our expedition into the Gokyo Valley, four months since tea at Bob and Linda's. I settle in with Cronin's book by the fire burning in the hearth of a house I'm building near the top of Spruce Knob Mountain, West Virginia. For seven years, home was a wooden, seventeen-foot-wide yurt in the forest. During those years, with a lot of friends, Jennifer and I built the Woodlands Mountain Institute; we did not just formulate its mission to advance mountain cultures and preserve mountain environments but we also built a wide variety of domestic and international programs and hammered together the institutional buildings. In 1979, upon my return from Nepal, I took six months off and started our own home. After 120 days without a break, the house shell and roof were up.

Settled now on the sofa, good logs crackling off their sparks and their warmth, hammer put aside for the night, I start reading *The Arun: A Natural History of the World's Deepest Valley*. The ecological scope is comprehensive for a two-year expedition – it tried to cover the zoology, ornithology, herpetology, and botany of the Arun Valley east of Everest. Cronin seems to know what he's talking about.

His first chapters summarize people and natural history. The description of Tumlingtar brings back memories of my three years working in Nepal's family-planning program. I remember in 1970 the Tumlingtar vasectomy camp and the very young physician who worked in the nearby hospital. To reduce the villagers' fears about the upcoming campaign, he decided to demonstrate with a sample operation before our camp opened. Unfortunately, he cut and tied his patient's testicular vein instead of his vas. Discharged, the villager walked home. The next day he was carried back on his bed, crying with pain, his scrotum ballooned with blood to the size of a volleyball. His story flashed, porter to porter, tea stall to tea stall, across mountain ridges. Throughout the kingdom strong men became terrified.

Khandbari Bazaar, the shopping town one week's walk from Cronin and McNeely's base camp, is memorable too. There in 1971, I helped set up one of twenty-five district family-planning offices around Nepal. Our second-floor quarters overlooked the bazaar square. On Wednesdays, the day of the weekly market, hundreds of people milled about buying and selling, the women dressed in bright colors. On my last Wednesday there, I paid the equivalent of four dollars for fifty pounds of the tastiest tangerines, roping the basket to the outside of the helicopter taking me out. That was the year before Cronin and McNeely walked through Khandbari, a town I never thought I'd return to.

In the eighth chapter we meet the yeti. Cronin begins with a punch, presenting his authority, the statement of a veteran village hunter: "Oh, yes! We have many kinds of wild animals in these forests. There are bears, and musk deer, and yeti, and pandas, and leopards, and civets, and monkeys, and many, many more."[9]

A village hunter's status and livelihood depend upon jungle knowledge – not knowledge of speciation or scientific abnormalities or where to bag trophies, but of where what animals are when, how each can be killed, and how each will meet the needs of life in the village. A village hunter is part of a long-term information network on the state of the jungle. His father and his father's father have passed on stories about a particular tree, the changing bed of a stream, the changing populations of a bird. Village hunters I knew as a boy talked of the dangers of overhunting and tried not to disturb the jungle too much, for they knew their children must use it too.

All hunters have their own styles of storytelling, for telling stories is part of a hunter's skills. Some exaggerate; others understate. Neither style can be trusted when a day or two's employment with outsiders is involved.

Cronin is clearly trying to be careful. But this man, Cronin's key yeti informant, is never mentioned again. Why didn't Cronin use this hunter to find out more? Why not go out with him and have him show yeti habitat? Why not follow up and probe for facts of yeti behavior? Why let this guy walk right out of camp? Was the informant credible or not? We really don't learn much about him. Was he a real hunter, or just someone who dabbled at hunting when he couldn't get other work? Most real hunters double as porters when they can get high-paying work on Westerners' expeditions. This expedition's research area straddled the trail to Makalu. The hunter could have known of Westerners' interest in the yeti from previous work for mountaineers. Maybe he'd worked on Tom Slick's second or third expeditions in the upper Arun Valley fifteen years before.

Or maybe Cronin didn't really understand the hunter. His book never reveals how fluent any of the team were in Nepali. Fleming said that they were ex–Peace Corps types from Thailand, seemed good at languages, and got along in Nepali. But other indications are that the team members with the real dual fluency were their Sherpa guides. Maybe those Sherpas were more interested in making their employers happy than in precise translations. If a village hunter mentioned *bun manchi,* might not a Sherpa translate "jungle man" as "yeti"? What was the actual Nepali word this villager hunter used? Was it really *yeti?* Rather unlikely – yeti is not an Arun Valley word.

The fire has burned cold. I set the book down and go outside to bring in more wood. The night above is sharp and pure. As I look into its celestial mysteries, my eyes travel to sharp dazzling points of light burning so far away, and again the yearnings are kindled to solve the mystery of the yeti. How do people fit within the natural system? Do our limits stop here on this planet, or do they go beyond? Are we the only people? Or are there other people or spirits here on earth, or out there amid the stars? Our ancestors believed in prophets who carried the word to them from out there. Who are our informants, and how do we know they are credible? Inside ourselves we cannot tolerate dissonance. Things must make sense. What signs do we have to tell the true from the false?

Inside, as I put more wood on the fire, the shaking and stirring of new logs added to old breaks off charred crusts, and from the now-exposed burning coals, new flames burst up. Kneeling by the hearth, I ponder the flames. Wood in a fire is not immediately consumed. It burns and speaks of the eternal, the unpredictable, of the changing of hard substance into lifelike flame.

The logs seem to burn and not be consumed. Spruce Knob is not Mt. Horab —but there are eternal truths to be understood, a mountain set apart from a civilization that was left behind. Do we take the time to stop and ponder the mysteries signed to us by flickering fingers that speak strangely to us, or do we discard and call such signs we do not understand random? My instructions from such signs are private —like everyone's. Fires are filled with life in so many ways, as the breath of life, oxygen, mixes with relics of life, wood. For this quest before me I must be sensitive to the relationships of spirit with body, fact with myth, people with place, and of wildness with civilization.

I sit back on the sofa and again pick up Cronin's book. After presenting the hunter, Cronin reviews other yeti discoveries, and summarizes their search. Then, their own discovery:

> Shortly before dawn the next morning, Howard climbed out of our tent. Immediately, he called excitedly. There, beside the trail we had made to our tents, was a new set of footprints. While we were sleeping, a creature had approached our camp and walked directly between our tents. The Sherpas identified the tracks, without question, as yeti prints. We, without question, were stunned. . . .
>
> The prints measured approximately nine inches long by four and three-quarters inches wide. The stride, or distance between the individual prints, was surprisingly short, often less than one foot, and it appeared that the creature has used a slow, cautious walk along this section. The prints showed a short, broad opposable hallux, an asymmetrical arrangement of the toes, and a wide rounded heel. . . . Most impressively, their close resemblance to Shipton's prints was unmistakable.[10]

That night all night I dream about creatures with broad sloping foreheads peering through bamboo thickets, shaggy yetis, jogging away through the jungle, or disappearing across snowy wastelands of Himalayan passes, hominoid footprints with bulbous toes sharply outlined in snow and holding absolutely no mystery and my camera jamming as I try to take pictures.

Over breakfast the next morning I share my dreams with Jennifer. Having saved, dollar by dollar, for years to start our house, and having just completed three years of graduate work at Yale Divinity School, paid for partly with loans that will be around her neck for ten more years, Jennifer is not impressed. She has her own dreams: building a relationship, a home, a family.

With twenty years of schooling at last behind her, Jennifer feels her life opening with new freedom to pursue her own quests.

"Dan'l, life is a collection of choices. We chose to get out of that yurt, so we took our savings, designed this house. From here we can see forty-five miles across the forests, we can see our future opening with possibilities. Let's stay with the choices we've made, finish what we've started. The house shell is up, but that's all. We have no running water and no electricity. Soon we'll be snowed in on a mountaintop for three months, carrying our supplies in and out by backpack. Today we must start getting in windows to keep out the weather. And with all this still to be finished you talk about chasing after yetis?"

By November 10, the windows are in, and that night the temperature drops to ten degrees. Each day, struggling with building, I plan another aspect of the expedition. Two years and two months away, surely by January 1982, the house will be finished, and that date is not so far away that I can't live in hope. In the meantime, Jennifer is getting a home, and we're talking about a baby.

By early December 1979, ceiling, walls, and floor are finished. Jennifer reads Cronin's book and agrees that type of search might be fun – an adventure combined with a vacation – certainly a break from the hard work of institution building. By Christmas we know Jennifer is pregnant. Her question becomes: "How will a one-and-a-half-year-old do in the jungle with ticks and bedbugs?" I've slowed down on house building and gone back to earning dollars. By November 1980, our wind generator is in and working, water flows uphill to the house from the spring, we have lights in the evening, a washing machine, a refrigerator. There are no electricity bills, no water bills, no taxes, and no mortgage. We are almost self-sufficient. Most important of all, we now have Jesse Oak, born at home on a sunny afternoon on August 20, in our upstairs room beneath the butternut ceiling. Jennifer had planned carefully. Her sister, the nurse, was there too. That morning we walked over the meadows. The day was everything she could want it to be.

February 1, 1981. The United Nations has offered me consultancy in Nepal to design a project to help small shopkeepers. A special rate from Pan Am Airlines allows Jennifer and Jesse to travel with me from Washington, D.C., to Kathmandu for less than $400 extra. Now is our chance to see whether a vacation in the jungle with a baby is possible. After finishing my consultancy, we float down a river on the Nepal/India border in dugout canoes, through

Exploring the Barun ridge near the site of Cronin and McNeely's discovery

gentle rapids, through drenching rain, to a "lost" temple deep in overgrown trees and vines. Going back, we head out overland, taking broken-down buses and crossing two landslides. Jennifer and I get diarrhea. Throughout, childcare in the jungle, on the road, and in the air demands a slower pace. But as a family we have a vacation: no bedbugs, no ticks, and Jesse remains in good health.

By November 1, 1981, I have been working full time for almost a year. Our combined family income is not quite $20,000. The house is starting to look finished, but there's no possibility of getting enough funds together for an expedition in January. We postpone that for a year.

In October 1982, a United States–based consultancy provides a surprise windfall. We use half of it for a furnace and put aside the rest for the expedition. In the three and a half years since the tea party with the Flemings, on work trips to Kathmandu, I've ferried into Nepal as baggage three sixty-pound duffels of yeti-chasing supplies. The expedition, planned for January, will include Bob and Linda – Bob is key – but not Dan Terry. Terry will be working with his family amid the civil war in Afghanistan.

Before we leave home, I make another survey of yeti references, twenty-three in all. Most were wishful thinking, with irrelevant items strung together, travails belabored in attempts to give substance to discoveries. Descriptions aren't helpful: a baggy rear end, a villager's tale of a shaggy face, long dangling arms, color varying from red to black to brown, a pointed head with a long sloping forehead, thick bulging eyebrows, feet that are on backwards, a shuffling gait.

Why didn't Ward take more photographs? So much more could be deduced if we had a close-up from him or Shipton of the other foot, another picture showing the length of stride. Other photographs would show how consistently bipedal the animal was. And how much had the Shipton print been altered by snow melt?

Was it really possible that a relic of human evolution could retreat into the high valleys? Maybe, but only if the animal had intelligence approaching that of humans, and was indeed furry enough to withstand the cold at those elevations. These are big suppositions. The durable evidence remains the footprints, particularly those recorded by Shipton and Cronin. I know that the valleys of the world's largest mountain range are not untrammeled wilderness. The Himalaya is not as isolated as the American West and certainly not as wild as western Canada – where there really could be space enough for a Bigfoot or Sasquatch. From Pakistan to Bhutan, never have I seen a Himalayan valley without at least one village, and never have I seen a Himalayan slope free of a human trail. With such human penetration, why have only footprints of the yeti been found?

The possibility that the yeti is still hiding in the Himalaya has gnawed against my rational mind for twenty-nine years. So much suggests that its existence is unlikely. But Bob saw those casts, and they were unlike anything he could explain. Inside me, that sixth sense still speaks, calling to search the last valley. What is it I search for? Is it the yeti? Or is it some hidden, wild part of me? If I find the yeti, will I also find myself?

Even though this is not Jennifer's dream, I think she understands better than I that deeper quest. My wild chase, although it might become a grand adventure, is going to demand a lot of her.

Like shadows, footprints are outlines of life. A hunter does not shoot an animal by shooting its shadow. Nor is the yeti discovered by photographing its footprint.

Chapter Eight

January 1983. Jennifer and I, along with two-year-old Jesse and his twenty-year-old uncle, Nick (just graduated from college and intent on adventure), are in Kathmandu for another tea at Bob and Linda's.

In two days, we'll catch the bush plane to Tumlingtar and start the trek to the Barun Valley. Taking Jesse into the densest jungle of the Himalaya gnaws at Jennifer. During those twenty-six hours in airplane seats and airports, she never challenged our decision aloud, but the questions in her mind were clear: What if something goes wrong? Do we really know well enough how to use our medical kit? Is it smart to pick the most remote of Himalayan valleys? Not answering these questions, I've made cracks about the wisdom of raising children in a skyscraper apartment. She points out that we've never proposed to do that. Yet she is here now in Kathmandu, caught up in the current of this adventure. Seeking clues that might help resolve our mystery, she asks Bob to explain what he knows about what Nepalis think of the yeti.

"Most Nepalis, like us, don't have firsthand yeti evidence, only the stories they've heard," Bob says. "Almost every Nepali has heard a yeti story or two. Some are outrageous. Most Westerners think of the yeti as living in the snows above the Sherpa villages, where yeti stories are most common. But I'd love to know whether forty years ago, before Westerners began asking yeti questions, before Shipton's photograph gave tangible substance to their legend, the yeti was really such a topic among the Sherpas. Anyway, the feature Sherpas always mention is that the yeti has backward feet, toes that point away from the direction in which it's walking, a deception it has developed to trick the uninformed."

"Has any Sherpa ever offered concrete proof of a foot with toes spun 180 degrees?" Nick asks.

"Certain Sherpas, usually a yak herder or shepherd out with the flocks, do report seeing yetis, but as far as I can determine those are always reports of reports. When I ask Sherpas, typically I hear, 'Myself, I've not seen, but my father saw when he was a boy with the yak high up in the pastures.' The most famous of these parental reports is from the Everest climber, Tenzing Norgay."

"But, Bob," Nick says, "isn't the consistently controlled falling forward that we call walking a way of moving that belongs only to humans? How could this highly developed characteristic, one of the most mechanically sophisticated features among all animals, which includes a lot more than feet, but also such paraphernalia as kneecaps, continue to work if the feet were turned around? Evolution doesn't produce something as intricate as walking, then turn it around 180 degrees simply for deception. The backward foot story seems physiologically impossible. Doesn't that prove that the yeti is just myth – just as reports that the yeti moves by flying carpet would?"

"You're right about the physics of walking, Nick. It is something only humans do well. The foot is an exceedingly complex body part. Remember, I'm only telling yeti stories, as Jenny requested. Be open-minded; maybe the stories are false while the yeti is true. Maybe the backward print of a yeti walking away is actually a print of one coming forward. Maybe the feet are straight forward and the story backward."

"The backward prints give a magical aspect to maybe a common, even well-known animal," I add. "The magic gives the larger-than-life attributes that make the yeti so usefully sensational in Sherpa culture. If the yeti is an ordinary bear or monkey, dressing it through stories makes it into a superhero. Much about the yeti is clearly myth and fabrication. Clearly too, there are hard yeti facts, such as footprints."

"Right," says Bob. "Sherpas use the word *yeti,* but they also use the Tibetan word *me tay.* The *me tay* is reportedly very fast, can outrun a human, and lives in rocky mountains, which is biologically strange, of course, since rocky mountains don't have much food, and further, if *me tay* did in fact live there, they would be more easily seen. One of *me tay*'s reported favorite foods is live frogs – which is also strange, since frogs don't live in high rocky mountains. Amphibians above 7,000 feet in the Himalaya are rare – there is too much temperature fluctuation. Anyway, Sherpas say that when you cross a stream and find much mud and disturbance in the water, you know *me tay* is up-stream rooting around for frogs.

"*Me tay* are reported to live above the line of cultivation, above 10,000 feet, so they don't really interact with farmers. Herders, not farmers, are therefore those who talk about *me tay* and their stories deal with disappearing yaks and sheep. *Me tay* can grow ten feet tall and are superstrong. When they attack, they come into a herd, sling a three-hundred-pound yak over their shoulder, and walk off. I've always found it strange, though, *me tay* never kill and eat these yaks where the remains can be found." Bob smiles wryly, leans forward, checks everyone's cup, then refills his own.

"This *me tay* sounds like a first-rate cover story of a mafia of yak poachers," says Nick. "They creep up during the night, make their tracks appear to be coming when they're actually going, zip in, grab a yak, maybe dye the coat to hide its identity, and bang, they're one yak richer."

Bob laughs. "Nick, you've solved the yeti mystery, a yak-rustling conspiracy in the Himalaya, organized crime!"

I reach over and pick up a biscuit. "Thirty miles from the Sherpa Valley, on the other side of Everest and behind the Great Himalaya, the yak herders in Tibet put a rather different twist on those stories. They too claim that the *me tay* lives in rocky mountains. It is brown, bigger than a yak, and walks at its pleasure on either two or four feet. But there is no mention of reversed feet, and I've never heard Tibetans distinguish between *me tay* gender or mention frog eating. The Tibetan *me tay* reportedly loves the high-altitude yellow mushroom. It's also a real digger, burrowing into the soil for both tubers and marmots. The Tibetan *me tay* is aggressive; it attacks animals that are grazing or caravans on the trail by rolling boulders down onto them, making the yaks or sheep stampede. But if it attacks people, it does so only one-on-one, using no boulders or rocks. When you're attacked, there is only one thing to do: run downhill. A *me tay* can't keep up, not only because its back legs are longer than its front ones – note, by the way, that this indicates it prefers four feet over two for traveling – but also because when running downhill its long facial

*Local herder
and his
animals*

hair falls forward, covering its eyes. But despite such attack stories, the animal is supposed to have a soft heart. Several times I've heard that *me tay* do not attack human children."

"Does the Tibetan *me tay* have the high wailing screech Sherpas attribute to it?" Bob asks. "The scream sounds supernatural. It fills a valley at night, driving everyone indoors. A number of people I've talked to have heard this sound. One can question stories, stolen yaks, backward feet, and such, but the most convincing local yeti evidence I've heard are these screech reports. Too many people, including Westerners, have heard this high wail, and they also describe it identically. Some thing, not imagination, makes this sound."

"Comparing descriptions of sounds is hard," I reply. "The Tibetan description I'm familiar with compares the *me tay* sound with that of a high-pitched horse, only they talk of it as vibrating. It can be heard both day and night. Is a horse whinny the same as the Sherpa sound?"

"I've never heard Sherpas compare it to a horse, Dan'l. But Sherpas don't use horses, don't even have them, whereas Tibetans use horses the way we use cars."

"Could the sound be wild horses?" Nick asks. "Maybe there are wild mustangs up in the cliffs."

"Not in Sherpa country, Nick," Bob tells him. "Habitat is also wrong for the Tibetan wild ass, which would be easily spotted. One of the goat types maybe, but not a horse. No, your yak rustlers is a better try."

"There must be other yeti stories," Jennifer says. "What do other Nepalis say?"

Bob shifts into his teaching mode. "From Nepali ethnic groups living adjacent to some Sherpa communities come reports of an animal called *needene*. All *needene* stories are of females, rather awesome figures with fantastic pendulous breasts sometimes two feet long. When *needene* run they flip these breasts over their shoulders so they don't smack into each other.

"*Needene* are on the lookout for children. When they find a child to kidnap, the animal first touches the child. That touch makes the child speechless. Then the *needene* carries the child to her cave where she keeps up to several children at a time. The caves are high in rocky areas, high above valleys. When *needene* leave the cave to search for food or more children, the spell of dumbness departs. Children then cry. Their sounds are not high-pitched screeches but long plaintive wailings. Down below in the valleys parents can hear their children calling. If the *needene* comes back soon, the children will be there in the caves, hungry. The *needene* brings them ugly insects to eat. If the *needene* does not return soon, the children will wander off searching for food, and their parents then find them. When children are thus recovered, they are confused, stumbling around among rocks and rhododendron. But if slowly fed ash soup they recover their former nature."

"Whoa! That's some yeti story!" Nick exclaims.

Bob smiles. "Yes, it's incredible. But when you push the story, it's clear these Nepalis consider *needene* a spirit, not a real creature. Figuring out how the Sherpas, on the other hand, draw the line between reality and myth is much harder; with them it's not clear which side of the line *me tay* is on. Usually, the *me tay* seems a real animal, but at other times their descriptions sound spiritlike."

Jennifer, the student of theology, breaks in. "For the Tibetans the line between physical and supernatural is not solid as it is for us in the West. Tibetans see both physical and supernatural forms as reality, as complementary and harmonious states in which a spirit can dwell alternately or simultaneously – or it can remain in only one. Reality, they believe, is conditioned by our imperfect understanding. That which appears concrete is an illusion, and these illusions create reflections that mask the true identity of that which is indeed real. Our Western inability to accept such dual and constantly changing realities may be the key to our inability to accept the yeti."

"Well," Bob continues, "the Nepalis along the rim of the Barun Valley, whose jungle we will soon visit, have another perception of the yeti. They call it *shockpa* or sometimes *po gamo*. *Po gamo* is a strong spirit that takes physical form from time to time. But it is aggressive, attacking people, even homes at night, also domestic animals. What it does after it attacks or why it attacks is not clear, but *po gamo* gives concrete form to villagers' fears of the unknown of the jungle. Villagers invest tremendous energy in protecting themselves from virulent spirits. Weapons don't help – forget the knife, forget the gun. Protection comes from substances possessing power, from even tiny amounts of gunpowder folded up in a piece of paper or from batteries. A worn out battery or even its carbon core holds enough latent power to ward off *po gamo*. Maybe each of us should carry a flashlight in our pockets as we enter the Barun. Our porters, I bet, will carry a dead battery somewhere in their clothes."

"Bob," I break in, "I've heard *po gamo/shockpa* stories over the years. Those stories describe a creature that's pretty real. Tashi, the head of our medical expedition field staff, camped once at the mouth of the Barun Valley, and during the night the walls of the hut he and six villagers were in began to tremble. Some animal was shaking the door by butting it with its head, shaking the walls by rubbing against them. Tashi and the others woke up and stayed huddled in their blankets, afraid the beast would crash in. Tashi is not an ignorant villager. He's a trained pharmacist and prides himself on his scientific understanding. Tashi suddenly sprang out of his sleeping bag, grabbed a flashlight, yanked open the door, and heard the *shockpa* run off to the edge of the jungle. He wasn't able to catch it in the spot of his light, but as he swept the darkness, the animal screamed, a piercing shriek that petrified everyone. All the men were riveted and motionless listening to that long-drawn-out shriek. 'Like the eagle's scream,' Tashi said later, 'but drawn longer, vibrating more.' He said the door of that hut didn't open again until well after the morning's sun had completely removed the shadows of night.

"Tashi thinks the *shockpa* is a real animal, one that can be caught. He reports that for many years in the village of Shakshila, above the confluence of the Barun and Arun Rivers, there lived a man who once fought a *shockpa* and killed it. The man was a lama, so it's unclear whether the fight was physical or spiritual, but after it was all over the lama had a physical *shockpa* arm bone as proof of his victory. He used the bone in his religious ceremonies. When he died the bone was sold to another lama. Tashi describes it as like a langur monkey's arm bone but longer and thinner."

"That story interests me," Bob says. "The Tamang here in central Nepal claim that their medicine men, *jankris,* are taught their trade by beasts from the jungle such as this *shockpa.* The Tamangs call these jungle people *bun jankri,* which translates as forest witch doctor. It is interesting, this repeated link between wild man, yeti, *po gamo,* or whatever, and the medical and spiritual community leaders."

"I see some intriguing links," Nick says. "There is no agreement and little interest even in what the animal eats or what it looks like or how big it is or its feet. Those are points they use to dress up a story, which only interest us — and undermine its credibility. Yet two consistent threads do run through these stories. First, the animal is celibate; there's no mention in any of these stories of sexual activity, or of a pair living together, or of sexual attacks on local village girls or boys. And second, the animal lives so often in high rocky areas. Why, then, are we on our trip looking down low in the jungles? Perhaps we'd have more success hunting caves in those high rocky areas."

Bob smiles. "Interesting, Nick. The cave hypothesis keeps coming up. More tea, anyone?"

Chapter Nine

The next day I walk into the Royal Nepal Airlines ticket office. "Please reserve all available seats on Monday's flight to Tumlingtar."

"Your names, sir?"

"Here, let me write them for you."

Taylor-Ide, Jennifer; Taylor-Ide, Jesse, youth fare, age two years; Taylor-Ide, Daniel; Ide, Nicholas; lama, Pasang; sherpa, Nuru; tent/duffel one; food/duffel two; sleeping/duffel three.

"But, sir, the last three are not names of people."

"They are our supplies. We wish to buy seats for our equipment. We have big bags that will fill an airplane seat and be held by a seat belt. They weigh too much to be taken just as luggage; isn't the allowance for accompanying baggage on these small airplanes only ten kilos per person?"

"I understand; you request baggage seats. But, sir, you don't actually need to put the bags in the seats."

"If we list the bags as people rather than baggage, then you won't sell these seats to other people and off-load our bags until a later flight."

"OK, I understand. Do you want these luggages registered as foreigners or as Nepalis?"

"What's the difference?"

"Foreigners may weigh up to 90 kgs. Nepalis may weigh up to 60 kgs. Foreigners cost double, but you get 30 more kilos."

"Count them as Nepalis."

Four days later, arriving at the airport an hour before the flight, we find that our three baggage seats have been sold. My protests keep getting shunted aside, and the departure time creeps forward.

"Sir, you cannot book a suitcase as a person. Of course such a seat will be sold to a person if a real person wants to travel."

"But I have done this type of booking before."

"I was not checking in that flight, sir. If you had been here two hours before this departure, before I sold the other seats, then I would not have sold yours. If you and I had some private talk, you and I could have made a special arrangement, sir. I am sorry. The plane is leaving in twenty minutes, sir."

We decide fast which bags to leave behind. Nuru, our cook's helper, is bumped. He will come on the next flight in two days with the delayed bags. We put two duffels in the seat reserved for him; our ten kilos each allows us two more. I talk to the pilot who says that the plane is a little under gross and he is willing to allow a few pounds more; that's another duffel. On this flight, then, we get five of our nine duffes.

Opening bags, resorting clothes, I put aside all the high-altitude gear for Nuru and the later flight. "Those two tents stay, Nick, and that duffel of food."

Jennifer is single-minded. "Whatever else you leave, bring everything of Jesse's. Bring everything. We don't know what he might need."

"Sir, the pilot is ready to take off now. The plane is leaving."

We carry our bags out to the aircraft and load them into the luggage bay. I cinch the cargo net tight and slip a ten-rupee tip to the airline staff member who helped. A fifty-minute flight east from Kathmandu, past the Solu Khumbu Valley of Mount Everest, and we land in Tumlingtar, one of the few places where the Arun Valley is wide enough to accommodate an airstrip. The Arun Valley, some say, is the world's second deepest – with 24,000 vertical feet from the summits of Lhotse and Makalu to the river. The Arun, unlike most of the rivers in the Himalayan chain, starts on the north and cuts through the tallest mountains on earth, a testimony to the power of running water.

Standing there in Tumlingtar and looking up, I am awed by the gigantic geologic uplift that the Himalaya represents, the largest on this planet in one billion years. Less than fifty million years ago, Tibet was lowland, oceanfront property. Then, over the past forty million years, big pieces of earth's surface started to move by a shifting of the planet's crust, breaking away from Africa and bringing up off the ocean's floor the plate that we now call India into violent collision with Asia.

The Himalaya are formed by three different types of meetings of these land forms. In some places, India slid under and lifted up the Asian plate; in still other places the earth's crust folded, like a carpet being pushed back; in other places Indian geology was inserted into Asia. The collision of one continent into another generated massive lifting up of a land mass about half the size of the contiguous United States from below sea level to heights over seven miles above the sea floor at which it started. (Mount Everest is now five and a half miles above sea level.)

Intense heat followed by major geological cooling melted and contorted many of the Himalaya rocks. By eight million years ago the structure of the Himalaya in its present form was complete. Although shifting still occurs as India rotates counterclockwise against Asia, and further uplift is happening, the processes of mountain erosion and decline are now also setting in, the washing of rains, the sliding of steep slopes, and the carrying down of rivers. The Arun River has flowed out of Tibet in the same streambed during all those fifty millions of years, maintaining and wearing down its bed while the mountains grew around its coursing waters.

Pasang, our cook, has hired a villager to carry in jugs of water while he starts supper. Nick and I set up the tent under an enormous fig tree behind the thatch tea shop just off the edge of the grass runway.

Then the shock hits. We inventory all our baggage. Jesse's only extra clothes are the spare T-shirt and one diaper that Jennifer always carries in her purse. Jesse's duffel of clothes has been left behind. He will have to run around bare-bottomed like a Nepali kid until his bags arrive. We are at an 1,800-foot elevation, so the climate here is tropical and he doesn't really need much covering.

"I think we'll keep the diaper unused," Jennifer says, looking at me. "We might need it to double as a big bandage if someone gets bitten by a yeti."

Two days later, the Wednesday plane bounces in across the grass landing-field. The goats that keep the field mowed scatter. Since I am friends now with the airport staff, security systems are more casual, and I approach the twin-engine bush plane while its propellers are still turning and join an employee unloading baggage from the nose compartment. He smiles and throws bags at me. The passenger door opens, and out step seventeen Japanese tourists from YETI TRAVELS & TOURS. Nuru, our cook's helper, has been bumped by their large group. But the airline employee finds one of our duffels in the back of the plane. I take it to our camp under the big fig tree. Jesse runs up dressed in the spare T-shirt, accompanied by two other bare-bottomed kids. The new duffel is food. Jennifer says nothing.

It will be two more days until the next flight, but Nuru is clearly at work; he got one bag here. Three more to come. We'll start to trek without Jesse's stuff, since it will take six days of walking to reach the Barun. If we leave now we can still fit in four hours of walking before nightfall. Nuru will walk faster than we; he should catch us before we reach the Barun. Bob and Linda will be along a week later.

I hoist Jesse onto my shoulders, and we set off. Fifteen minutes out, the trail cuts up sharply. With Jesse on my shoulders, leaning, wiggling, getting restless, can I really keep up the pace? I release his legs, let my arms drop. He's going to have to learn to ride me like a horse, holding on with his legs. He turns and calls back to his mother and the reply comes from her between puffs. "Jesse, Mama can't talk now. She's walking." The hill is steep and taking its toll on Jennifer and on all of us. Four hours later we walk through the market square in Khandbari, where in 1971 I bought the tangerines. An hour later, as the setting sun reddens, we arrive at camp. Pasang has been there for an hour, the tents are up; supper's nearly ready. I swing Jesse off my shoulders as Pasang smilingly holds out a mug of hot tea.

After supper we light a candle in what the Eureka Tent Company calls a six-person tent, although three adults and a two-year-old getting settled fill it up. As I roll out and unzip sleeping bags, Pasang calls from outside, "Sahib, sahib, Nuru aiyo." I burst out of the tent, incredulous. Nuru's here! After we left Tumlingtar airfield, an unscheduled charter arrived. Nuru and our remaining duffels were on that. Guessing there would be extra space, he even included a forty-pound basket of fresh carrots, turnips, and cauliflowers. Now we are prepared for three months in the field.

The next day, with the village of Bhotebas three hours behind, we cross the first ridge and look out over the upper Arun Valley. The village of Num is below; the village of Hedangna lies across the valley. At the head of the valley is the fifth-highest mountain on earth, Makalu, its subzero rock and ice soaring five miles above sea level. Snow blows off upward, the snow plume like a white flag above puffy white cumulus. Makalu is notorious for its terrible weather; only four expeditions have walked on its summit. Beyond stands Lhotse, fourth highest, and behind that, Everest.

I swing Jesse off my shoulders. He runs after three yellow butterflies with black lines in their wings. The air here smells exceptionally sweet. Sitting with my back against a rock, I suddenly crave toast and a cup of tea.

A porter comes up the trail from the direction of Num, ascending with short strides as he rounds the bend and climbs the carefully placed stairlike rocks. His body is bent under two gigantic bundles of tree bark held onto his back by a woven rope strap passed around his forehead. Cinnamon! Stopping to rest his load on our stone wall, he releases the strain off his tump line and gives a long, high whistle, the universal sign throughout Nepal that your load is heavy.

"Where are you going?" I ask.

"To Hille … then to Dharan by the big truck if prices in Hille are too low."

"Did you cut the cinnamon, or are you carrying it for someone else?" I ask.

"It's mine, from some trees I know. Slowly I've been gathering it. I do not

Jennifer & Jesse

DANIEL TAYLOR-IDE

take too much from one tree because then next year I cannot go back. Nowadays, some people are too selfish. They take all the bark from the same tree; then the tree dies."

"Big load you have. It must be two people's load," I answer.

"Three loads, sahib."

One hundred eighty pounds.

"Why don't you get one of your children to help carry? Three people's load is too much for the bones and joints of an old man. Your knees will soon hurt like doors that swing on rusty hinges if you continue to walk downhill with that much weight. Then you must stop walking and will have to just sit by your house. After so many years, and walking down so many hills, three loads is too heavy for a man like you."

"Last year, sahib, one more of my children died. Many children have died, so I have left my other two children at home to stay with my wife."

"What happened last year?" Jennifer asks.

"Last year the sickness of children came. For six years it had not come. But last year it came back. You know the children's sickness, the one with fever."

"What does he mean?" Jennifer whispers to me.

"Measles," I whisper back. "Villagers call it the sickness of children because only the children get it. It sweeps these villages in waves every five to seven years, infects all children who have not had it, then comes back when there's a new group of children who aren't immune."

"Two children still are left, one son, one daughter. To God I pray my son does not die, because the sickness of children came last year. He got it and almost died, as did one daughter last year."

"If your son has had the children's sickness, he will never get it again," I reply.

"Yes, that I know. But my wife and I, we worry . . . and besides, he might get another sickness. So thankful we were it was not our son who died, but three daughters we have lost and maybe more someday. My wife is younger than I and still strong, soon will be having another baby. Is that your son down there running?"

"Yes, that is our son," I answer. "You should take your son and daughter to town. There the doctor has medicine to protect them from the sickness of children and also other sicknesses."

"You be careful, sahib, with your son. Why do you bring such a lovely son into this bad place? Why not keep your son home where he can be safe?"

"What happened to your three daughters who died?" Jennifer asks in Nepali.

"The youngest died last year. She and my son both had fever at the same time. The daughter was three, my son was eight."

Nick has been calculating the reported six-year cycle. "Why didn't your son get the strong fevers six years ago, when the children's sickness came before?"

"My wife and I never understood that. Last time six years ago another daughter, age six, died, but our son did not get sick."

"The almost two-year-old boy and the little girl would both have been nursing; he was clearly getting preferential treatment over the newborn girl, probably still also protected somewhat by his mother's immunities," Jennifer whispers. "Dan'l, his family must be doing something terribly wrong when measles strikes. Their children get hit hard. What are they not doing? Hydration? Shouldn't we tell him something?"

"Sahib, now can I go?" The porter is getting uncomfortable; I wonder if we've been asking too many questions.

"Yes, my friend, you walk slowly with that big load. Use a stick when you walk downhill; that will save your knees with such a load. Buy some of those rubber-thonged sandals with cushioned soles in Dharan. They will save your knees. We also will go now."

The porter lifts the tump line up from his shoulders and puts it over his head, positions the webbing across his forehead, and, holding it where the strap passes both ears, bends into the 180-pound load. As he starts off up the hill, two bony and aging legs pump underneath. The cinnamon bundles creak and squeak as they adjust to their own weight; their sweet smell, reminding me again of breakfast toast, lingers in the air. The man weighs less than the load he carries. It will take him another week of carrying to reach Hille. To get his price, he might travel all the way to India with his bundles. I hope a "friend" does not get him drunk one night in one of those border towns – the bundles will be gone by morning.

After supper we sit talking. We have made a 6,000-foot descent from last night's camp on the ridge to 2,600 feet here by the banks of the Arun. Pasang and Nuru are close by the fire eating their supper. The steep walls of the canyon narrow here, providing as ideal a spot as I've seen in the Himalaya for a hydroelectric dam. A strong wind rushes down the canyon above the water, carrying air that was cold and dry as it started falling with the river from Tibet, but has now grown moist after passing over the thick vegetation and the warmer water of the Arun Valley.

As the mists of sleep settle over me I think about these hardy peoples living in harmony with their land, living for generations in the same place. It is easy to believe that they must be sensitive to that environment, allowing them to cope with change without destroying the land that gives them almost all that they have. The cinnamon porter's careful harvesting of his trees certainly suggests such knowledge. It seems the more people understand how harsh their life is, the more careful they are. They put away reserves – like squirrels putting away nuts. Knowledge of hardship breeds resilience. Unless, of course, they are desperate and cannot put anything away. Then they will even eat the seeds needed to plant next year's harvest.

The next day we stop for lunch on a high knoll looking up an extremely steep valley. "There must be 300 homes on that slope and thousands of terraces," Nick exclaims. "Look at them. The hillside is almost collapsing under the pressure of human settlement. Why don't families reduce the number of their children? Small families are obviously better."

"A small family may not survive," I tell him. "Take the Nepali family in that mud house below us, a family representative, perhaps, of 80 percent of this country's population. More children mean more help not only in planting, weeding, and harvesting the fields, but also for full-time herding, which may mean they can keep a water buffalo or two, and a buffalo means a regular milk supply and young water buffalo to sell. More children provide maybe a full-time water carrier, and families need help carrying water when the spring near the house goes dry and water must be brought in jugs a two-hour walk from the river.

"More children mean more labor to clear terraces, and as they get older to work as porters bringing cash income. Cash makes a big difference in their lives. Here, more children mean more labor; in America, more children mean greater costs, as children must be invested in to be able to compete."

"It's more than economics," Jennifer adds. "Remember what we heard from the cinnamon porter? Think of the insurance many children bring to that family. Despite deaths, some children will probably survive. There will be children to care for parents when they get old.

"And think of the mothers' hearts. With so many of the children she bears dying, the life of a Nepali mother must be a continual saga of sorrow. Think of her fears each day while she watches them play yet knows that tomorrow those lives might be taken away."

Rested, looking up at the knoll that seems to rise off the ridge like a rhino's horn, we can see that the trail we must walk makes a short steep climb up ahead. The four of us start off again. Tonight our camp will be at the Barun.

Chapter Ten

As we walked up the Arun Valley and neared the Barun, we could hear a roar ahead. We are among the first Westerners to be allowed into the lower Barun Valley. For three years I've checked out the Barun on every map I could find, none of which was made by an actual survey team. Even in 1983 most maps of the Himalaya are derived from field sketches drafted by British spies who sneaked into the closed valleys in the 1920s or before. Barun maps are even more speculative, based on deduction: If the river falls 11,000 vertical feet while traveling only fourteen miles from the glaciers of Makalu and Lhotse to the Arun it must be traveling so fast as to cut a straight line. Are there really no bends in this river? Is there really only one tributary?

Looking down into the gorge, we can see it for ourselves. The Barun is only twenty feet across. But the trembling of the rocks under my feet tells me this is a river, not a creek. It descends within a channel cut through rock, a river without banks. But there is a mystery here. The walls show that the water level rises at most only five feet during the year – not much for the fiftyfold increase in volume it likely carries during the monsoons. So to carry the flow the river must work like a natural pipe. It doesn't need to be wide; the monsoon just makes the water rush harder, like a fire hose when the pumper truck turns up the pressure.

I'd talked to Cronin on the phone about the Barun Valley. "Full of bears and bamboo," he said. "Unbelievable. We hacked a trail for days and got only miles." He was right. Looking up the valley, I see that the slopes are too steep to ascend – more than 60 degrees. If we're going to go up into the Barun, we must go high and around, climbing thousands of vertical feet. My altimeter says I'm standing at 3,100 feet and my map shows that the ridge tops are 10,000 feet, rising to 14,000. Someplace between the river and the ridges we have to find a trail.

We pay off our six porters. Eager to return, they literally run back down the trail. It took us five days of trekking to come this far; their families will probably greet them tomorrow. Here at the confluence of my dreams I sit with Jesse, Jennifer, Nick, Pasang, and Nuru. Depression strikes. How can our feeble contingent unravel the mystery we've come to solve? Grow up, Dan'l. The yeti is about as real as Peter Rabbit – both never die, eternally slipping under the gate just as you are about to catch them.

The narrow Himalayan valley ahead of us is ugly. Seven landslides are within sight of our camp. The river roaring yards away sounds more like the flushing of a high-pressure institutional toilet than a watercourse of adventure. The villages perched on epauletted slopes up and down the valley are the most primitive I've seen. Even the living conditions of the people are depressing, made worse by their increasing numbers, failing crops, and sliding fields, communities struggling to survive another season and avoid another famine. For the land and people, there seems no hopeful future.

The reality is that none of us knows what we're doing. I yearn for some hard knowledge – and know that such seldom ever exists. Where is Fleming? Seeking this animal is his idea too. What should I do? This isn't Eden – nor is there a mother with camomile tea waiting for me when I awaken from this fantasy.

Our first and second days pass with busywork, setting up camp, checking supplies, the simple routines. At the end of the second day, in the dwindling light, reorganization work is basically complete, so I walk the cliff above the confluence, wishing an answer would somehow reveal itself. I feel guilty about having brought the group here. We've reached the end of the known trail and now we must head into the unknown jungle. I look at the running river, wishing some magical instructions would be hiding in a cleft in the sandbank under that large fir tree by the shore. But I know the answer; I must listen to the local people. They know what is in their jungles.

Early the next day, still in my sleeping bag, I hear Pasang getting the cookfire going. I slip out to chat with him. As I step into the freshness of the morning, I see standing on a rock fifty yards away a silent, scraggly bearded man of the jungle dressed in green, a muzzleloading rifle upright beside him. His eyes are uncovering the secrets of our camp. He seems both afraid of us and curious. Holding out a mug of tea, I motion to him to come down. He vanishes into the bushes. Pasang works the cookfire, blowing on the coals. Two minutes later, the stranger strides into camp. How has he moved so quickly and silently from the rock above to where he walked out of the bushes? Where is the muzzleloader?

I can't take my eyes off his feet. They are feet of the earth. All through my childhood I have seen barefooted mountaineers, their feet thick with calluses, toes splayed wide like bird's claws, feet forming to the ground they touch. But these feet are different. The toes are not on top of the earth; they have slipped aside several pebbles and reached to the stone underneath. There is something about those feet that suggest the dexterity of hands – also, that this is a man who has a way of always seeking a secure footing.

Nestled in the coals, Pasang's teapot gurgles as hot water swirls the tea leaves around. It is that cold time of day after sunrise, before the sun has burned through the damp, chilly air rising from the river. I hunker down by Pasang's cookfire. The stranger watches Pasang pour milk into a fresh mug of tea and ostentatiously add a double serving of sugar. I look at him by way of his feet. The toes move. Is he nervous – or is he poised for action?

Pasang finishes stirring in the double helping of sugar and holds out the mug. The jungle man squats, joining us. We are an incongruous trio: a man who owns a muzzleloader, therefore certainly a village poacher; a former Tibetan nomad now working as a cook; and a white hunter seeking something. Soon Nick joins us, closing the circle on the other side of the fire. Pasang stirs up two more mugs of sweet milky tea for Nick and himself.

"Where is your village?" I ask.

"Shakshila."

"Where is that?"

"Up the ridge."

"Where have you come from?"

"Oh, sahib, I've just been walking."

"What is your name, my jungle friend?"

"Lendoop."

"Why do you carry a gun, Lendoop?"

"I don't."

"What was that we saw you with?"

"Why are you people here? Why do you come?"

"We are looking for animals in the Barun Valley."

"You won't find them."

"Why?"

"Because you cannot go into the Barun."

"But we have permits to go there."

"That doesn't matter, you still won't go."

"Why?"

"There is no trail. You sahib folks cannot walk without a trail."

"Why?"

"Because there is no trail."

"Can we make a trail? It is only jungle."

"You won't know where to put the trail."

"Can we find people who will know where to put a good trail, people who can help us make it?"

"How much will you pay?"

"Twenty rupees per day."

"You won't find anybody."

"How much is required?"

"Thirty-five rupees per day."

"Maybe we'll pay twenty-five."

Talk stops. Lendoop looks into his mug. It is empty. Pasang moves to fill it. Lendoop smiles with the second helping of sugar. Pasang adds a third.

I resume my questioning. "What animals are in the jungle?" I ask.

"All types."

"Like what types?"

"Serow" (a donkey-sized, red-brown mountain goat with white legs).

"What else?"

"Ghoral" (the Himalayan chamois).

"Others?"

"Red panda, leopard, wild boar, barking deer, musk deer, bear, snow leopard, tahr, three types of monkeys."

"Blue sheep?"

"No. In Thumdum (two valleys east) there are these animals."

"Any jackals?"

"Sometimes, not always."

"What animals do you hunt?"

"I don't hunt."

"Are there any small cats in the jungle?"

"Yes, two types of jungle cat."

"Any fish in the river?"

"In the Arun, yes. In the Barun, no. The Barun is too fast. The Barun is a dangerous river."

"Are there wild men in the jungle, *bun manchi?*"

"No."

Lendoop looks at the bottom of his cup. Pasang fills it again, and again adds three spoonfuls of sugar.

"Any villages in the Barun Valley?"

"How can there be villages? I told you there are no trails," he says scornfully.

"Do you ever go into the jungle?"

"No, there is no need."

"How do you get your meat to eat?"

"We kill a sheep or goat."

"Isn't it cheaper to shoot a wild animal with your gun?"

Lendoop is silent for several seconds. This conversation is going nowhere and Lendoop is clearly a smart man. He knows what I want. Finally, he breaks off a twig and with it draws several arching lines in the dirt. Pointing to the longest, he says, "This is the Barun. Big mountains are here, high above the valley floor, all ice and snow. Makalu is here. Another big mountain, Lhotse, is here." At each of these places he makes a check mark. "Halfway down, another river, the Mangrwa, joins in like this. At the top of the Mangrwa there are no big mountains. There is a low pass into Tibet. It is easy to cross, and there are never any border guards. After the Mangrwa and Barun join, there are some streams closer to us, like this, the Hinju and the Piranee."

The sketch is simple and also different from any U.S., British, or even secret Indian Army map. Here before me, I suspect, in this sketch in the dirt, is accurate cartography of the Barun.

"How long would it take to walk to where the Mangrwa and Barun meet?"

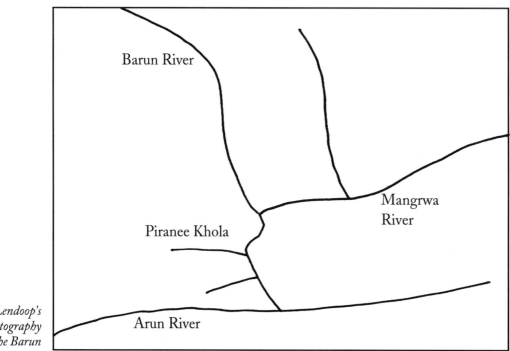

Lendoop's cartography of the Barun

"You cannot. There is not a trail."

"How long does it take you?"

"One day."

"How long if you take us?"

"If you are strong and we make a trail, three days."

"Three days? We can walk to Khandbari in three days!"

"No you can't. It took you four days to get from Khandbari to here, and one day before that."

He is right, of course. Our movements must have been daily communicated throughout the valley, particularly among people headed to the Barun. Probably not even once a year do Westerners probe this far into the Arun.

"Do people ever find *shockpa* or *po gamo* in the jungle?"

"No," says Lendoop. "*Shockpa* is not an animal." The statement is simple and ends firmly. Like a glass of ice-cold springwater on a hot day, the news runs through me and feels like the truth. Is it the end of my quest? With his teacup now empty, Lendoop suddenly stands and walks out through the brush. I remain, squatting by the fire.

All this way to search for "the something," and now finally we're here and the animal doesn't exist. I have kept saying that the villagers would know. What a horrible waste of money. Nick heard the big question. His Nepali is good enough to understand Lendoop's "no." As I talk with Nick, wondering whether he's angry at being brought here for nothing, he responds that this is all part of the quest. The value of this expedition lies in solving a mystery, the answer to which is hidden somewhere. There is an explanation to the yeti mystery more than debunking it as myth; something made those footprints. Lendoop's "no" is not the end of the search, only another layer in the plot.

ALTHOUGH WE STATE THE METHOD DIFFERENTLY, OUR RESPECT FOR village perceptions is what a self-appointed group is now calling the cryptozoological method, the science of learning what native peoples know about animals. Richard Greenwell, secretary of the International Cryptozoological Society, told me before we departed, "Dig for the information hidden in local knowledge. Sometimes this knowledge coincides with our own . . . and sometimes it doesn't . . . The fun of cryptozoology is trying to determine if native peoples are right or wrong."

That evening two other hunters come into camp to drink tea by the fire. They always hunt together, they say, because they share a muzzleloader. Early one morning eleven years before, they were stalking mountain chamois along a streambed, hoping to get close to the animals while the noise of the stream covered their sounds. By the stream's edge they saw two baby *shockpa* splashing water on each other. Their fur was gray and lay both ways on their bodies.

Other informers come the next day and report *shockpa* screams at night, long vibrating screeches. Other visitors deny the existence of *po gamo* or *shockpa*. Others claim that *shockpa* are ghosts. Others bring no jungle tales but come for the sake of curiosity and tea. Except for a few real hunters, nearly everyone is clearly afraid of the jungle and seems to travel there as little as possible even though they live literally on the jungle's edge. Most of their jungle tales seem to be stories heard from others.

Only the hunters who saw the two *shockpa* babies possess Lendoop's aura of jungle savvy. They come back on the fourth evening, and want money for telling their story. Their stories fit my expectations, captivating variations of the *po gamo–needeene* themes. But when I ask if they'll guide us into the jungle, to the river where they saw the babies playing, they say no and leave. They never return.

Nick points out that among the half dozen we've heard, no two descriptions of *shockpa* match, whereas descriptions of wildlife and jungle uniformly dovetail. Lendoop returns to our fire each morning and drinks more tea. Over the next four days, Lendoop's descriptions ring with the most precision. His observational powers appear keen. Accompanying him after the first day is Myang, one of the Shakshila village headmen.

After five days listening to reports, we find no other person willing to take us into the jungle. Lendoop and Myang have staked out their territory in this community as our guides. Few others even talk seriously about the jungle. Those who suggest they know the way never return. How are such decisions of territory made and passed through the local population and village hierarchies? Or am I imagining that a decision was made and really there is no authority?

In any case, few local people seem to know the jungle. Clearly, it is a strange place, a place to stay away from. Like people who live by the sea, among whom there are few real seafarers, these traditional people remain fearful of the great environment "out there," which they view more as a mysterious forest, not something to interact with. And except for a few like Lendoop, for them the jungle generates scary and dangerous forces; it is a place to be avoided. The jungle is entered only to gather medicinal herbs, grass for animals, and bamboo and timber for homes.

Our tents are astride a trade route that has linked India with China for a thousand years, and links each village with its neighbor, bringing supplies and jobs. In this narrow valley the trail is the artery of life along which everything flows. While our camp is here, every trader, pilgrim, or messenger traveling this byway must walk around our tents. These wayfarers are not hunters or shepherds. They are the same people who wore down the dirt tracks of Europe with commerce during the Middle Ages, people with practical missions. Such trails are not walked for fun. Life doesn't offer that cushion of time.

But there is always a little opening for curiosity. Each day for the five days we've been here women and children cluster around camp. They come from villages up to half a day's walk away, coming as women throughout the subcontinent do, in groups. On the sixth morning, we're awakened by quiet whispers on the other side of our tent walls. "Jesse." "Jesse." "Where is he?" "Is Jesse awake?" The women wait for the blond phenomenon with the white baggy bottom to appear.

Jesse steps out of the tent, pushed by Nick. Inside we listen as the women say, "This is Jesse." Peeping out, we watch Jesse walk toward them, then run toward them, toddling, a bobbing stride that women universally seem to enjoy. There is something about children at this age that makes all adults their parents. Twenty women and children stand back looking at Jesse.

"His clothes, have you ever seen such shades of brown, green, and yellow?"

"Look at how big he is! They say he is two years old."

"Look at the yellow hair. See, the sun shines in it like straw after harvest."

Soon we are up, and after breakfast Jesse has his bath, as he has each day of this trek. With all the new sights and events to explore, this two-year-old gets dirty quickly. His mother wants to wash away chances. Each morning, Pasang heats wash water in his giant pot over the fire. Sitting in a small yellow plastic basin, Jesse splashes. Jennifer soaps him down with the first tubful, then rinses him with a second. Such copious use of water and soap is new to these women. Amid the grunge of the adults, both Westerners and villagers, Jesse's crystal cleanliness sets him apart more than his hair or clothes.

Jennifer giving Jesse his daily bath, as Nick sleeps

This morning we break camp. As the tents go down, a trader we have never seen before walks into camp. He looks around, sees Jesse in his bath, and says, "That must be Jesse." Like the yeti for us, Jesse is gaining for them legendary status. It is indeed time to move on, time to head into the jungle.

DANIEL TAYLOR-IDE

Chapter Eleven

I hoist Jesse's lively thirty pounds to my shoulders. The seat in my backpack, with straps and supports designed and redesigned during six months of training walks through West Virginia woods, remains unused. Jesse will not go into it even with stories of danger ahead.

Taking short steps, my legs find a sustainable stride for the steep climb out of camp. Resting his hands on my head, Jesse steers me through knee pressure on my chin, less effort for him than what he started out doing, pulling on my ears. My head drops forward to loosen my rider's pressure on my windpipe. I understand how horses get broken. That's how parents also get made. There is something satisfying for a parent in obeying a child's command. Carrying him gives me comfort. When I wonder if I'm leading my family into danger, stretching safety too far for my dream, following Jesse's lead helps; giving him the reins makes this his expedition too.

Almost an hour out, we catch up to Jennifer and Nick. They had left after morning tea, before we struck the tents, before the porters had left. Jesse's knees come forward, biting into my chin, his signal to stop. "Mama, down, down on the ground, I need that stick. I need it." Jennifer stoops, then hands him the stick.

Now swinging his stick, Jesse directs me up the trail around three more switchbacks. I stop to take a breather, stepping off the trail onto a crag over-looking the Barun far below. Jesse slides off my shoulders without objection. A breeze moves refreshingly across the rocky outcrop. From the mix of gear in my pack, I fish out a 200MM lens and a tripod. Jennifer and Nick catch up, ac-companied by Lendoop, muzzleloader on his shoulder, small canvas pack on his back. Strung out behind him are the six porters we hired the day before from the village of Shakshila, carrying fifty-pound loads, lighter than the cus-tomary sixty-six so they can negotiate the jungle more easily. From here, for the next three hours, Lendoop walks in the lead. Sometimes I lengthen my stride to try to catch up with him, but he stays consistently fifty feet in front. The most I can catch of him is his voice: "Trail is good, sahib. This way."

Now the steep climbing stops. We're traversing the slope, have climbed above the first rock cliff, and are headed into the Barun Valley. Ten-foot-tall grass surrounds us. Tall grass like this in a pristine Himalaya? What happened to the trees? Just before we entered the tall grass, crossing a stream, I slipped on a rock, soaking my left foot. Sitting down amid the grass, wringing out my sock, I see the Barun jungle not far away. After four years of planning, I am there; we are here. I lift Jesse back up. Lendoop takes off. Jesse and I follow, winding our way toward those tall trees. Swinging his stick, Jesse leans out from my shoulders and swats overhanging clumps of the tall grass from his face. Around a bulge of the hill the slope levels. There, squatting in his green hunting clothes, arms cocked akimbo on knees, is Lendoop, sitting like a frog on his rock amid a grassy sea. With a big grin he croaks in self-satisfied glory: "Sahib, today we camp here. Now we stop."

"Impossible to camp here, Lendoop, impossible. The day is not even half gone. You and the porters are getting thirty-five rupees per day carrying light loads. Camp must be farther."

"Sahib, porters can go farther, but you cannot. Baby and memsahib are important. We must make our camp here. This is the last place tents can be set up."

As evening falls, Jennifer, Nick, and I sit against the slope outside our tent. A stillness settles through the Barun Valley. As he does every night, Jesse helps Pasang push sticks into the cookfire. Pasang has taught him not to pull them out once lit. Through the quiet, a croaking comes from the porters' camp. Nick goes to investigate. He returns, his face trapped between a grin and a gri-mace, "Jennifer, don't go; they've caught eight frogs from the stream, skewered them, and are now doing a live roast over their campfire." As the croaking stops, peace settles again with the evening dew on the tent flies. Below our camp the Barun continues its steady roar.

Next morning the sun shines strong on the south-facing slope across the valley. I set up the tripod and tighten a high-powered spotting scope to the swivel. Back and forth, contour after contour, I scan for animals that may have come out into the warmth after a wintry night. My scope frames a troop of langur monkeys. This survey of a south-facing slope from a safe distance across the valley is part of the plan we made years ago, during the first tea party with Bob. Years ago, too, that museum curator writing from London suggested the langur could be our mysterious something. Now, sitting here in the Barun, langurs are all the life I can see.

After a leisurely breakfast that I find frustrating, Lendoop hands Pasang his empty teacup, gets up, and walks to the edge of the jungle. Now the trail-building begins. Back and forth Lendoop swings his *kukri*, a large curved Nepali knife. Our first barrier is a wall of bamboo, each stalk an inch thick. In a continuous motion Lendoop fells the stalks, and, with the same swing, stacks them on the left, carving a channel through the tall greenery. How do animals get through this stuff?

An hour later we cross the ridge we've been climbing and drop over the west-facing side. The bamboo disappears. Lendoop now moves steadily forward into hardwood forest, among gigantic trees where decaying vegetation lies more than three feet deep. Twice I have suggested that by going higher the slope would be more gentle. "This is the way, sahib," he replies. What way? I wonder. He is simply bushwhacking; it makes no difference. Why not take the more gentle slope? I look for signs of the trail he is following, cut stalks of previous trails, or blazing on trees. I see no signs. "This is the way" is all that he says. What does he follow? Does he really know where he's going?

During the next two hours we traverse small streams every several hundred yards. Usually in the Himalaya at this time of year the streams are all dry. One gurgles now below my feet somewhere under the rocks and decaying vegetation. Jesse hears it too. "Water, Papa. I want to drink some water." How do I find it for him? The stream runs right under trees and moss. Why are so many streams running here? This is a steep slope; water should drain fast, but this stream doesn't sound like it's running fast. Why are little streams still flowing in February, five months after the monsoon? Does the three-foot-thick

*Jennifer and Myang studying tracks on the approach to Piranee Khola;
Lendoop on left (photo by Nick Ide)*

sponge of decaying vegetation soak up the water during storms and gradually let it out? I stop and measure again. The decaying vegetation here remains nearly a meter deep – I've never seen it so deep anywhere in the Himalaya. This is as close to pristine as still exists in these mountains – no trails, the jungle floor thick with decaying leaves, moss, branches, whole trees even. In other places fallen trees would have become firewood.

In the jungle it is hard to see any animals, and most of the animals except monkeys are shy. Grandpa taught me to depend on Himalayan streambeds as my wildlife census sheet. Without visible streambeds, how will we survey for wildlife? My plan has been to locate any tracks left at drinking spots. Now after three days of working our way through the jungle I haven't seen one suitable spot, although Lendoop claims he sees tracks in the leaves and moss of the jungle floor. Must I wait for a winter storm to bring light snow down low?

For a half hour or so the roar of a stream has been growing steadily louder. Now, perhaps only twenty yards away, the air is cold; plants drip with a spray that soaks the air. I can't even talk to Jesse over the roar. He's tense, knees tight against my ears. I step forward another couple of strides, pushing apart wet branches. We look into a monumental shaft of rock. Hurling down through the rock shaft is a waterfall that cascades into a pool the size of a large room, dug out of the rock by the force of the falling water. After it lands, the water in the pool swirls peacefully, slowly. But just five yards in front of my feet the water takes off again, slops over the outer ledge of the pool and then shatters downward, making another waterfall that splashes back up into a spray and fills the air with mist.

Piranee Khola has carved its raceway into a stone cliff flanking the Barun Valley. Looking up the shaft framed with green jungle, a crescent of refracted light glistens in colors against a blue backdrop of sky, a rainbow in the prism of scattered water. Since our first meeting a week before, Lendoop has spoken of the edge of this pool as the only place to cross the Piranee torrent. That edge is the ledge of stone before me under the slow-flowing water that launches the second waterfall. As we have twisted our way through the jungle this morning, he has hit the spot dead on. He is indeed following a trail I cannot see.

LENDOOP HAS GONE INTO THE ROCK SHAFT AND NOW STANDS KNEE-deep in the safety of the peaceful pool. To join him, I must traverse a narrow and mist-soaked ledge. Up and outward from the other side of the pool, I see another ledge that climbs out of the shaft up into the jungle beyond. But first I must cross the ledge before me.

I step onto the wet rock, balancing, left hand outstretched, fingers seeking support from a bush growing out of the wet wall. Jesse's knees tighten; his arms wrap tensely around my forehead. Surprised to see us step out from the bushes, Lendoop charges toward us across the mossy slippery ledge. "Sahib, sahib," he yells, "don't come!"

Jesse flings himself back on my shoulders away from Lendoop's charge, pulling me off balance. My left foot slips on the ledge as my right hand grabs Jesse's leg to keep him from flying from my shoulders into the gorge below. With both feet now sliding out from under me, I hold tight with my left hand to the bush growing from the rock. I spin on that handhold and face the wall.

As my head snaps around, my eyes stop on Jennifer. Jesse's mother has just stepped through the bamboo and looked into this rock gorge. Six feet away, her face is a universe of expression, eyes wide, mouth open. I watch her silent scream. I watch her as she watches her son. Jesse, feeling my fall, has grabbed my hair, locked his knees under my chin, and pulls with his arms, holding himself back from being flung into the waterfall below. The Piranee Khola never misses a splash.

Roots deep in the well-watered rock, the bush holds. My fingers clamped in its branches, I pull myself first stable, then upright on the ledge.

"Sahib, don't come. Dangerous, very dangerous here. I, I carry Jesse." Lendoop stands shaking beside me on the ledge.

Adrenaline races. Anger rises. The two waterfalls thunder with too much strength for me to yell. I storm past Lendoop, across the mossy ledge. With the magic of a mountain guide, he melts into the rock face so as not to take up space as I pass. Arriving at the still pool between the waterfalls, I look back at Jesse's mother. Her eyes are still wide. Not fifteen seconds have passed since Lendoop charged.

An hour later, climbing through the jungle on the other side of the Piranee Khola, we break out into a clearing, the closest approximation to flat ground we've seen in three days of walking, a hundred times bigger than the depression between the roots of the giant oak where we unfolded the tent last night. Here at 8,000 feet, in a clearing between three giant chestnut trees, will be our mountain camp. Jennifer christens it "Makalu Jungli Hotel."

The sun shines bright, the first rays that have broken through the jungle

The author carrying Jesse into the Barun jungle

canopy in three days. The ticks are out too. They crawl up our legs. One homesteads with a sharp bite in the warmth of my crotch. We set up the tents quickly, and we retreat with Jesse to safety inside nylon. In West Virginia Jennifer worried about a tick becoming blood-engorged and lodged in Jesse's ear. This thought kept me awake the night afterward wondering whether that would rupture his eardrum. Over my pant cuffs I pull on a double layer of socks, then spray insect repellent up and down my pant legs. Jennifer and Jesse are in the tent, reading *The Cat in the Hat Comes Back.* Outside, we begin creating a camp. Porters are paid, the toilet site scouted, a cooking canopy built. A tick finds the opening in the neck of my shirt and crawls down to warmth in my armpit.

As night falls and the temperature drops, the ticks leave, nestling underground in the warmth of decaying humus. Camp is lovely. Around the cook-fire we sit on stools, a civilized luxury conveyed by porters. Tonight Pasang breaks the rice and lentils routine and serves us all spaghetti.

Dusk hardens into night. The rare and spectacular one-meter-long *Petaurista magnificus,* Hodgson's flying squirrel, maroon with a yellow stripe, glides over camp, seeking berries, insects, fungi, nuts, even dead animals to eat. Ever descending to lower slopes, at dawn it will return by climbing to the top of a tree, gliding almost horizontally back onto the hill, then finding another tree, climbing it, gliding off again, each time landing nearly a tree-height higher than the time before. Moving this way, gradually it will ascend the hillside while spending minimal time on the dangerous ground, where predators might lurk. When the sun returns, the flying squirrel is safe in its nesting hole in some tall tree on the slope above camp. Now, as it feeds, from time to time it beeps out its call.

As we lie in our sleeping bags, through the darkness comes the call of the tawny wood owl, the highest-altitude Himalayan forest owl. Appropriately mysterious, its *hoo-hoo* (the second *hoo* dropping in pitch) resonates through the jungle. Sixteen hundred feet below, the Barun River vibrates steadily like the roar of big trucks on an American interstate.

The air of night, clean and very cold, descends through the valley, settling off the glaciers of Makalu, Lhotse, and Everest. Wrapped in Arctic ice and wind, three of the world's five highest mountains are within twelve miles of us, summits standing sentinel, four vertical miles above our 7,700-foot-high camp.

Our most accurate picture of where we are remains Lendoop's map drawn

Jennifer & Jesse

in the sand a week before. We lie exactly where we planned to come after another spaghetti meal four years before: just below the snowline, in uncharted jungle, at a moderate altitude, and on a north-facing slope where we can observe animals across the valley.

The three-day walk in has shown plenty of undergrowth and food for "the something" to eat — if we only knew what it ate. In this uncharted valley, people are seasonal visitors. The animals have probably had the Barun Valley to themselves for more than a million years. Were there animals here when the Himalaya rose from the ocean and folded upward 40 million years ago? Then at least there could have been strange prehominoids. What were the plants here then? How fast did the ocean bottom change into jungle as India collided with Tibet? Is this dense Barun like the Himalayan jungle of 2,500 years ago when people first walked the Arun?

Chapter Twelve

The first morning at Makalu Jungli Hotel our senses fill with the sounds and smells of a pristine Himalaya, a wildness before people, where people have not yet pushed the limits. A special energy fills camp. We are the ones who are going to push the limits and find the unknown.

Our task today is to locate ourselves in the Barun Valley. We need an idea of the terrain beyond Lendoop's sketch. We need to find good lookout points from which to survey the south-facing slopes, protected places to work where we won't be seen. Maybe Terry was right; maybe we should search the caves. The jungle is so dense here, how can we see across the valley to the other side? Should we set up an observation platform atop a tree?

Myang, Nuru, Nick, and I set off up the slope through dense jungle. The two sahibs do not pretend to know the way. Neither Nick nor I can sense the ripples of rocks, and roots under the brush. Neither Nick nor I can swing a kukri through a one-inch-thick bamboo stalk to carve out the trail. Myang, using his authority as a village headman, appointed himself to stay in camp with us. Lendoop has reluctantly left; the porters wouldn't go back to Shakshila without him. So it is without Lendoop that we probe the jungle. Myang and Nuru lead the way, swinging their kukris. We agreed that since Myang is barefooted he and Nuru will turn back when the snow gets too deep or too cold. Anyway, when snow covers the undergrowth, kukris shouldn't be necessary. Nick and I will then keep climbing alone. How high will that be?

Our route slashes up through the bamboo. The jungle turns to oak and maple; hundred-foot-high trees at 8,000 feet. Never have I seen such virgin monuments in the Himalaya, even at 4,000 feet. Little light penetrates through the leaves to nurture young plants sprouting in the moist rich humus, so our walking is easy. We ascend rapidly 700 vertical feet. The oaks thin out, and birches come in.

We continue climbing. The jungle has turned dense again in maybe the last 100 vertical feet, a mix of birches and bamboo; I can't see more than six feet. Swinging hard, Myang and Nuru slice open an alley. The bamboo falls easily. Something in the soil or climate caused the species here to change; the bamboo is only as thick as jumbo kindergarten pencils and maybe eight feet tall. An ant must feel about like this when negotiating a well-fertilized suburban lawn.

Several hundred feet higher the bamboo is again twenty feet high and one inch thick. Here is yet a third species. The stalks are packed extremely close, each tightly sheathed in leaves, unlike the taller bamboo below whose leaves lie loose away from the stalk. Do these tight-wrapped leaves give the stalk protection in the cold?

In this large bamboo, we encounter a network of animal trails, two-foot-high tunnels going off in various directions. In one I see red panda droppings; in another serow. These tunnels seem too large to have been made by panda, and it seems unlikely that so many paths were here before the bamboo. In this bamboo patch there are a lot more stubby shoots coming out of the stalks than in the patch below. In winter these shoots could well be the highest succulent food on this north-facing slope. That would account for the trellis of trails; animals come here to feed. Might those be musk deer?

Little is known scientifically about any of the large Himalayan animals (remarkable when so much is known of large animals in other parts of the world). But a Nepali scientist, Bijaya Kattel, has studied the musk deer, a deer that looks as if it were the offspring from the union of a kangaroo and Eeyore, if Eeyore's long droopy ears were considered fangs. Mouse-brown colored in the Barun (although the color varies a lot over its range), the musk deer stands about three feet tall, weighs twenty pounds, and has significantly larger hind quarters than front, with a dramatically arched back. Unusual among deer, the musk deer has no antlers, but rather both males and females have two- to three-inch-long tusks. The world would have ignored this tiny deer (as it ignores the other Himalayan ungulates such as barking deer, ghoral, serow, thar) except for the presence of its abdominal pod that secretes a waxy, aromatic musk. Perfumers prize this scent as do Eastern medicine makers. The pods bring $50 each at night in the contraband local market and ten times that in Hong Kong or Paris after the middlemen finish.

The musk deer is a cute little animal, reminiscent of Eeyore in its personality, too, approaching people when it is not hunted, sticking close to home, each with a range of about ten acres. The males protect their territory heroically through fights during the winter mating season, sneezing to warn their ladies of possible danger through all their time together. These deer scour the high forests looking for shoots, moss, and grass; and when snow covers the ground they turn to eating twigs and lichen.

The killing methods by poachers of this little animal is simple. Thin, strong vines are twisted, then knotted with a slip knot and strung into a lasso. The loop end lies on the ground, the other end attached to a sapling that is bent over. When snared, the twenty-pound deer is yanked into the air where it dangles until it dies or has its throat cut. Strange that this deer should die by being strung up in a tree. It is one of the few deer that naturally climbs trees, lithe and with good balance (unlike Eeyore), finding an inclined branch or trunk coming out from a steep slope, then balancing itself on up to nibble on a favorite food, the green/gray hanging lichen, *usnea*, what tourists call Spanish moss.

Sad in any case that this animal would be poached so humans can smell more attractive to each other – especially sad when one remembers that the vine snares do not distinguish between male and female or young and old, and only the males over two produce the musk pod. At least three musk deer must usually die for a poacher to claim one with a harvestable pod.

One thousand vertical feet higher, with snow one foot deep, the tree types change again. Thirty-foot-tall rhododendron are mixed with the smaller bamboo and some small birches. Here we enter snow, and Myang and Nuru turn back. As Nick and I continue upward the snow gets deeper, up past our knees. It soaks us from the waist down, turning to squishy puddles in our boots. A wind blows gently off the Makalu ridge, making wet clothes feel colder. Step follows step, each foot feeling as though it's lifting a concrete block. Climb, breathe, sweat, breathe, climb, breathe, sweat, breathe. Cold soaks through to our bones. We're used to the oxygen volume in our lungs at 3,000 feet. Here at 12,000 feet, with one-third less air pressure, our blood cells search the air pockets of our lungs for the oxygen molecules to keep body fires burning.

Climb, breathe, sweat, breathe, climb, breathe, sweat, breathe. Another 500 feet higher, and the depth of the snow reaches our waists. Lungs pump. Each breath sucks on empty. Lendoop's animal list included virtually all the eastern Himalayan species. Many of these I've never seen before: serow, thar, clouded and snow leopard, Tibetan wolf. I would really like to see something of the clouded leopard, the rarest of all the Himalayan cats.

Breaking trail through this heavy snow is legwork, hard on the thighs. With the slope angle maybe 45 degrees, stalks of bamboo and rhododendron in the snow provide the only firm grip. In this snow the soles of my shoes slide like bald tires on ice. I bend my legs forward, really almost kneeling, making a slot in the snow. Grasping the closest bamboo or rhododendron, I pull my legs up into the slot and probe into the snow to catch some foothold beneath. With my handhold I pull myself upright, kneel forward, pack down the snow again, and search for another foothold. Again, again, and again.

Shivering, sweating, sucking for air, I wonder whether I will distinguish the symptoms of hypothermia from those of fatigue. It is almost one o'clock. We haven't eaten since eight A.M. The trail Nick is breaking is especially steep. The snow is above our waists. Without the rhododendron, bamboo, and birch holding the snow, avalanches would sweep down. How's Nick doing with the cold? How can he be climbing so fast? My feet find nothing to stand on.

"Hey, Nick, we gotta stop. I gotta eat something." We both carry five *chapatis* (whole-wheat flatbread) smothered that morning with peanut butter and jam and then rolled up. Half a day inside our backpacks must have thoroughly blended the peanut butter and jam. To get out of the snow Nick climbs into a rhododendron tree with comfortable-looking branches. I join him in a nearby fork five feet above the snow. We unwrap our squished chapatis.

Despite the added wind these few feet higher off the ground, it's great to be out of the snow even for this short while. Leaning against the rhododendron trunk, I prop my feet on a branch above my waist; out from my boots water runs up my legs and into my underwear. The warmth of that water from my boots is soothing; from my waist down everything's been cold, it seems, for a long time. I chew on a chapati. Bread, jam, and peanut butter melt in my mouth. My blood seems to warm. I decide to stay in this tree for at least half an hour.

Having finished his food in fifteen minutes, Nick drops into the snow and starts again up the slope. I pull out another mushed chapati and try to think about something besides being cold. Is there any redeeming quality to this deep, wet snow? Maybe the theory proposed by a Nepali botanist, Tirtha Shrestha, answers that question.

Shrestha believes this belt of high bamboo and rhododendron serves as Nepal's premonsoon irrigation reservoir. From December through March throughout the Himalaya the interlocking mat anchors billions of tons of snow onto steep slopes. Acting as a giant umbrella, the canopy foliage provides shade for this snow. Thus, protected from melting and held to the slope, snow accumulates for four months despite the sun of the near tropical latitudes. By early spring, a water reservoir is held in place, snow packed six feet deep. From May through June, increasing heat from the plains of India climbs to these ridges and under the canopy of leaves to melt the snow. As the water is released it seeps downward, stoking springs and keeping the land below moist.

This is Shrestha's trickle-down theory of pristine Himalayan ecology. It holds that if the high rhododendron/bamboo belt is cut by an expanding population seeking firewood, timber, or agricultural land for corn and millet, the results will be not only deforestation and soil erosion but also loss of this water. With the canopy protecting the snow cut, moist fields will give way to dry earth – until the monsoon comes in June, when the waited-for water will rush down unabated, carrying topsoil in its current, especially in the early monsoon before grasses grow back and hold the soil. Then the water itself will disappear without the water-soaking sponge of humus that once was there.

Today, though, it is hard to value this wet snow. The climbing is too difficult; even animals won't be moving in this snow and leave tracks. Should I tackle my fourth chapati? The water bottle in my pack is low. Is there enough left to wash down the last chapati and still make a plaster of paris cast should we find a footprint?

Nick yells from above, out of breath, his teeth chattering as he calls. "Dan'l, you'd better come up. Something here *you* need to see."

What's his excitement? What did he find? It sounds as if Nick doesn't know either. But he's got something.

Suddenly warm and excited, I drop from the tree into the snow. Climbing fast, no longer aware of having to suck for air, I feel as exhilarated as I did once before at a high altitude, when, climbing without oxygen, I crested a ridge, and a buddy dropped over my face an oxygen mask flowing at six liters per minute. That time my senses, loose as in a dream, soared, power injected into a vacuum. Cresting now another ridge, Nick points to tracks beside my feet – sharp, reasonably fresh yeti tracks. My senses soar again. Like a mother recognizing her child, the identity is instantaneous and beyond doubt. It belongs to a big animal, maybe five feet tall. There is the thumbprint. Looking at that print I can almost see the animal's face. I see its long, hairy arms, its sloping forehead.

Archetypical signatures, the tracks march toward us with unbroken regularity from the top of an almost vertical, moss-covered cliff. The stride looks human, the unmistaken left-right-left prints of a two-footed trail, the monogram of a barefooted person walking a snow-covered sidewalk. I pull the tape measure from my pocket. The stride is twenty-eight inches; the length of the footprint seven and a half inches. Neither Nick nor I has said a word since I got here.

"Can it be anything else?" Nick eventually whispers.

"Impossible. What other two-legged animal walks in these jungles? Have you ever seen so clear a bipedal stride? It couldn't be four-footed; any overprinting of back tracks on front would mess up some place, like there where it had to step over that branch. These tracks are all clean, sharp, no mistakes. It's bipedal. It's gotta be bipedal."

"But those tracks are too perfect," says Nick. "See the thumblike mark on each print? It's too perfect – the human-shaped foot. You don't just stumble onto a discovery like this the first day out."

"What do you mean 'too perfect'? You want to find something that biologically doesn't work? What's wrong with making the discovery the first day if we're looking in the right place? Why did I remember the water today and forget the plaster of paris?"

Pulling my camera from my pack, I start taking pictures. The moss on the cliff is ever so slightly disturbed. Clusters of bamboo grow by the edge of the rock face. On the base of some of the bamboo stalks are scratched nail marks. At the top of the cliff, other stalks are broken and hang down like bangs of hair. Did the yeti use these stalks to pull itself up?

Scratches in the mossy wall show where feet were placed during the ascent.

It was a fastidious climber that went up this fifteen-foot face. Never in my years of mountaineering have I seen a human climber so delicate. This animal has balance and considerable strength.

Kneeling in the snow, Nick and I examine the tracks. There are no slip-ups, no evidence of overprinting by a quadrupedal gait. The tracks seem consistently left-right-left bipedal walking. Each track shows the thumblike print, although some thumb prints are clearer than others. Some imprints are a lot sharper than others. What causes that selective disfigurement?

"Those are thumb marks, not claw marks," I say looking over at Nick. He grins back.

The tracks continue up the ridge. We follow alongside. They move from the left side to the right, then to the center, then back to the right, then again to the other side. As we walk, the snow above our knees, it becomes clear that the maker of the tracks is seeking a route on top of submerged rhododendron branches. Somehow, the animal senses where these branches are below the surface of the snow, branches we cannot see, branches that keep it from sinking through. The animal is using these branches like in-place submerged snowshoes. Every so often, one of its feet sinks through deeply where it misjudged. In that deep snow, the prints are no longer clear, their precise outlines obliterated by the downward force of the creature's weight.

Most of the tracks, though, are less than an inch deep. The animal must have been walking on this morning's snow or snow from the evening before. Tracks under trees are sharper than those in the open. But melting has not rounded the sides or put different angles on different sides of the track. If we return tomorrow we'll then see how these tracks (and ours) have changed. Melt rates vary with snow type, altitude, and sun. I glance at my watch; it's 4:12. Nick and I head down to reach camp before dark.

Chapter Thirteen

The following day it's my turn to stay in camp with Jesse, Jennifer's turn to go high. I fret at staying behind. What will they find? Is the yeti out there? What to do with Jesse? Yesterday's sunny weather has gone and we have limited options playing all day inside a tent. We read *Winnie-the-Pooh;* we go out and play in the thickets; take a climbing rope and make a swing from the limbs of a jungle tree. Anticipating, planning, trying to orchestrate what to do with Jesse is worse than letting him shape his day. He's only two – but he clearly knows what he likes and doesn't like to do. Finally I let go and do what he wants to do – go out into the jungle and look for animals. We dig inside rotting trees for beetles.

That evening, Jennifer and Nick return from climbing to the tracks. Nick sets down his pack. "They're almost melted, Dan'l. Even our tracks from yesterday are melted. The magic is gone. If our tracks melted so much between yesterday and today, that yeti must have passed only hours before us."

"It was good to see those tracks, but really there wasn't much there. The nicest part was catching the mood of that high jungle, but your tracks aren't convincing." Jennifer sounds tired. She takes the mug of sweet tea and two Fig Newtons offered her by Pasang.

I turn to Nick. "How long do you think those tracks were made before we saw them yesterday afternoon? Would you agree that they're probably about the same time lapse as Shipton's tracks thirty years ago – except his were on an open pass in direct sun, and ours were shaded by rhododendron?"

"It is really amazing, Dan'l, how fast tracks melt, even in the shade. I never would have guessed. The tracks we saw yesterday were sharp, the toes clearly defined. Today they're round snow bowls. The only thing you could sense was the right-left bipedalism."

Jennifer has regained some energy. Holding Jesse to her, she says, "We followed its trail up the ridge a half mile or more until the animal dropped off into bamboo. While tracking it, I stepped on a branch on top of the snow, a branch the animal had also stepped on, since we could see that the moss on the branch was disturbed. The branch bent under me as it must have for the animal. I'm 110 pounds. But when Nick stepped on it, the branch cracked, actually splintered. He's 150 pounds."

"So this beast is less than 150 pounds," Nick says, "Then we started looking at other branches. We found a four-foot-high branch that crossed the path. An animal on four legs should be short enough to walk under it, but any two-legged, hundred-pound-plus animal would find the branch blocking its path. So, how did our animal go? There were no marks of four feet, so it doesn't seem to have dropped to all fours. The branch was too high to go over without leaving deep marks for takeoff and landing. But when we looked on the back of the branch, there was a scratch, as if made by a nail, a scratch in the moss on the top back side as the yeti grabbed hold with its front paw and swung under."

"Dan'l, the scratches were like those on the bamboo on the cliff," adds Jennifer.

That night wet snow starts to fall. Wet snow is quiet and settles on a tent like dew, no ting ting like rain, or click click like hard, dry snow. Around midnight I awaken, sensing that all is not right. The snow is pressing down the tent walls, about to collapse the poles or rip the fabric. I pull on my boots, and go outside to scoop the snow away.

We have hoped for low-altitude winter snow to help us find evidence of animals here. The next day Nick and I leave camp in different directions to search for signs. Neither of us finds much; the animals aren't moving. The new snow makes walking a slippery business. Back at Makalu Jungli Hotel in the evening, we do not even have dry camp slippers for our wet, chilled feet to retreat into. The snow melted some during the day, and six inches of slush stand in camp while our slipper tops are four inches tall.

We take the next day off. Too much wet snow has fallen. We can't climb back up to the ridge, and we don't want to walk out into the jungle. Climbing down to work the lower elevations is not worth the effort. We will let the cold weather firm things up. Toward noon the snow turns to drizzle; in the evening the rain turns again to wet snow. Without the trees and bushes holding the snow on the slope there would have been avalanches all around. Life, like our camp slippers, feels soaked and cold.

As Pasang is getting afternoon tea ready we hear shouts coming up the hill from Piranee Khola. I run to the edge of the clearing. Bob is here! Lendoop and Lhakpa have brought him in. We tell him about the discoveries. He excitedly probes for more facts. "Did you see nail marks in the snow? No? Are you sure? Then how come you found nail marks on the bamboo, also on the cliff and on the branch? Are you suggesting you found an ape that moves its nails out while climbing cliffs and holding branches, and like a cat with claws, draws them in while walking? How can you be sure there weren't nail marks in the snow? How are you sure there were no hind-foot overprints? Did you take adequate photographs to prove these points? How do you know the route showed intentional selection for rhododendron branches under the snow? Maybe it was just happenstance. Did you photograph that?"

The next morning Lendoop, Nuru, Bob, Nick, Jennifer, and I fan out through the jungle all day searching for caves and evidence. Jesse stays in camp with Pasang. Three different rock crevices show bear scat and bear hair on the walls. We find droppings of Himalayan chamois, red panda, maybe leopard, and more bear. There is no sign of primates.

Our sixth day in camp, freezing rain leaves an ice film on the rocks and builds a crust that breaks under every step, into slush beneath. Bob looks around camp fondly for some project to sustain his optimism. "We'll learn more and lower the probability of breaking legs if we stay in camp and talk. Why don't we go into the large tent and I'll ask Myang, Lendoop, and Lhakpa some questions?"

We crowd into the tent. I sit in the back listening. Bob and the three others sit facing one another in a lopsided square. Bob's Nepali is fluent, his knowledge of local names for plants and animals is almost complete. He starts by joking with Lendoop, Lhakpa, and Myang about the sex life of jungle animals. This bear with that goat – what animal would that make? That monkey with this rat? The jokes give him a list of jungle animals, similar to mine of two weeks ago at the confluence, but with three new ones, wild dog, and two civets.

Bob starts slipping in oblique references to *shockpa*, but in the stories that come out, the animal's description is inconsistent and unclear. It doesn't sound as though they believe these *shockpa* stories; they're just passing along village tales, a snippet from one person's account, a piece of another's.

Lendoop says, "Sahib, I am many times a hunter. How can there be such an animal living wild in the jungle? I never see its eating sign. How does it move? I never see its prints."

"Well, Lendoop," Bob asks, "if not *shockpa*, what was it that Dan'l and Nick found tracks of up on the ridge?"

"I didn't see the tracks, sahib. Maybe *rukh balu.*"

"What is *rukh balu?*" Bob asks, trying to sound offhand.

"Two bears are in this jungle. One is *bhui balu*, ground bear. It is black, strong, very aggressive, and when dead requires six men to carry out. The other is *rukh balu*, tree bear. It also is black, but climbs trees, is very agile moving high in the branches and it is shy. Two men can carry tree bear when dead. The bears are different, not the same bear, sahib."

Bob repeats, "Ground bear, tree bear, different sizes, living in different places. One is aggressive, one is shy. How else do they differ?"

"Well, sahib, it is strange," Lendoop answers. "Front paw of *rukh balu*, tree bear, is like the human hand. This bear hand can grab, holds things like people. It has a claw on the side of its paw, here sort of like my thumb is."

A bear is in this jungle with a forepaw that makes prints like a human hand? Are tree bear prints the yeti prints? No wonder the yeti has never been found. Everyone is looking for a known animal or an ape – while the animal that makes the prints is unknown, may have been seen many times by mountaineers, explorers, and scientists, but remains unrecognized. A small black bear, *rukh balu*, hiding high up in the trees. As it hides in those treetops, investigators pass underneath. If they saw the little bear they would count it just a cute cub of *Selanarctos thibetanus*, a species they already know of. They wouldn't realize that this was an adult bear of an unknown species. The explorers were looking for a wild man, an Abominable Snowman. But all the while, a little black bear was high up in the trees, a little bear with unusual forepaws.

"Sahib, the *rukh balu* is very shy. The only time we see it outside jungle is when it comes to our fields to eat ripe corn at the end of the monsoon. Back in Shakshila I have a skull from a bear I killed raiding my fields five months ago."

Lendoop is getting too much attention. Lhakpa breaks in with one story better. "Sahib, in my grain room, to scare away the mice and evil spirits, I keep one *rukh balu* skull plus its dried front paw and back paw!"

Bob leaves camp the next day with Lhakpa and Lendoop. All three are excited. Bob is going to see the skulls and paws. Jennifer, Nick, and I must thrash around in cold, wet, heavy snow another week looking for more field evidence. As he leaves, Bob again brings up the old questions: "Are you sure your tracks on the ridge had no nails? Bears have nails. Certainly a tree-climbing bear would have nails. Why are you sure the animal was walking on two feet? Why not four feet? Take a look at cat tracks; they place their hind feet precisely into their forefoot prints. When you get back to West Virginia, have your house cat walk through the snow; it'll look bipedal."

"No, Bob, those prints had no nail marks. The snow was firm. If there'd been nail marks they would have shown. The tracks were bipedal. I know they were."

"Then what made your tracks?" Bob asks. "What, if any, is the relationship between your track maker and the tree bear?"

Early the next morning Nick and Jennifer awaken at dawn and try to leave the tent silently. The walls are weighted again by half a foot of new wet snow. This time poles have been bent, and the fabric presses down on some of our gear. Jennifer and I heave against the tent wall to unpin her gloves. When she and Nick leave I burrow back into my sleeping bag. Outside, the noise they make stuffing four empty tin cans into their backpacks wakes up Jesse. Soon he is crying, "Mama, Mama." I hear Jennifer and Nick having a quick mug of hot tea by the campfire before adding two pounds of peanut butter to their packs. I wrestle with Jesse, trying to distract him from opening the door flap. Soon I hear Jennifer and Nick tramping up through the bamboo on their way to the ridge.

Today's plan is a bona fide crackpot scheme, one that would never pass a scientific review board if our methodology had been screened by professional researchers. The plan is to spread peanut butter on tree branches and hang it inside cans punctured with holes so the wind can waft the aroma around the ridges. In tomorrow's snow we hope to find prints of animals attracted by the smell – if not yeti prints then at least bear prints. I know bears like peanut butter. They have fantastic noses that can smell for miles; Grandpa used to say

Bob Fleming quizzing Lendoop and Myang about Barun Valley animals.

that a Himalayan black bear could smell a rotten animal fifteen miles away if the wind was blowing that way. The peanut butter smell should carry for a mile. This way we can bring in some bears and compare their prints to those we found in the snow. Jennifer and Nick place the peanut butter and cans up on the ridge. Then we wait.

The next day is cool, the old snow firm with an inch of new on top. Good condition to find tracks; we hope to cover a lot of territory. Nick and I separate. My job is to search the base of the snowline for signs left by animals entering or leaving. Nick goes high to check the cans on the ridge.

The going for me is easy. Scouting an east-facing slope, I find an absolutely massive fresh leopard scat filled with brown hairs and some big bone chips. Was it from a meal of Himalayan chamois? Was it snow leopard or common leopard, maybe even clouded leopard? Later, amid a large stand of maples, its head just peeking over a fallen tree, a chamois stares at me, then bounces away. The lighting was funny. Was it really a chamois, or was it a juvenile serow? I'd much rather it be serow – the more I think about it, the more I think it must have been. The photograph I took will tell.

I enter the thick bamboo belt. Crawling through the two-foot-high tunnels

I see fresh red panda scat. The hind end of an animal flashes ahead of me and disappears along the tunnel. White legs – a serow? Or was it just a flash of light? Musk deer? Suddenly I am afraid. What should I do if a bear comes at me in this tight bamboo tube? I reach into my pack for my canister of tear gas mixed with oil of pepper. I don't know of anyone who has used this mixture on bears, but some researchers in Yellowstone are now carrying it. I open my water bottle, moisten my bandanna and put it around my neck ready to draw up over my nose and mouth for a mask in case I have to shoot off the canister. I wiggle on through the tunnel.

A couple of hundred yards further, I break out into a sort of clearing where wind or huge amounts of snow have matted down about an acre of the inch-thick bamboo. I can't continue through the tunnel, which is mashed down by the crushed stalks. I must either go back the way I came or crawl out and across the mat. The mass of stalks appear almost woven together. I decide to try going further and climb up on the bamboo. It heaves up and down like a trampoline, and I have to be careful not to let a foot slip between stalks and wedge inside the mat.

About two-thirds of the way across, both of my feet slip, inward and to-gether. Two bamboo stalks skewer my backpack straps as I fall, leaving me hanging by those straps about five feet off the ground, like a parachutist caught in a tree. My head rides just below the top of the bamboo. Somehow in the fall my glasses stay on. Sunlight fills the hole I've dropped through. My left arm sticks up above my head, just about the top of the bamboo. The feel-ing inside is one of deep loneliness. I'm not scared, I'm not worried. I feel as though I'm alone and the last person alive on the planet. Could a bird flying over spot my hand waving? Why don't researchers carry messenger pigeons in their packs?

I try to move. I'm hanging in the air and pinned from all sides. Inside this bundle of bamboo I can't reach and grab anything. There are no footholds to push against. The bamboo is so tight around me I can't even drop down. I turn and look up at my watch: 1:32 P.M. The digital display flicks almost hyp-notically through the seconds: 1:32:41, 1:32:42, 1:32:43. . . .

Slowly I work my left arm down along my side and inch it into my left pocket, where I keep six feet of parachute cord coiled into a little bundle. Slowly I work that hand back out and upward until the parachute cord is inches in front of my teeth. Then I work my right hand upward. Carefully, using one hand and my teeth, I untie the cord. Don't let it drop, don't let it drop. I stare at the beautiful red, black, and yellow diamond weaving of its braids, inches in front of my face. So beautiful. Artistry in some factory making beauty even of nylon cord. Sweat streams down my face and falls on the cord.

I start a bowline knot at one end. First, the flip out of a small loop. Then, up out of the loop comes the rabbit (as we used to say in Scouts), goes around the tree, and ducks back in. Sweat runs down my cheek, inside my collar. I pull the rabbit tight. My legs dangle amid the bamboo below. My shoulders are starting to ache from hanging in the pack straps. I drop the looped end of the cord down to fit my boot like a stirrup.

Now the other end. I pull up eight inches of cord, bend it into a bight, then loop that around the biggest, smoothest stalk among those within a foot of my face and start feeding the rest of it through the loop. Feed it once, wrap it through, feed it through again, wrap it through again, feed it through: a Prusik knot. Pull it tight. Drop the stirrup back down. I swing the cord until my foot is inside the stirrup. Gradually I ease weight onto it, standing. Will it hold? Yes, the knot is tightening and does not slide back down the bamboo. Is the loose end of the Prusik pulling through? It might. To catch the loose end should it start to slide, I bring up both hands and tie a figure-eight knot.

The beauty of a Prusik is that it slides up a rope (or bamboo stalk) when weight is off but locks when weight is on. It won't slide back down. Seating the knot harder on the stalk, I take one step in the stirrup. Wedging myself against other stalks, holding with one desperately tight hand, I support my weight in a wedged position so the weight is off the cord and I can loosen the Prusik. The cord obligingly slackens. I bend my leg, slide the Prusik up the bamboo, stand in it. It holds. Six inches gained upward. Next step, eight inches. Next step seven inches more. For each step the hardest challenge is to find a way to wedge myself into the bamboo to keep from falling while I free one hand to slide the Prusik farther up the stalk. Finally on top of the bamboo mat, lying on my back, I look at my watch again: 3:17. Nearly two hours to shinny up a few feet of bamboo. No, dummy, you can't even subtract anymore: an hour and a half.

Exhausted, sweating, ravenously hungry, I roll over on top of the mat and pull a squashed chapati out of my pack. With the chapati inside me, I remain on my back, watching the clouds sail past, not moving on the bamboo for fear of falling through. Up above circles a giant bearded vulture, the lammergeier,

Tree bear nest made in bamboo clump three feet above the ground

looking for carion – its long tail identifies it as it rolls and turns, the acrobat of the high ridges. The biggest bird in these mountains, nine feet across in the wings, the biggest bird in any mountains except the condor. The lammergeier, like the griffon, soars on the rising currents of mountain ridges. But it soars more spectacularly.

I lie on my back watching. The wings are flat across like the griffon, not in the V of the golden eagle. Up twists one wing – and over to the other side the lammergeier rolls. Up twists the other wing – over the other way the big bird rolls, effortlessly like an acrobatic pilot in a Pitts Special. Although the undersides of both birds are white, a lammergeier can never be mistaken for a griffon if you watch it turn. The more aggressive ones will sometimes even chase the eight-foot griffon; aggressive even in the search for food it will drop bones on rocks, eat the marrow and the shattered bone fragments. As I watch, overhead into my view comes another lammergeier. Is this the time of their courtship? Yes, down swoops the first lammergeier, displaying his prowess like Bob reported, down it swoops, then with a dipping of its long, long tail, suddenly upward the male bird shoots, straight up. It holds its long tail outward – and over it rolls, an inside loop.

The doggerel of old Miss Marley teaching English at Woodstock comes back to me:

What is the mind of the vulture
That sits and thinks
And stares and stinks
And has no culture?

How can such a soaring bird not have culture? Like many teachers, Miss Marley might well have listened more closely to her pupil, Bobby Fleming. First they do some twisting flight together in the sky, then the two vultures above fly off straight and level together, neither of them now a spinster. I too must hurry back to camp. I'll be less likely to fall through this bamboo mat again if I slither the rest of the way across on my stomach.

In camp over supper, Nick reports, "I lost the trail in all that fresh snow. I couldn't find the cans and I've no idea whether anything found them, but I did find something strange, a clump of bamboo. Maybe forty stalks of it were broken off evenly at a three-foot height. The stalks were an inch and a quarter in diameter – that's hefty bamboo, no way could I ever bend it. Yet these stalks were all snapped forward into the clump and each stalk again broken to make what looked like a nest. What was once a clump of bamboo ended up being a bamboo basket three feet off the ground."

The next day Nick and I climb to the site he found. Together we try to break inch-and-a-quarter bamboo. Impossible. Yet the animal that made this five-foot-wide nest seems to have snapped off the stalks just where it wanted to. As Nick reported, the breaks seem carefully planned. Why? To get a sleeping place up off the snow? For protection? Protection from what? Is this the work of a tree bear (or a yeti?) seeking protection from snow leopards or from aggressive ground bears?

Then, eight feet above the first nest, we see another. A second animal has made a smaller nest, only three feet across, also of bent bamboo. To do it the animal must have sat in the rhododendron tree, reached out and brought bamboo over, bent the stalks around this fork in the tree. Twenty-five feet away in another rhododendron tree is a third nest, also smaller than the first, made in a similar way. Is the bigger nest mother bear's, the two smaller ones up higher for her offspring? Did each animal make its own nest, or did the mother make all three? Did they stay only one night, or did they use these nests as a base for several nights? Are they in the bamboo because they were eating bamboo shoots? Everything is guesswork. But now we have more than footprints.

Snow is falling. Digging into the nests, we sift through the snow searching for hairs or to uncover imprints of feet to tell us what animals were here. I look across at Nick. His lips are blue. His face is bluish too, and he is having trouble talking.

"Nick, you're in bad shape. Gotta get you back to camp. Gotta get you warm, or you'll be cold for a long time."

"I think I can make it back alone, Dan'l."

I force him to drink the rest of my bottle of orange drink, still warm from being rolled up inside the down vest in my pack. I give him the vest and a dry ski hat. He walks off down the mountain slowly, eating our last two candy bars. Will he warm as he walks? He knows he has to be careful. The trail's good. The warm sugar drink will help. The dry hat and down vest will hold in more heat. With hypothermia, the most important thing is to identify it before it really happens; then adrenaline helps the recovery. Wet snow is still falling, and I return to my search for clues.

I find nail marks on the tree trunk four feet above the second nest. Knowing now what to look for, I find more nail marks on some of the bamboo stalks. Then I find three stiff black hairs about two inches long wedged inside against some bark. I find two more under snow in one of the tree nests, caught by bamboo splinters.

Hiking back down to camp, looking now for nests, I see two gigantic clusters of limbs high up in adjoining oak trees. Both are at least six feet across and maybe sixty feet above the ground. Studying the nests through binoculars, I see whole oak branches snapped back and stacked up in a crotch in the oak. The limbs are broken off regularly, much like the bamboo. On the trees I find scratches that slant diagonally. Why aren't they straight, reflecting the angle of pull as an animal goes up or down?

Then I realize that this animal did not climb the way I would expect a bear to climb, clawing its way up the tree like a cat, or like American black bears. Each oak has a strong four-to-six-inch-thick vine firmly growing up the trunk. There are deep nail marks on the back side of each of these vines. The animal appears to have grabbed the vine with its front paws, then leaned back and, pulling against it, placed hind paws on the tree trunk and climbed the way a monkey climbs a tree or a telephone company worker climbs a pole. The animal Lendoop calls "tree bear" certainly acts apelike.

Lendoop is waiting in camp, having come back in after walking Bob out. He is eager to take us to Shakshila to show us his bear skull. He says we can make it from here in one day.

"But three days were needed for the trek in, Lendoop. What makes you think we can walk out in one day?"

"Memsahib is very strong, sahib. This memsahib walks all day like a Nepali woman – she even carries heavy load." I have to laugh. Lendoop knows only the physical side of Jennifer's strength. Given the eagerness in her heart at the prospect of walking out, she'll be doubly strong now, happy to leave this drizzle and snow. At the Barun's 3,000-foot confluence she'll be warm again.

Everyone except me is eager to go. Lying in my sleeping bag our last night in Makalu Jungli Hotel, I listen to all the noises telling the tale of the night. I might come back to this place, but I can never come back to this experience. Jennifer in particular has been great. Exploring this jungle with Jesse, I remember my times with Grandpa and Dad.

Before dawn I wake to hear Jennifer quietly stuffing her belongings into her duffel. Outside, there is the rattle of pots. Pasang and Nuru are working on breakfast and at the same time taking down the cooksite. I hear Pasang ask Lendoop to strike the porters' tent. Quickly I unzip my sleeping bag and start yanking on my boots. Big strong Lendoop will get the job done all right – and bend the poles if he tries to take the tent down alone.

Half an hour later I look around. It is amazing how fast the camp closed. Everything is packed, and by eight o'clock we're ready to leave. The four porters who were to come from Shakshila to help us haven't arrived, so we put together double loads for the rest of us. No one wants to wait for them. Lendoop smiles as Jennifer tightens the cords on her sixty-pound pack.

The sense of friendship deepens among us as we start down the trail. Each person slips, and each supports one another. The route is especially difficult as we descend the wet slope to the Piranee Khola. The days in the jungle have made us into a team. We walk closely together. We are getting out together. We are having fun, the jokes passing from member to member. Pasang's hundred-pound basketful rattles with the cacophony of spoons nested inside pots nested inside larger pots, shifting and banging against enamel plates with each step. Throughout the Barun Valley, yetis, bears, pandas, and crimson-horned pheasants must be hearing our marching band, our passage out.

Our four porters are waiting by the Piranee Khola. They had stopped here for their morning rice. Steam and smoke from their fire and mist from the two waterfalls rise together up the narrow gorge. We redivide loads by the pool and drink hot sweet tea by the porters' fire, before going on. The downward momentum for home carries us pounding forward like the current of the Barun, both seeking the confluence with the Arun. Knees tired, we arrive there too late in the day to visit Lendoop's house.

The next morning Lendoop and Lhakpa stand eagerly outside our tents to take us to Shakshila. I had hoped that they would bring their skulls to our camp. My knees are still sore from yesterday's pounding, but it would be an insult to ask that they bring the skulls to us and not share tea in their homes. It is their turn to host us. Having heard so much about Shakshila while he cooked, Pasang wants to see the village – maybe he's looking for some local brew too. Breakfast over, we are escorted uphill.

First we stop for tea at Lhakpa's. Then we stop at Myang's for boiled eggs. Myang's wife can't take her eyes off Jennifer and Jesse. When Jennifer speaks to her, she blushes and doesn't respond, although we saw her repeatedly at our earlier camp by the confluence. But she brings her two children out of the back room and we pass along several of Jesse's T-shirts and a pair of shoes.

At Lendoop's there is much ceremony. But before we can enter his house he explains the presence of an immense boulder in his yard. Half the size of his house, the boulder rolled down the mountain the fall before and lodged across his front porch. "I'm lucky," Lendoop says. "Natural disasters always miss me in the jungle and also my family. I'm a lucky man." His luck is clear: That house-sized boulder would have pancaked both family and house. Inside, with window shutters open, light streams across the hewn logs that shine with the marks of an adze crafter who knew his skill. Years of footsteps have worn the roughness off the handmade cuts and given the wood a glowing patina. As we sit on Lendoop's enormous ground-bear skin, a trophy from one of his hunts, his wife brings us food. Then Lendoop brings out his bear skull.

In the sun on the porch, I photograph the skull. Lendoop wants to sell it to me for 300 rupees, but I have already bought Lhakpa's, and the front and hind feet as well. Lendoop's skull is similar in size and shape. One skull is enough to discover if the tree bear is really an unknown species. Soon we will know. In a month we'll be back in Washington.

Chapter Fourteen

March 14, 1983. Tumlingtar Airport, East Nepal. The seventeen-passenger Twin Otter bounces like a rabbit as it settles on the grass field, its long, Canadian-made landing legs hopping up and down like the Saskatchewan white-tailed jackrabbit, absorbing the wallows and bumps. Then the plane turns and taxis toward us across the stubble, nipped short by goats and water buffalo. The whining turbines never stop as arriving passengers get off and Jennifer, Jesse, thirteen other passengers, and I climb aboard and the fuselage door closes. Before we have cinched our seat belts, the plane is already taxiing to the end of the big grass airfield perched on a shelf overlooking the Arun River. Turbines roar. The Twin Otter leaps forward at the release of the brakes and picks up speed; across the grass its landing legs chatter as we become airborne and head toward Kathmandu.

The plane banks and turns to leave the valley, its turbines wailing at full throttle to pull us over the western Arun Valley ridge ahead. Sitting on the back bench, with all the regular seats full and baggage in the aisles, I suspect that the plane's weight is at full gross generously calculated. Looking down the aisle into the cockpit, I see the ridge directly ahead, filling the windshield. Will the pilot circle to gain the altitude? No, with a reserve yet of airspeed, he pulls back further on the control yoke, and the plane rises on its tail into a maximum-angle climb to clear the ridge. With the increased pitch one of the two navigational radios slides out of the instrument panel. Reaching over, the pilot catches the radio with his right hand while still holding the yoke with his left. We're going to clear the ridge straight ahead – unless there's a downdraft. The copilot turns in his seat and glances down the aisle. Our eyes meet. Smiling, he reaches up, unhooks the latch, and pulls shut the cockpit door.

I look out at the Himalayan peaks as we climb higher. The window plastic is blue from age and tropical sun. Scratches cleave the light into red, yellow, and blue stripes. Tiny random rainbows lattice the windows. I get a crick in my neck from bending to look out. Why don't aircraft manufacturers, even on the big jets, make their windows three inches higher?

The Twin Otter climbs through fluffy cumulus. According to pilots in the Kathmandu cocktail circuit, Himalayan clouds are agricultural and grow rocks. So every time we enter a cloud, this pilot follows practice and turns south toward India to make sure he's flying away from the mountains. Once through the cloud and back on Visual Flight Rules, he turns back northwest toward Kathmandu. Although flight routines may be unorthodox, Royal Nepal Airlines has over its forty years accumulated an outstanding (and very comforting) safety record.

Winds from the winter rains are blowing hard today – bluish-white clouds billow and reshape outside the windows. The plane bounces and banks sideways, caught by varying updrafts and cross currents. Each time, with smooth skill, the pilot brings us back to the straight and level. Our tiny craft seems to be cascading like a bowling ball down a badly (very badly) warped alley in the sky. One by one the passengers pull out the airsickness bag tucked in front of them. Looking forward two rows, I see Jennifer grow greener. She hates planes, but I've never seen her reach for the bag.

After forty-five minutes, Kathmandu Valley comes into view. My relief at arriving plunges with the Twin Otter as it drops into a tremendous downdraft. My carry-on bag jumps from between my feet and scoots like a hockey puck down the aisle toward the cockpit. It lodges sideways against a sack of oranges sticking out from under a villager's seat. Three rows in front of Jennifer, a villager lowers his airsickness bag and pulls out a rag to wipe off his face. This is an exceptionally bad trip. It's not a bowling alley; it is more like a roller coaster.

As we walk into the terminal, Nick jumps out from behind a pillar. He had left us two weeks earlier to see another part of Nepal while we continued to do fieldwork. He cannot hold back his news: "There's a tree bear at the zoo!"

Jennifer and I are unenthusiastic. After seven weeks in the field, a hot shower is the only thing we care to think about.

Undeterred, Nick continues. "One afternoon last week, with nothing to do, I went back to the zoo. Jennifer, remember that bear in that cage by the pond? After searching for bears in the jungle, I decided to stare at this bear. Watching it for a while, I wondered: Could this be a tree bear? It's small – of course we don't know how small tree bears are, but this bear is small. I searched out the zookeeper. He said the bear had been at the zoo for two years, that it had not grown since it came. If it isn't growing and it's still small, the bear could be a tree bear. Don't you think?"

"Yeah, Nick, but small and not growing doesn't mean much. Maybe the bear is a runt. After all, zoo food must be lousy." Nick's excitement makes me tired. After forty-three nights in the same sleeping bag, I want that shower and a bed. I want clean sheets.

The next day we visit the zoo. The bear is indeed small. As I pitch peanuts through the bars of her cage, she holds her mouth accommodatingly open six inches away on the other side. I try to fathom through crushed peanuts and saliva the amount of wear on her molars. Are her cusps sharp or rounded down? She loves peanuts, the shells as well as the meats. Would she go for peanut butter? As I reach through the bars with a little stick and try to brush off her teeth to examine better her cusps, her jaws snap shut almost on my fingers. Now as I work with another stick, she curls her front paws around the cage bars, grabbing for my fingers. Is that inside claw dropped low enough to make a thumblike print? She's using it like a thumb, gripping the bar with the dropped claw. That inside digit is definitely out of line with the other four. I can conclude little about her age from her teeth beyond that all her juvenile teeth are gone. It's close quarters; her breath smells like boiling turnips.

The zookeeper works backward to figure her age. "Sahib, she has been in the zoo for two years, and when she came she was not a cub. She has always been a good bear, never mean. Since arriving, she has not grown. Maybe now she is five years."

This is exciting. This bear is far too small for a normal five-year-old Asiatic black bear. She certainly weighs less than 150 pounds, and is not mean as Asiatic black bears are usually known to be. Either this is a runt or it is a different type of bear. How heavy should a five-year-old female Asiatic black bear be? Is there absolutely no mention in the scientific literature of tree bears and ground bears? All these are points I must check. Bob and Linda can't help; they're off with other fieldwork. Jennifer, Nick, and I keep these questions to ourselves, along with the others that still have no answers.

Given our budget, we cannot afford a hotel layover and have to fly thirty-two hours nonstop back to the States. Jennifer sets aside eighteen diaper changes and prepares for the contingencies of lost suitcases and long waiting lines. As we fly over the Baluchistan Desert, I look down on the vast sands of southern Afghanistan, where our yeti Volkswagen engine burned out fifteen years before. In Rome the airport employees are on strike, giving us a surprise forced layover, and thanks to a college classmate of Jennifer's, a night in a bed rather than on the airport floor.

Two days later, we drive down Constitution Avenue in Washington, D.C., and find a parking space right in front of the Smithsonian National Museum of Natural History. Pulling open the heavy glass doors with brass handles polished by thousands of tourists' hands, I remember childhood dreams of contributing to this collection, of bringing something to this repository of accumulated knowledge. Insecure yet excited, Jesse, Jennifer, and I walk on the other side of the ropes that funnel the tourists toward the dinosaurs.

We take the elevator to the third floor, the laboratories and scientific collections of the Mammal Division. The curator, Richard Thorington, is out. His assistant leads the way along the labyrinthine hallways of the Mammal Division, past case after case of specimen boxes, boxes stacked like giant white blocks against the walls. Inside these boxes on sliding trays lie the other mammals of the world, waiting for their appointed moments to define knowledge for the furless, upright-walking species that once shared the planet with them more equitably.

I try to look serious, but it's hard to look like a scientist while carrying my specimen in a red nylon stuff sack and accompanied by a two-year-old kicking a ball of paper along the floor of the hallway. "Papa, after this can we see the dinosaurs? Will this be fun? After this can I get a hot dog from the truck out front?"

With Jesse's straightforwardness, the tension vanishes, time suddenly runs easily. Our quest is a family quest; it is right we walk these halls together. Why pretend to be the scientist I'm not? What's wrong with coming to look at lab specimens with your kid? If this skull is ever added to the Smithsonian collection, it'll be just as much a two-year-old's contribution as mine. Maybe one of the serious types here will pick on me because I dabble in science. But why? I'm just asking questions.

Nothing is threatening about Bill, the assistant who walks with us. Together we follow a couple of hallways and come to the two drawers of Asiatic black bear skulls. *Selanarctos thibetanus* is what they call our bear here.

The skulls Bill takes out of the wooden drawers are meticulously washed, each carefully penned with an identification number. The ink is black; the bones are sanitized and white. Each skull sits in a little flat box owning its spot in its drawer – these bears don't have to fight for territory. From the red nylon bag I pull out our specimen, unwrap the protective newspaper padding, and reveal our skull, yellow, with dried muscle and tendon still attached.

In my left hand I hold a mystery. With my right hand I pick up a large white skull whose identity is known. Lifting up the skulls, I look into the bony faces of these two bears, at the big eye sockets, at the gaping holes that once sustained their sensitive noses. Looking, I almost expect flesh, sinew, and breath to return, filling out these bones with life. So many unknown holes perforate these skulls, entry and exit channels where once nerves and veins ran carrying out their appointed tasks. My fingers explore skeletal ridges, concave and convex undulations of bony structure. How insulting to a once-fierce bear now to play so with its head. I look into our skull's gaping nose hole; nostrum they call it here. I doubt the bear had any name for this, its most important sense. What would it think when the message went from the nose hole back through the nerves to the brain when it smelled peanut butter?

Jennifer and Jesse stand patiently. Bill shuffles about after a few moments, then says, "I know very little about bears. My specialty is shrews. For each family and genus there are certain key features in the skulls, and I don't know what features are critical for bears."

Bill's words put me at ease. Of course he doesn't know what to look for. The last time anyone walked into the Smithsonian with a skull from an unknown bear was a hundred years ago, when the Kodiak bear was discovered. Jennifer and Jesse stand off to the side while I search through the trays, looking for some definite difference. But all the skulls in these two drawers differ. Some have a hole in one place behind the eye socket; others have the same hole in another place; one skull doesn't even have a hole behind the eye socket. How can brain hookups be so random? (Do the differences in any way affect brain function?) The most dramatic differences are among the skeletal ridges, which resemble mountain chains of bone right down the crest of the skull. Some skulls are smooth along the top; others have a ridge that sticks up half an inch or so. Sherpas say the yeti has a pointed head. Is that point really just a ridge crest on an unusual bear?

Bill relaxes too and lets his curiosity show. He pulls out trays of skulls from other Himalayan bears; sloth bear skulls, *Melursus ursinus;* and Himalayan red bear skulls, *Ursus arctos isabellinus.* Their skulls are broader than ours – nose holes smaller, eyes bigger. Only the fit between our skull and the black bear specimens is close. That means the genus for our skull is certain, *Selanarctos.*

Bill suggests that among *Selanarctos* teeth are probably the most critical indicators. How do our teeth compare? Our skull has the *Selanarctos* configuration of molars, premolars, canines, and incisors and are worn enough to prove it was mature. But our skull is small for a bear with that much cusp wear, about 20 percent smaller than the skulls in the drawer, and its molars also look smaller. We don't have calipers with us, but a red plastic ruler from Bill's desk shows that our bear has uniformly smaller teeth than any specimen they have

Villager carrying home a small, field-dressed tree bear killed with a deadfall trap

(photo by David Ide)

from the west Himalaya. Our molars are the same size as those of *Selanarctos* specimens from Iran and Japan, the far edges of the species range.

Our bear then must be a small adult *Selanarctos.* But why are its key features so small? Is there in its habitat some nutritional deficiency? Or does an over-population of bears in the Barun deplete food supply and produce stunted bears? Or is our bear abnormal and a runt? Or is there a subspecies difference in the eastern Himalaya, the heart of the *Selanarctos* range, where specimens would be expected to be bigger but are in fact smaller? None of the skulls here is from the eastern Himalaya, so we don't have anything for direct compari-son. Or is the explanation as villagers say, that there are two species of *Selanarctos:* the known, *thibetanus,* as represented in this collection; and a dis-tinct, smaller tree bear, previously undiscovered? I wish we had brought one of those large ground-bear skulls from the Barun to prove the existence of the larger bear. And we need more small tree bear skulls to get an idea of variation. Why didn't we buy Lendoop's tree bear skull as well as this one from Lhakpa?

I spend the next day in the Smithsonian mammal library, reputedly one of the world's foremost collections. I find amazingly little on *Selanarctos.* In only two hours of searching, on one eight-and-a-half-by-eleven-inch piece of lined white paper, I list the citations for all known references. In another five hours, I've read all of them – except one book that is in Russian and four other docu-ments referred to but not in the Smithsonian collection. The world's written knowledge of *Selanarctos,* a bear with a 5,000-mile range, from Iran to Taiwan and Japan, from India to the Soviet Union: one book, eleven articles.

According to these accounts, western Himalayan bears weigh from 200 to 400 pounds, ranging from a light female to a heavy male. These weights are too high for the tree bear the villagers have described as that which "two men can carry." The five-year-old female in the zoo was at most 150 pounds. And the lower small *Selanarctos* weights are reported from the periphery of the range – Japan, Taiwan, Iran. Himalayan specimens of this bear are supposed to be big. Such small size is not typical of Barun bears.

The weights given in the literature fit those we heard reported for ground bears. Five or six men could carry 400 pounds, especially if they field-dressed it. But descriptions of bear size for other species emphasize that weights have little significance. Mature North American grizzlies, for instance, vary from 300 to over 1,000 pounds. Half-size bears usually indicate poor nutrition, not gene differences.

Other discrepancies exist between what the literature says and what villagers report. *Selanarctos* is aggressive, attacking humans, unlike the Himalayan red bear, *Ursus arctos isabellinus*, which usually leaves people alone. But Lendoop said tree bears aren't aggressive. And our bear can't be a red bear; our skull didn't match the *Ursus arctos* skulls.

Late in the afternoon, in a footnote from 1941 in R. I. Pocock's definitive *Fauna of British India*, I find a short report describing a tree-living Asiatic black bear, *Selanarctos arboreus*. Back in 1869, J.E. Gray, Pocock's predecessor as curator of mammals at the British Museum, suggested that *Selanarctos arboreus* differed from *Selanarctos thibetanus*. He based his assertion on field reports and a specimen submitted to the museum by Oldham, a naturalist working out of Darjeeling, a hill station in India.

Arboreus, a small black bear that lives in trees – the tree bear exists! Its skull is still in the British Museum. Here before me in this article is proof. The tree bear is reported and known.

I read on. Seventy-two years after Oldham presented his bear skull to the British Museum, Pocock examined it more carefully and compared it with others there. He found nothing distinctive enough about it to warrant classifying it as a separate species or even subspecies from *thibetanus*. But in those intervening years both Oldham's field notes and the bear's skin, which he had also given the museum, disappeared. Maybe the notes held data that were critical? Pocock had only Oldham's assertions, Gray's classification, and one skull, a skull that, like ours, seems to be not dramatically different from others, only smaller. Maybe Pocock and modern taxonomy are wrong, and Gray and Oldham were right?

The name is exciting: *arboreus*, "tree." Had Oldham seen the bear in trees? Was he simply translating the village term *rukh balu?* Darjeeling, after all, is only sixty-five air miles from the Barun Valley. Darjeeling's altitude and habitat are similar; could the name be, too?

Although the library will soon be closing, I've got to find Gray's original article. Does the Smithsonian have it from 114 years ago? I go to the back shelves. Good libraries are so wonderful; an obscure scientific datum just sits on the shelf waiting, being dusted regularly, patiently waiting. Seventy-two years it waits in one room in England. Pocock looks at it. Another forty-one years it waits. Now I seek it in another room in the United States. Has anyone else checked out this mystery in all those years? In libraries around the world, such data sit, waiting a century or more for one person to build knowledge using that particular iota.

High on a gray metal shelf I find the annals of the *Royal Zoological Society*, bound in black leather, embossed in gold print. More than a hundred such volumes fill this sturdy shelf against the back wall. Here is the volume from 1869. Here is independent evidence that 114 years ago, before the tree bear possessed our fantasies, another Westerner gathered reports of a bear in trees and sent a specimen home to his museum.

My eyes race through brittle yellow pages, reading, rereading, unable to comprehend the text one sentence at a time. Then, laughing at my hyperactive imagination, I slow down. Oldham's evidence is, in truth, scant. They found a small bear they thought to be different. Why did they think it different? Oldham does not say. He collected the skull and skin. From them, Gray concluded that the different size and coat were important, but Pocock did not. His analysis of the skull seventy-two years later found no unusual features. Why did Oldham and Gray call this bear *arboreus?* Does the name come from information Oldham gathered or from information provided by villagers? The annals of the *Royal Zoological Society* do not say.

Suddenly, the tree bear information we gathered clicks. Except for two characteristics – the peculiar foot and its smaller size – everything distinctive about the tree bear is behavioral. Villagers do not claim that the tree bear is taxonomically different; that's something museums worry about, not villagers. And our concern, like the villagers', is behavioral, especially a behavior that makes mysterious footprints in the snow.

Sitting in a wooden armchair by the government-gray water cooler, again I go through the *Selanarctos* articles, taking notes. Reported findings are congruent with ours. When walking in snow *Selanarctos* sometimes uses submerged rhododendron branches to support it from falling through. More consistently than the other bears, *Selanarctos* places its hind paw into the forepaw track, making the track appear bipedal. Among Himalayan bears, *Selanarctos* is the most agile and delicate climber.

Looking down the five floors to Constitution Avenue, newly found facts and old ideas mix in my mind to create confusion. I see hot dog trucks selling to the late afternoon tourists. What have we found? I don't know. Our family's been away from the gentle hills for more than two months. It's time to head back to West Virginia.

Chapter Fifteen

April 4, 1983. The postman leaves twenty boxes of developed slides from Kodak in our big red mailbox. My curiosity grows all day as the slides sit on my office desk. What will they show? Will any of the rolls be all black? Taking the boxes home, I wait until Jennifer and Jesse have gone to bed, put another couple of logs on the fire, and brew up a pot of hot chocolate.

Down from the attic comes the projector and screen. I flip through the slides. Box after box looks good – sharp pictures, good colors. Box thirteen: the tracks in the snow. Uniform prints are marching up the slope, clearly out of high-altitude bamboo. There, the tracks detour to one side off the ridge, then cross to the other side seeking support from rhododendron branches beneath the snow. Over here, crossing the cliff, are the delicate but perceptible disruptions of moss on rock.

The next slide shows a close-up of the tracks, of the thumblike imprint. Another slide shows it again, standing separate from the four digits across the top. Two months ago that "thumbprint" was instant yeti proof. Only primates have thumbs, so the maker of that track must be a primate. I relive the excitement of our discovery. The fire burns low as projector and screen shine forth their tale. Softly the refrigerator hums from the kitchen. Memories rush through my veins, and with them a vision. Beyond the footprints on the screen, a hominoid walks through the snow. It stops, disappears into bamboo, then peers back out, in its paw, a white bamboo shoot held like a cigar between thumb and forefinger. Embers burn. The vision dances on.

I flip more slides across the screen. I stop. There in the track before me shine nail marks. Nail marks mean bear. Two months earlier – even a few minutes earlier – there weren't nail marks there. Alone, in the privacy of my living room, I flush with embarrassment. I swore to Bob there were none. Of course my brain was starved for oxygen that day we found the tracks, my body fatigued from the climb through wet, deep snow. Why didn't I sense that my judgment might be gone? Why didn't I at least hedge my bets?

New ideas and old ideas about the tree bear, about the yeti collide in my head. Explanations no longer fit, no longer run smoothly. Is everything, including our prints, explained by bear? I lean back, thinking. The footprints tell their tale on the screen before me. But there might be further evidence in the attic.

Tiptoeing upstairs through our bedroom, I go into the attic and unwrap the two paws bought from Lhakpa. On my way back through the dark bedroom, I grope around in my top dresser drawer for my pocket emergency kit. From it I pull out the small green Bic lighter I laid in the track to indicate size when I took the photograph. Back downstairs, I move the projector table closer to adjust the size of the image on the screen. With the projector four feet away, the size of the lighter on the screen is the same as the lighter in my hand. Now, the paw print on the screen must differ only by the amount the snow melted from the size of the bear's paw.

I pick up the left forepaw bought from Lhakpa in Shakshila and hold it against the picture of the print in the snow. It fits perfectly, no distortion. The print in the snow is identical to the dried paw in my hand, nail marks match nail marks. The only difference is that the snow print is longer – and that is extended because of the hind paw overprinting.

I did not see a tree bear make these prints shining before me on the Himalayan ridge, but now I am as certain of the maker of these tracks as if I were seeing the bear make them before my eyes. On the screen is a yeti footprint. In my hand is a tree bear's paw. I now know that at least one yeti identification is indeed a tree bear.

Will Shipton's and Cronin's photographs of yeti prints fit too? Both are in a drawer at my office a mile away. The clock hands slide over the top past midnight. I turn off the projector lamp, jump into my old red vw van, and bounce along the dirt road to the office. On the way back, a flat rear tire cools my excitement.

The April night shines clear and cold as I open the van door and step out. The house is half a mile away, the wind generator spinning above it with a gentle "thwup, thwup, thwup" of its blades. Spruce trees sway softly and whisper their messages as I change the tire. The moist wind, a hint of spring that is coming, strokes my neck and around my face, and runs on to rustle the brittle grass of last year. I work slowly so as not to disturb the night with harsh metal sounds.

An hour later, the tree bear track is again alight on the screen. I compare it with Shipton's original photograph. The Shipton print remains a mystery. It's too big for a tree bear, and there are no obvious nail marks. The ordering of toes is not uniform. The thumb is placed differently.

I hold up Cronin's Arun Valley photograph, taken less than three miles farther up the ridge from the spot of our prints. Drawing any firm conclusions from it would be risky. The print sizes correspond, although not closely: discounting for possible snow melt, our track is 6.7 inches long and 4.8 inches wide; theirs measures 9.0 inches long and 4.8 inches wide, but the bear that made ours might simply be smaller, or, more likely, the overprint a little more complete. The thumblike inside digit is in the same place. The quality of their photograph is poor, grainy with fuzzy lines. Snow was soft for them and therefore conditions were not as good that day as on our discovery. A crisp, clear photograph from them will tell more.

With new logs now on, the fire burns strong. I settle into the sofa, our slide still shining on the screen. By the projector light I read the captivating narrative again:

> Shortly before dawn the next morning, Howard climbed out of our tent. Immediately, he called excitedly. There, beside the trail we had made to our tents, was a new set of footprints. While we were sleeping, a creature had approached our camp and walked directly between our tents. The Sherpas identified the tracks, without question, as yeti prints. We, without question, were stunned.

Why was Cronin so sure their print was not made by a bear? Hadn't he picked up tree bear stories? The villagers he encountered were virtually the

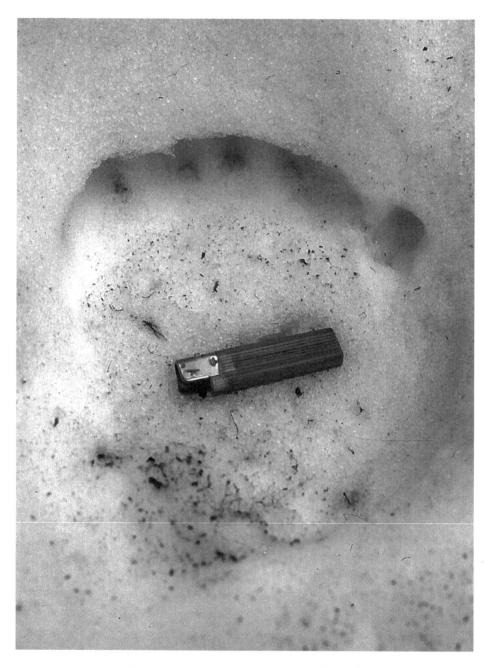

The author's yeti print complete with nail marks

same as ours on the other side of the Barun ridge. But then I hadn't picked up the tree bear reports either. It took Bob's skillful questioning to do that.

NICK RETURNS FROM NEPAL A WEEK LATER AND CALLS FROM WASHINGTON. IT is clear over the phone that he has more than memories of our month in the jungle to tell. He knows nothing yet of our visit to the Smithsonian or the revelations on the slides. Ten minutes after entering the house, he is telling of *his* discoveries.

"Prints I found in the snow in Langtang Valley were bipedal, just like the ones we saw on the ridge – with the thumblike marks too. And I found more bear information. In Tarkegaon I found a skin, the skin of a small black bear, about the size of the zoo bear. The man who had the skin was the one who had killed it, so I asked him specific questions. He used the words *rukh balu*. I've got pictures that I'll show you when they're developed. I took pictures of everything. But the surprising thing is, villagers also claim there's a large ground bear. Another villager showed me a ground bear skin too."

Do two bears really exist in the eastern Himalayan jungles? In how many valleys are they? Is Nick's Nepali good enough for his reports to be trustworthy? Clearly, one of the most important variables in such research turns out to be language skill, something few yeti hunters have had.

Two months later, in June 1983, I receive a letter from Fleming: "Since we were together in February, on three treks I've picked up further village reports of tree bears and ground bears: the southern slopes of Himalchuli, the Rowaling Valley, and Sikkim." Fleming's reports, therefore, confirm what Nick found.

Since March I've written twice to Cronin, but he hasn't replied or answered his phone. I send off two more letters, one to Cronin and one to McNeely, who works in Switzerland, telling them about our hypothesis. In July, working from field notes, I pull together what is known about tree bears.

1. Tree bear reports are now known from the Barun Valley and four additional regions. The villagers in these Wve regions are of diVerent ethnic groups, speak diVerent languages, have diVerent cultures, and have little known contact with one another. All their descriptions of tree bears and ground bears across these regions agree in major details.

2. A live small bear exists (and has existed for two years in Kathmandu zoo). It appears to fit in all respects to physical descriptions of tree bears. Of particular interest is the dropped inner claw on the front paw.

3. We possess an apparently mature skull and two paws from another such small bear.

4. In 1869 Oldham reported a seemingly similar bear in Darjeeling, sixty-five air miles from the Barun Valley, and called it *arboreus*.

5. Nick photographed the skin of another such alleged tree bear in the Helambu Valley and also claims seeing a ground bear skin. Fleming has found reports also from three other regions.

6. Photographs we took in the Barun indicate that this new bear makes tracks in the snow that appear strikingly primatelike in that they seem to have a hallux and appear bipedal – fitting yeti stories in many respects.

7. Nail marks and hair remnants suggest that there is a bear that is almost apelike at climbing trees and makes intricate nests using strength and dexterity to break 1¼-inch-diameter bamboo stalks at uniform heights or oak limbs at great heights.

8. Some of the characteristics above are reported for *Selanarctos* but not all. This incompleteness is not of great concern, since this genus has never been thoroughly described scientifically. Most evidence being drawn from anecdotes by British hunters before World War II.

Major questions must be answered. Is the tree bear a new species or subspecies of *Selanarctos*? Are tree bears and ground bears the same? Are tree bears females and ground bears males? Or are tree bears juveniles and ground bears adults? Or are tree bears runts and ground bears normal? Do tree bears really not breed with ground bears, as villagers claim?

It seems incredible something as large as a bear should exist into the modern age and remain scientifically undetected. But maybe it isn't so surprising. The epoch of exploration ended in the past century; Nepal was closed during that exploratory period. Once Nepal opened in 1950, no one ever looked there for new mammals. But how did a major multidisciplinary team like Cronin and McNeely's spend nearly two years in the same area, inventorying flora and fauna, and miss this bear?

What is most puzzling about the Cronin/McNeely data is that their descriptions of bear activity (both what they published and what Cronin spent half an hour telling me on the phone) fit so neatly with ground bears. None of their descriptions mesh with tree bear evidence – except their yeti print. They never report "nests" or shy bears – and that is all the bear evidence we found. The only bears they reported were large and aggressive. One particularly mammoth bear, Fleming remembered, they tried to kill. Why are ground bears their most common bear and for us the rarest one?

As I wrestle with the yeti questions it becomes increasingly clear that the larger biological context of the Himalaya is poorly understood. The reasons are twofold: first, wilderness in the Himalaya is essentially gone; only a handful of valleys remain, the Barun being the furthest one west that is still pristine across multiple biomes; second, although specific aspects of the Himalaya, such as its anthropology, history, and mountaineering, have been explored extensively, and although focused research has investigated key species such as the tiger or crocodile or has undertaken taxonomies of birds and plants, it is only now, with local scientific leadership, that we are moving beyond the narrowly focused research and the historical explorations from the decades before 1940 to explore broader issues. We are just beginning to understand the fascinating interactions among the ecological zones that are stacked one upon another in the Himalaya.

A whole new understanding of the resilience of life is opening for me. With the urgent focus of biological research on the tropics there remains therefore much ignorance about life at high altitudes, especially animal life. We do know that the soils and ecology there (like in the Arctic) are clearly fragile. Whereas it may be easy to scar that landscape, it is not adequately recognized how hardy and adaptable the individual species are. Botanists have gathered plants. Physiologists have studied the human capacity to adapt and live there. Despite this research, the interaction and the knowledge of the resilience of high-altitude systems is incomplete.

The species of these high-altitude, colder climates have remarkable bioresilience. High-altitude species must adapt to vast and rapid climatic change, temperature fluctuations of 100 degrees Fahrenheit in a matter of hours. Not only must vascular systems respond adequately to prevent rupture from freezing, but they must maximize the times of warmth (when biochemistry is most efficient) for metabolism, respiration, and photosynthesis. Reproduction must also adapt, avoiding complex rituals, preparing (as high-altitude flower-bud primordia do) a year before they procreate. Gender differences lose their decoration and become more functional. Food sources, which may be deprived half the year and sometimes up to eight months of the year, must efficiently harbor nutrients in roots and rhizomes or body fat and secret caches – and dramatically minimize metabolism through hibernation or reduced activity. Compared to the tropics, the biodiversity of species in colder climates and at high altitudes is less but the resilience of each individual species may be greater.

As our planet spins into an approaching era of dramatic eco-change, the capacity that it will bring forward to respond effectively to its newly unfolding environment cannot only be measured by biological diversity. So many species, especially the numerous tropical ones, fill small and fragile niches. As pollution increases and as climate changes, these highly specialized species (and ecosystems) will lose their adaptive advantage. To select an extreme example, the greater New York City ecosystem may well be more resilient and ecologically determinative than the Costa Rican rain forest – two areas of roughly equal size. At least we need parameters that allow rigorous consideration of comparative biological reslience, given the magnitude of the changes under way.

The biological strength that comes in the tropics from biodiversity may be complemented by the resilience of the fewer species in the colder climates. Research must increasingly look at the whole planetary system. Like the bounce of any ball, we will not rebound from the impact of the coming changes if we do not utilize the flexibility of our whole sphere. Hope for a planet rapidly changing in the very basics of ecology – that is, its temperature, atmosphere, soil and water quality and quantity, and distribution and density of species – may also lie in nurturing those species that give it resilience, as well as protecting those species that give it diversity and precious genetic strength. For me, as for those who create national parks, nature is first attractive because it is wild: animals, grand mountains, untested rivers. Preserve the majesty. Then awakens a recognition of biological value. Count the species. Value is measured by diversity. Although large numbers of species could suggest great wealth in the Himalaya (835 species of birds exist in Nepal, roughly equal to the number in all of North America), additional dimensions are now needed. My quest for the yeti is opening new views for me on how often otherwise-separated perspectives reveal the complex interlinkages of a whole planet.

Chapter Sixteen

Fourteen years earlier I walked through these glass doors, the C Street entrance of the U.S. State Department. That morning in 1969 I was showing up for the first day of work on my first "real" job. Graduate school and the Vietnam protests behind, I was no longer standing against the Establishment; I was joining it. I wanted to do something patriotically positive and so I joined the State Department to work on the population problem in the Himalaya.

I remember my feelings of fourteen years before as I walk through these doors again. They still have the same delicate black strip bordering their edges. My earlier feeling is the same: this room is all breadth and no depth; its ceilings are too high and it feels like a post office, not the entryway to U.S. foreign policy. Then, as now, I straighten my hair with my fingers, my comb lying on the backseat of the cab from when I pulled out my wallet. But today, just off the plane from another medical research expedition to Nepal, I'm also sweating from the rush of finding a cab after an interview for "All Things Considered" at National Public Radio. Fortunately, Noah Adams didn't ask, "Is your new bear the yeti?" How would I have answered that?

Vice President Bush is hosting a state luncheon for King Birendra of Nepal. What will it be like to see His Majesty in the United States and on a state visit? The last time we spent time together in the States we were both graduate students. Surely he will be more formal than on our many visits together in Nepal. Where can I put this suitcase?

The revolving glass door still spinning behind her, Lila Bishop – whose husband, Barry, pointed out Jennifer to me in that crowd in Kathmandu – comes to my rescue with a smile and a hug. "Dan'l, what are you doing here with a suitcase?"

"This suitcase? Why, Lila, it holds one bear skull and two dried bear feet. We've got to represent the villagers at this high-class luncheon. Didn't you bring something too – maybe some nice smelly yak cheese?"

Lila hugs me again, then leads me by the elbow to the elevator, where we stand at the back while I use Lila's comb. After the doors open she straightens my bow tie. I pick up my suitcase. The dry paws rattle. Secretary of State Shultz steps out of a door and into the hallway and walks ahead of us, followed by two aides. After some confusion with the woman at the name-tag table, a question to Security about bear parts at such a reception, and some embarrassment, it is agreed that I can stash my suitcase behind her table. Lila and I enter another room, another world. A harp plays with a string quartet. Massive gilded picture frames dominate the walls. The furniture, the light fixtures, everything feels so French. Barry, vicechair of the Committee on Research and Exploration at the National Geographic Society, quickly joins us.

"Congratulations on the discovery. I read it in the *New York Times*. What do you have to prove it?" Lila tells him about the suitcase out in the hall.

As we move through the receiving line, Barry spots Russell Train, president of the World Wildlife Fund, and introduces us. Train invites me to make an appointment and moves farther down the receiving line.

"Dan'l, how are you going to prove this bearish assertion?" Barry's bluntness is renowned. "How is a nonscientist like you going to make this stick?"

"Well, Bob Fleming is involved . . ."

"Bob's a scientist for Himalayan birds, maybe the best, but bears aren't birds. For bears Bob won't do."

"Bob started with birds, but he's solid on other aspects of natural history. I'd much rather have Bob's breadth than some hot bear expert who doesn't know the Himalaya and can't speak the language. Anyway, there just aren't any real Himalayan bear experts. Moreover, the really interesting leads are coming from local villagers, not from scientists. They know what's in their jungles."

We greet the vice president and His Majesty and resume our discussion.

"You have a taxonomic question here, Dan'l. A natural historian, even the best, is not the person you need. And without a bear expert, you can't raise money to fund further research. I'm not telling you this because you have to convince me. You don't. I want to help."

"Barry, it's not that complicated, and we don't have outside funding to do a big scientific process. All we need is to collect both types of skulls from the same habitat. That'll prove two bears."

"Where have you ever seen anything that simple?"

Barry's right. We need help, but I don't want to make room in this project for others. Bob knows the jungle and Nepal. With a bear expert and a Nepal expert, what's left for me? Jennifer and I would be out the thousands we had spent on our search so far and the excitement of the continuing discovery.

"You need one of the Craighead brothers. John's health is better than Frank's, so I'd start by asking John. Either of the Craigheads has the guts to take on a new idea – and the skill to help you do it right. If a Craighead participates, others will pay attention. You'll learn a lot working with one of them, and as a side effect you'll make a good friend."

MARCH 1984. I'M BACK IN WASHINGTON WITH MY LITTLE GREEN SUITcase to meet with Russ Train. Inside the case are the skull, the two dried feet, and 300 slides of the Barun Valley. The cramped offices of the World Wildlife Fund off Dupont Circle feel friendly – no grandioseness here. Train welcomes me warmly to his long, narrow corner office, introduces Curtis Freeze, a zoologist working on World Wildlife's Amazon project. "Please tell us about your bear."

"The story is simple, really. Nepali villagers claim two bears exist in their jungles, a small tree bear and a larger ground bear. The ground bear seems similar to the known Asiatic black bear. But their descriptions of tree bears don't fit with scientific descriptions of any known bear. It's easy to discount these reports, but we have a skull, a tree bear skull, a skull uniformly smaller than Asiatic black bear skulls in the collections at the Smithsonian or in New York's American Museum. And besides physical differences, there are differences in behavior. We discovered some remarkable bear nests in oak trees and bamboo."

"What do you actually know?" Freeze asks.

I open my case, take out the skull, and pass it to Train. "There are three key features. First, the reports are remarkably uniform in five separate valleys. Second, there's a variety of hard evidence, such as nests, evidence that doesn't fit with what is known of *Selanarctos*. And third, the actual skull we have is uniformly smaller than the other skulls collected from the central Himalaya."

Freeze presses. "You have a skull and you have stories. Skulls and stories do not prove hypotheses. What will you do to prove your assertions?"

"The research needed isn't complicated. We have one tree bear skull. Now we need a representative ground bear skull. Since the ground bear is a known bear, getting such skulls should be easy. It's just that we need both types of skulls from the same habitat."

"What qualifies you to do this research?" Freeze asks. "What do you know about bears?"

"I don't know much about bears. A bear expert or even a taxonomist is not needed to challenge a hypothesis. A bear expert is not needed to bring in more skulls. We, the nonexperts, were the ones open enough to uncover the possibility of this discovery."

"True, but maybe it's precisely because you are inadequately qualified that you've jumped to erroneous conclusions."

Train joins in. "Let's see Dan's data. The World Wildlife Fund focuses on preserving animals, not finding new ones, but maybe there is something here. Why don't you submit a proposal? Let us look it over. But please understand we have many requests and can make no promises."

I thank Train, pick up the suitcase, and leave, convinced that we're not going to get World Wildlife support. The meeting was flat, no excitement from either Train or Freeze. At the core, they didn't take the possibility of a new species seriously. I've got an hour before my appointment at the Smithsonian. Over a too-expensive hot fudge sundae at an ice-cream boutique off of Dupont Circle, I sort out my thoughts.

What is it that bothers me so about the conservation organizations? Is it just that they're not interested in my bear? By now I have knocked on the doors of most of the major ones, introducing my bear. No, it's that they remind me of the worst aspects of the missionaries I knew as a child. Conservationists feel that they know the truth, that they have seen the future, that you achieve enlightenment only by accepting their way. Theirs is a narrow orthodoxy. To them the loss of any species of flora or fauna is a sin. Desecration of nature by any human waste, a sacrilege. The consumption of natural resources, an abomination. Environmentalists tend to be dogmatists rather than not open-minded scientists.

This rigidity has resulted in the isolation of the environmental movement. Those who do not join in true belief become opponents, in the courts, in boycotts. The environmenal movement has walled itself off from its natural allies, farmers, fishermen, loggers, those who make their living off of the land – or those, like me, who want to explore new ideas or try unorthodox solutions. Environmental priorities are in opposition to jobs and economic growth, suffering and human welfare, children and stewardship of the future. In truth, environmental action is not a separate crusade, the preserving of a world apart from people. The new world environment is more and more a world of people – and the orthodoxy that sees the environmental task only as preserving wildness ignores where the world has now evolved to.

I scrape what remains of the chocolate sauce from inside the glass dish. I know that I'm hurt, finding reasons to criticize. This bitter, hot chocolate is so good. My emotions are bouncing me around because I was rebuffed. I scrape the corners of the glass once again for the last of the bitter chocolate. If I want to help build a bridge between people and nature, I must not blame others. I must learn to listen better. I head to the Smithsonian to see Richard Thorington, curator of mammals.

I knock at a half-open door. "Come in, come in. Ah, Taylor-Ide, the fellow with the Himalayan bears. I'm Dick Thorington." A smallish gentleman rises from his desk, takes two steps toward me with outstretched hand. "Sorry I wasn't in the office when you came before. Glad Bill could help you. Let's check your skull, see how it compares with ours. I'd like the opportunity of looking it over."

Thorington leads the way through the maze of hallways of the Mammal Division. "Here we are, *Selanarctos*. Let's take a look." Down falls the front of one box. Out slide the wooden trays: skulls, courtesy of more than a century of scientific fieldwork; nineteen bears from across 5,000 miles of Asia – bears from the Baluchistan Desert, bears from northern Kashmir, bears from southern Russia, India, northern Burma, China, Japan, and Taiwan.

"Hum, general bone configuration similar, occipital crests almost identical, nostrum remarkably the same." Thorington holds our skull in his left hand, a large skull from Kashmir in his right. "Here underneath, dentition between the two skulls is identical; molars, premolars, incisors. Yes, it's all there."

"But, Dr. Thorington," I reply. "Here; use the micrometer, measure the molars. Measure all the molars of your central Himalayan skulls. The teeth of the smallest of those Himalayan skulls, even the juveniles, will also be larger, significantly larger, in all dental measurements than our skull. Doesn't uniform size differences indicate some sort of separation?"

Thorington takes the micrometer and checks the molar sizes. "You're right about the size difference. But intriguing though such uniform differences may be, they don't prove anything. True, central Himalayan bears such as yours should be large, like these other central Himalayan bears from Kashmir or Assam. And instead, your teeth and skulls are smaller, like the skulls from Taiwan or Iran. The logical explanation for this difference is that your population is nutritionally deficient, not taxonomically different. The first assumption should be that something in their diet, or not in their diet, prevents these bears from getting as large as one might expect."

"But your nutritional argument neither explains the villagers' claim for the larger ground bear nor their behavioral descriptions concerning the tree bear. These descriptions certainly contradict what is known of *Selanarctos*."

"But keep in mind, Daniel, this other evidence you present I must treat as only hearsay. It is not scientific evidence. This skull you bring is scientific evidence, something we can compare. As scientific evidence, your skull is inconclusive."

"But what about the bear nests we found? They are evidence. They are exceptional."

"I haven't examined the literature. Such nests may be exceptional. But even if bears have never before been reported to make nests, rather than jumping to the conclusion that you've found a new bear, it would be more appropriate to assume that a known bear has adopted until now unknown habits."

"But what about what the villagers say?" I reply.

"Villagers aren't scientists. What might be two bears to villagers could be one bear to science. Villagers express ideas that are completely implausible scientifically, like the yeti, for instance. You have to be careful. You aren't saying you've found the yeti, are you? Villagers use language differently from the way scientists do."

"I hear what you're saying," I reply. "And I appreciate the differences between how villagers use language and the way scientists use language. Any suggestions?"

"Yes, I think your question needs investigation. Something about this skull, something I can't pin down, seems different. In features it is similar, but in its *feeling* it is more delicate. The skulls in our collection feel massive – even the small ones. But such subjective judgment is nothing to base a scientific decision on. You need to go back to the field.

"To show that you have a new bear you will need skulls of both the known and the new. The two skulls have to be morphologically distinct to be separate species. If they are both distinct and sympatric, that is, from the same habitat, then you probably have two species, one of which would be new. If the skulls are morphologically distinct but not sympatric, they may or may not be species but only subspecies differentiated. If you cannot provide distinct skulls, you probably don't have two bears."

"OK," I reply. "That taxonomic question is interesting, it may even be important scientifically, but for us it is the behavioral differences that matter. There is an animal out there that is doing things we never thought *Selanarctos* could do, especially in the prints it makes in the snow."

"Well," Thorington replies, "you'd better be really careful about those prints in snow, what you say about them. Yeti claims can make you lose credibility very quickly. You've got to prove that there are real behavioral differences between the two bears, just as you've got to get more skulls for taxonomic differences. What you have now is only a hypothesis, not a conclusion."

"Could it be that this is like two of the Nepalese wren-babblers? In all physical features the two species look virtually alike, with nearly identical plumage, but one is considerably smaller, has a different song, different breeding altitudes. Two babblers, physically indistinguishable, are known different species – it is behavior that tells them apart. Two bears that look the same could be still different. There are such parallels known among animals."

"Check out your hypothesis. Such a species or even subspecies difference is an interesting possibility, especially for mammals. So far your evidence does not prove that, but your hypothesis is particularly unusual and worth testing. I'll send you a letter to that effect. Such a letter from the Smithsonian Institution may help with your fund raising."

I leave with thanks, promising to keep Thorington informed.

Chapter Seventeen

At two the following morning, Jennifer, Jesse, and I arrive home on Spruce Knob. Jennifer and I have talked the whole business through once again in the car as we drove. It isn't the bad news; I get that regularly in my work. It's the loneliness of not finding people willing to risk steps into the unknown.

Time to bring in the suitcases before going to bed. As I step outside and pull the front door shut, a deer snorts, then snorts again. Crashing comes from down the hill by the blackberry bushes. Stillness returns to the night. Washington is only two hundred miles away, but it seems more like light-years, farther certainly than the Milky Way shining overhead, which is very much still a part of my cosmos. A breeze rustles the tops of the three spruces down the slope by the spring. A sliver of a moon hangs over the ridge called Spruce Bars, not throwing much more light than the stars.

So many people seem only interested in further domesticating the little compartment of knowledge that they have chosen to live in. Thorington had strong grounds for skepticism. He remained scientifically honest and still willing to accept that the world we live in remains unknown, undomesticated. How can people stand on the shore of the uncharted and watch waves that rise from mysterious deeps come and crash at their feet – and think they can hold such oceanic unknowns back with concrete reality?

Opening the tailgate, I make one trip with Jennifer's and Jesse's small suit-cases, another with my bag and the duffel of toys, and a third and last trip with a bag of groceries. The car is empty. I close our front door on the Milky Way and go to bed.

Jesse wakes me at six-thirty. I carry him downstairs to let Jennifer get some more sleep, and I start to put away the suitcases and groceries left by the door. Where is the little green suitcase with the bear skull and the Barun slides? Maybe it's still in the car. In my pajamas, I dash outside into thick fog; water drips off the metal roof like a light rain. There's no green suitcase – only an overlooked grocery bag. Then I remember. On the trip down, when Jesse was crying, we stopped to rearrange baggage. I took the suitcase out and set it on the ground at the edge of the interstate. I must have forgotten to put it back in the car. Picking up the brown paper bag, now sodden from the humidity, I walk back into the house, under the dripping roof edge. Jesse is crying again. My soaked pajamas cling to my sides.

Jennifer hears me on the phone asking for the Virginia State Police. She comes downstairs, takes Jesse, and, holding him on her hip, stands listening to my conversation and looking out our picture window into the wall of fog. I reach the State Police barracks in Woodstock, Virginia.

"I need your help, please. I lost a suitcase, a green one, in the Shenandoah Valley alongside Interstate 81 early this morning when I pulled our car over to attend to my crying toddler. Could you alert troopers to search for this suit-case along the road? It's small and dark green, looks sort of like an overgrown briefcase. . . ."

"What's in it? Well, this may surprise you, but there is one bear skull, two bear paws, and 300 photographic slides. All are extremely rare scientific speci-mens, specimens from possibly a new bear in the Himalaya Mountains. These are the only artifacts of this bear now known to science. . . . Yeah, I know it's hard to believe someone would leave a suitcase like that beside the interstate in the middle of the night. Oh, you have a little kid? She doesn't like to ride in her car seat? Well, maybe you understand how I got distracted by my son's screaming last night."

Jennifer turns as I hang up. "I can't believe that. After all we have gone through for that bear skull, for those slides. Now they're sitting along the interstate somewhere. This search will break us yet!" Her voice reassures me of her trust, her continuing support, in spite of this. She offers some ideas:

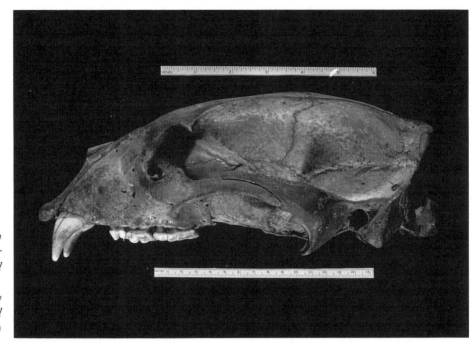

*Side view
of tree bear
skull*

*(photo by
Michael
Meador)*

"Did you have our name on the suitcase? Do you remember where it was we stopped? Was anything else in it? You'd better call newspapers and radio stations throughout the Shenandoah Valley. Maybe they can help get the news out."

I can't look at her or Jesse. All our family money, all our family time – months of it, mostly good times, but still gifts that they've given to my project – cast aside. I turn, walk past the old bed in the living room that, for lack of funds, Jennifer has made up with big pillows and bolsters to look like a sofa, and go out the front door into the morning fog. Into the white cloud I walk aimlessly over the 400 acres I know so well. Wet and cold, my shirt clings to my skin. I have struggled for these mountaintop acres like I've struggled for that bear. In the high meadow north of Noah Warner's barn, a hawthorn tree rears out of the cloud like a bear. I steer a course around the prickly tree. Clouds like these can hang on the mountain for several days. Everything will be wet and cold, the cold that settles into the bones. The evidence is gone, our funds are gone. Nothing is any longer credible about my yeti/bear. I have nothing now for going on except the people who know and trust me. Now that I've lost this suitcase, why shouldn't friends lose that trust? Who is left to turn to for funding?

After an hour or more, I take the trail from the beech woods back toward the house. Jennifer has a strong fire crackling in the fireplace and the furnace on, too. A Mozart horn concerto plays on public radio. Walking to the phone, I call the Woodstock barracks again.

"Yes, I'm calling to follow up on a report I made this morning regarding a green suitcase lost last night along Interstate 81. . . . Oh, it was you I talked to? Any news?"

The troopers had searched the road from Toms Brook to New Market and no sign of anything. Nothing had blown off the side of the road into the grass. No reports by other travelers. I called all the service areas. Maybe someone picked up the suitcase but threw it away when they found a bear skull, two paws, and hundreds of slides inside.

Mid March moves slowly to mid April. A lot of rain, no flowers, and no news of the suitcase. For a month I had been calling radio stations and talking newspaper reporters into doing stories. The address on the suitcase is that

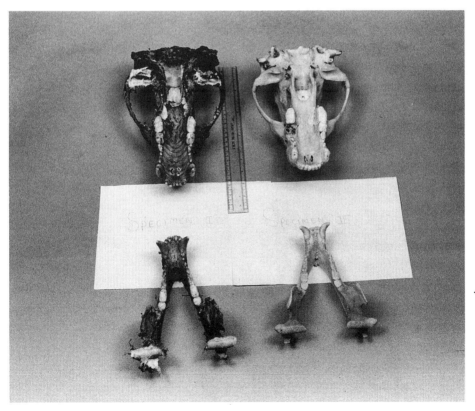

Dentition on field-collected and museum tree bear specimens

(photo by Michael Meador)

of my parents in Baltimore; I talked to the mailman and the UPS delivery man for that route. For a month someone has always been standing by our phone. It's become ridiculous. Jennifer doesn't object. In the beginning she got a new idea every day or so, some new angle to try. But we seem to have run out of ideas.

A telephone call comes from the Nepalese ambassador in Washington, D.C. The Smithsonian is hosting a reception at the National Zoo to kick off U.S. fund raising for Nepal's King Mahendra Trust for Nature Conservation. The World Wildlife Fund is organizing who should be invited, and there will be quite a guest list. His Royal Highness, Prince Gyanendra Bir Bikram Shah Dev, the king's energetic brother, will be the chief guest.

The National Zoo – what a great place for convening a wildlife gathering. The guests move around the patio in front of the lecture hall. Across the walkway are the pandas. Someone did a superb job of designing this. Philanthropists coming here should be reaching for their checkbooks. Is there anyone here who might be interested in helping find bears?

Ed Gould, curator of mammals at the National Zoo, introduces me to Jack Ziedensticker, the Smithsonian zoologist who used to run their tiger project in Nepal. "Jack, meet Daniel Taylor-Ide, the fellow who came up with the new information on *Selanarctos,* pretty interesting stuff." Inside, my gut is a knot. I hope I don't have to reveal the loss of the skull.

Jack is clearly skeptical. "How can there be a new species of *Selanarctos* out there? The Himalaya has been thoroughly studied for more than a hundred years. An unknown bear couldn't remain hidden that long. Bears have vast home ranges. Bears interact with people. We're not talking about a small bird with a small localized habitat."

"Well, that's the point. In a way, this isn't news. Villagers in eastern Nepal have been talking about two bears in their jungles for many years. No scientist knew their language well enough to hear what they were claiming and also knew enough Himalayan natural history to know what these claims meant. Now skulls have been collected. Nests and footprints have been observed. All these and the village reports suggest a taxonomic problem with simply including this within *Selanarctos.* I'm not saying it's definitely a new species; I'm saying there are differences: taxonomic differences maybe, and certainly unknown behavioral characteristics that are particularly interesting. And all these contemporary data are supported by a citation in the 1869 *Proceedings of the Royal Geographical Society.* A naturalist by the name of Oldham collected a bear skin and skull in the Darjeeling district, less than sixty miles from our site. Oldham named this bear *Selanarctos arboreus,* indicating presumably that it lived in trees, an interesting confirmation of modern villagers who talk of 'tree bears.'"

I doubt that I've convinced Jack, but our conversation ends when a friend, Mary Wagley, arrives with a warm hug. It is remarkable how some people can get so hostile over this bear stuff. Increasingly I suspect that, although no one mentions it, it's because of the possibility that it all points to the yeti. The yeti is scientifically preposterous. There's something – why else would things suddenly get so emotional?

Two weeks later, washing dishes, back home on our mountaintop, I reach over the sink and pick up the telephone on the first ring. It's the newspaper editor in Woodstock. "Dr. Daniel Taylor-Ide? You remember we ran that second story on your lost bear artifacts last week? Well, there's a fellow on hold now on my other phone line who says he has your suitcase. This guy won't give his name or phone number and wants to know what reward you'll pay to get it back. Oops, the light just went out."

The receiver in my hand, too, suddenly goes dead, its twisting black cord curling into a black box that goes nowhere. My heart races; my skin is hot. Is this someone's cruel joke? I want to run outside and shout out my pent-up woe. Was the phone call real? Where did I put the number of the newspaper in Woodstock?

The phone rings again. "Sorry I cut you off. I was trying to salvage the other call. Yes, the guy seemed for real. He spoke simple English and seemed afraid. I asked him twice for his name. He wanted to know how much money you'd pay. Then suddenly his phone went dead. Sorry we lost him. I think he got scared I might be tracing his call. Maybe he'll call back. How much reward will you pay?"

"Pray he does call back. Tell him $250. I'll have to borrow even that. I'll pay more if necessary, but I think a higher price might scare him off; he might think there's something illegal among that stuff. Whatever you do, please, please get that suitcase."

"I'll try. Stay there and let's wait this one out."

An hour later he calls again. "That guy called back. He said to show up at the ARCO gas station at the Shenandoah Caverns exit off Interstate 81 at 7:00

tonight with $250. He says show up there and wait. He'll get there as soon as he gets off work. I promised repeatedly there was nothing illegal done and nothing illegal in the suitcase. He was real scared you might have cops with you. I told him you wouldn't, that there wouldn't be anyone else anywhere around. I told him you won't ask any questions and will hand over cash for the suitcase."

The bank is closed. I call two friends whose business is on the way to my rendezvous. They take the money from their petty-cash drawer. Racing down Interstate 81, Jennifer, Jesse, and I arrive at the ARCO station at 6:40. We wait: 7:00 passes, 7:05, 7:10, 7:15. At 7:20 an aging, once-blue pick-up pulls through the station. The driver looks all around, then drives away. At 7:25 the pick-up comes back. "Kenny" gets out, reaches into the back of the pick-up, and pulls out the suitcase. I hand over the money. My shirt is soaked with sweat. I feel twenty pounds lighter. The suitcase is back. Inside our car, it sits in Jennifer's lap.

As we leave the gas station Jennifer opens the suitcase and separates the family slides from the bear slides. "Too many good memories are tied up in these slides to lose them again. I don't care so much about the skull or paws, but the slides are family memories; let's not run risks with them."

Chapter Eighteen

We need more bear skulls – one from a ground bear and another from a tree bear. Several months later, I head back to Nepal on another medical expedition. Thanks to another airline discount, Jennifer and Jesse again come too. When my work is finished, Jennifer and Jesse head off to a resort for a vacation, and I catch the plane to Tumlingtar to start the ten-day round-trip trek to Shakshila to gather more skulls.

Landing at Tumlingtar at four o'clock and trying to book my return, the official tells me that among all the flights only one seat is still available to Kathmandu. It is in six days (five and a half really). If I don't make that flight, there's not an open seat for a month. I have only six days to make the trip to Shakshila and back; last time it took us five days one-way. I make the booking and leave.

In the thatch-roofed tea shop next to the airstrip, villagers loiter and visit in the late afternoon. This spot is a waystation on the ancient north-south caravan route linking India and Tibet, and also on an east-west trail from the Everest region. Behind the tea shop is the fig tree we camped under eight months earlier while we waited for Jesse's clothes and our duffels to arrive from Kathmandu. In the tea shop villagers and government officials gather, pausing with friends over glasses of sweet milky tea, exchanging comments with the shopkeeper, or watching the perpetual caroms game. Four players are flicking their fingers to ricochet black and white checker-sized disks into each other and, they hope, into the four corner-pockets. From thornbushes behind the shop, a dove coos. The air with evening settles cool.

But my evening goal is ten miles away, 4,000 feet higher, the sheltered glen below Bhotebas village. I must hurry. Jennifer and Jesse will be waiting for me in Kathmandu. I can't miss that return flight. But I must get those skulls.

Leaving the tea shop, I see a young man step out of the dry-goods store fifty yards away. He appears to be angry as he strides out on to the trail. There's no village before Khandbari, so he's probably going that far. Probably going home. Maybe the four miles and the 2,500 feet to Khandbari Bazaar can be shared. He's walking fast. His wife should be starting his dinner of lentils and rice – they'll be waiting hot on his arrival. I hustle to catch up; he'll make a good trail partner. As he makes the first turn up the trail, I glimpse enough of his profile, the forehead, the nose, to know he is a Brahmin, one of the priestly caste. He's well dressed, but not a government official – probably then a schoolteacher.

I gain on him until I am ten yards behind, then slow my stride to his pace, adopting the flow of his upward climb. Neither of us says anything, each caught in his own thoughts. We Westerners learn our climbing on staircases. As children we hold to the bannister, standing straight, taking one riser at a time, at each step the knee joint engaging and disengaging, each tread a staging ground for the next. Nepalis learn to climb on slopes without planned or symmetrical breaks. Their legs move rapidly in short strides up the slope. Where they should place their feet is not regimented by a carpenter's cut – their selection of steps is based on what makes the climb easiest for them. Their bodies bob above their legs as they climb, leaning in and out from the slope, their strides adjusting with its angles. Nepalis flow uphill like water running – except for those city-bred, staircase-taught Nepalis, also spotted by their clothing.

The eager Brahmin knows I'm walking behind, knows I'm carrying a pack. He can probably describe me even though he never looks straight at me; he glances at me sideways, his eyeballs only turning with the trail. But once I've settled into his pace, and we're like any travelers walking the trail together, I settle into his thoughts and he into mine. His thoughts filter down with the cadence of our identical pace. He knows he is walking fast, but I'm keeping up and also carrying a pack. I can imagine the questions he's asking himself. Is the foreigner going to Khandbari? Yes, probably. Where else could he be going at this hour? Does he know he won't make it before dark with a load that size? Who is he? Peace Corps? No, Peace Corps people carry dark green sacks; his is brown. And Peace Corps people have smaller packs; they know how to live in these hills. This foreigner can't be trekking; the area past Khandbari is closed to foreign trekking. And foreigners take porters when trekking; where is this man's cook?

I smile. The Brahmin is clearly puzzled. Twice he briefly breaks his pace, about to slow down and let me catch up. His curiosity isn't surprising: As a Westerner, I don't fit. Nepali life is ordered, like the caste you are born into. And here in Nepal I am not just a white among browns. There is something indigenous about me, but what is it? Is it the way I walk or the feelings that flow uphill from me to him?

Accelerating upward, he answers his curiosity by testing me, starting the old porter's game. I accept his challenge and speed up too. The point of the game is to push each other to determine which person can't hold the pace. As in chess, where the king is never captured, only pinned in checkmate, winning the porter's game involves pinning your opponent by wearing him down and forcing him to suck for air. When you hear him opening his lungs, you've discovered his limits and can play with them. Speeding up, slowing down is the end game that wreaks havoc on body rhythm, tires legs, wears down blood sugar, forces the pace to be dropped.

For young Nepali males, walking trails this way is regular sport, the way dragging Main Street is for young, rural Western males. When you can play by the delicate unstated rules, you are "in." I could concede his game with a joke, with some acknowledgment of his strength. Then he would slow the pace and we could walk and talk together. No, let's go head-to-head, toe-to-toe. This is classic sport. I concentrate on timing my breathing, opening my lungs, and relaxing my throat. I shorten my stride but make my feet fly. Shorter strides use fewer calories than longer ones. This guy ahead of me is good, but he's a Brahmin schoolteacher, not a porter. Keeping up with him is tough, but although he walks this hill every day, I'm in shape and fresh. I've just finished carrying thirty-five-pound Jesse plus forty pounds of emergency and camera gear through Helambu Valley on the monthlong medical expedition. The Brahmin probably thinks this bulky pack weighs sixty pounds; actually it's half that: a loose sleeping bag, a sleeping pad, a change of clothes, some food, and ten pounds of cameras.

But he too is in shape. He kicks in a sudden spurt as we start to cross the rocks and almost makes me lengthen my stride and climb boulder by boulder. If I do, my legs will soon use up all my blood's oxygen, and I'll have to suck more in. I must hold my body's burn rate steady. Loosen that throat, let the air flow free, flex the lungs.

After picking up the pace still more on a flatter grassy stretch, he suddenly slows down. I can't allow myself to catch and pass him – that's racing. My game role is to play on the end of his string. I must slow my own pace and my metabolism. He's gambling that I'm so tired I won't get a second wind when he speeds up again. But I choose to keep up my burn rate. I lengthen my stride and slow my pace. That's inefficient because it makes leg muscles work with disadvantageous leverage, but the extra effort keeps the fires inside burning steady – and I'll be ready for the spurt that will soon come and will then shorten my stride.

Twenty minutes later we reach a fig tree just above a turn in the trail. Off to the right behind the tree stands a small thatched tea stall, rock bench under the tree for travelers to set their loads on. Turning suddenly aside from the trail, the Brahmin stoops and goes in under the thatch eaves, greeting the squatting shopkeeper beside his fire and teakettle. The Brahmin turns and studies me as I walk past. The tea stall has given him an excuse to disengage and get a look at me. Consciously he doesn't know what he's looking for, but he knows that he'll find something. Most of his questions will be answered if he can watch me walk. After rounding the next bend, I slow my pace, glad to have an excuse too; he had me on the verge of breaking.

Fifteen minutes later I hear him approaching from behind, striding out, each step reaching for new trail. From the forcefulness of his walk, I guess his intention is passing. But let us be friends. As he goes ahead, I greet him.

"Going to Khandbari?"

"Yes."

"Before dark?" I must keep my questions short, make him do the talking. No one can walk, talk, and breathe well at the same time. Words will slow the pace.

"Yes, but you can't get there by dark," he says.

This fellow talks the way he walks – with a swagger. Already it's so dark that many people wouldn't travel without a light. Now let us walk together, holding each other to the pace.

Up the trail we climb, our strides building friendship. He confirms he's a schoolteacher. Every morning he walks four miles and 2,500 feet down to his mud and thatch school. The trip down takes an hour. Every evening he walks home; the uphill trek takes an hour and a half. This evening he stayed and played cards – and lost forty-seven rupees. He's angry at the government worker who won his rupees; then, the more he talks, angry at the government that employs him; then, to forget his losses, he shifts the blame to the king of Nepal.

The king of Nepal is also a god of Nepal, reincarnation of Vishnu. While European monarchs established their legitimacy through divine right, rulers in Nepal became the divine, both potentate and pope, divinity making the monarch not just absolute but unchallengeable. Thus, traditionally, the king of Nepal as the starting point of Nepalese society is beyond question – much as the number *one* in elementary mathematics is unquestionably the starting point among numbers.

But just as people eventually learn that there are also negative numbers and fractions, some Nepalis' perceptions of their king are changing. Angry words like those coming from the schoolteacher are new to Nepal. Like the ideas of change they espouse, some come from outside. The once-isolated valleys of Nepal now share the moods and attitudes of an aspiring world. The information transfer just seems to happen, much as the two of us have shared our moods while we've walked. The pace of this change is accelerating, and this Brahmin on an isolated Himalayan slope, like the rest of us, is caught in its onslaught.

"That government worker took my money! Why, why must everything I work for go? Why must my work disappear?"

"Because you played the wrong card. You played the knave, but forgot that the king was stronger." (The pun works in Nepali as it does in English.)

The schoolteacher laughs. "Yes, the king is stronger. He takes my money – but he is taking my country too. He is taking my country, giving it to those who are beyond the law, even giving Nepal to rich Indians."

"He is not taking your country," I reply. "It is his country. You gave him the country when you crowned him king. The gift of your country to your king is part of your ancient custom. The people of Nepal give the king the country each time they crown him. If Nepali people are honorable, how can you now take the gift from him?"

"I am not taking the gift from him. He gives it away. Actually not he – those close to him are selling it away. These people enter into business deals with others outside Nepal who come in to take Nepal for themselves – our trees to India, our temple idols to Europe, our cloth to America. We gave Nepal to the king as an investment, as a resource so he could help us."

"No, you didn't give the country to him so he could help you. That is a new idea, not part of your historical contract. Nepalis have always given Nepal to the king because Nepal belongs to him. You, his people, belong to him. What he wishes you must wish too. What he wants, you must provide. He is your king and your god."

"Who are you?" the schoolteacher asks. "Why do you talk like this? I am only speaking the way your man, Thomas Jefferson, taught me to speak."

Since my childhood mission experiences I have wondered about the penetration of foreign ideas into parochial village life. I decide, for some perverse reason, to distance myself, to sense more fully whether this cultural intrusion is resented. I reply, "Why do you say my man, Thomas Jefferson? He is not my man. Jefferson is American. I'm a Russian. I'm . . ."

"Then, your man Lenin," he says, unfazed by my fabrication and giving me no sense of antagonism toward the outside. "I talk now about people owning what is not theirs. I don't care who you are. You seek to use Nepal and her people for your own happiness. You seek to take for your own purposes, take to your own country something of Nepal. Just yesterday some French tourist tried to talk one of my girl pupils into going to France with her. She gave this girl a bag of bon-bons, asked her name, then while the girl's mouth was still full of candy, asked her parents if she could take the girl home to France! You all seek to take your pleasures from Nepal. You Russians are trying to . . ."

"That is why you need the king. Who else can hold Nepal together? Who but this king can bring a Brahmin like you, here in eastern Nepal, a man with no fields, cursed with big ideas, a man who so desires money he gambles when it is illegal – who but the king can bring you, an eastern Brahmin, together with a Brahmin from western Nepal, a Brahmin from a village where almost everyone is a Brahmin, a Brahmin who is poor because there the rain never comes and who, because he is isolated, doesn't have ideas of change in his head? Who else can bring you two Brahmins together? Certainly not yourselves – you don't even speak the same language. Certainly your gods can't bring you together, for you don't practice the same rituals, though you are both Brahmins.

"The king alone is holding Nepal together. If two Brahmins cannot get along, how can a Sherpa from the east and the mountains and a Tharu from the west and the jungles ever possibly get along? Those Nepalis do not share even the same religion, will not even eat together, cannot even talk to each other . . . but still they both respect the king. If Nepal ever truly enters a time of trouble, only the king will be able to rise above the many self-serving factions in this country, have the authority to speak for national interests, and act for the best interests of the country."

"Who are you anyway?" he answers. "You must be some kind of spy walking here in the mountains. How do you know so much about me, so much about Nepal? How do you know I'm a Brahmin? How do you know I want money?"

"I am no spy. I was simply raised in these mountains and I come back often as a friend. I know you as well as you now know the ideas of the West. Knowledge flows both ways in the modern world. You are a friend of Nepal, too. Therefore, in this new world, we are brothers. I know you are a Brahmin the same way any Nepali would. Your face tells me, even as the string you hold under your shirt would. Of course you hunger for money. Why else would you play cards? Why else would you be so angry and blame the king when you played the knave?"

He laughs. "You are a brother of Nepal, dear Russian."

I wince. With this new fabricated layer to our conversation darkness has grown around us. The schoolteacher enjoys such debate. In villages like his, among those with book learning, it is popular now to talk revolution. Life in Khandbari must be monotonous. But like the changing seasons, debate and the proposal of new structures give hope. Now, though, I am in over my head and my Russian ruse could backfire on me.

Politics in Nepal – a country the size of Tennessee, with 18 million people, the population of greater New York City – is a lot more complicated than the picture the Brahmin paints. The political players are always changing, not only in their levels of influence but also in their colors. There is no black, no white. Varying shades of gray merge with shifting influence to make politics impenetrable, like night on the trail before us.

Our pace has slowed as the Brahmin talks. I cannot see ahead. With each step I know only that the trail leads still farther, not the end of this mystery. Although I am moving toward something, I'm conscious only of the present, the stride I'm now taking. My senses probe for clues about the trail, clues from his footfalls two paces ahead, clues from the lighter line of the night-illumined, packed earth. My feet, not my eyes, find the way, feeling for firmness along that lighter line, ready to lift upward if there is no firmness. The Brahmin stumbles rarely.

My lungs have become freer with our slowed pace, and they flow open and full. This strenuous walk has relaxed the barriers of my mind into the limit-lessness of the night. Like the liberating high of long-distance running, when the body falls away and all senses float, my life now is also all sensory. Dark-ness opens my imagination. Rising above the trail, a bamboo grove against a sparkling sky looks like great claws bending high and over. I tell myself to re-lax. Night, bamboo, and politics are all very safe, if impenetrable; I must stride into each step of the trail as it comes.

"I don't like your Soviet bear," the schoolteacher suddenly says.

Making tea alongside the trail

"Why?" I answer absently, as I concentrate on the trail. We are now on the back of a ridge where moonlight hasn't reached. I follow the Brahmin's dark form.

"We Nepalis never trust Soviets. We like your words, how you say you help working people, but we know you do not help people. Maybe, as they say on Voice of America, you don't help people anywhere. You only want to take control of the world. You act big because inside you know you are small. In world history you have never been great. You own a big country, but it is big with emptiness – and you know this. You know Russian life is no good, but you keep pretending it is."

"No, I reply. My country helps people. We help Nepal. We help the people of Nepal in foreign study, by training them in Moscow. This year we're sending forty students to become doctors, twenty students to . . ."

"Don't tell me about Soviet doctor training. My cousin-brother studies in Moscow. He came home to Nepal last month for his father's funeral. He told me your doctor training never permits him to touch Russian patients. Hah! My cousin brother is studying in your country, but you show him surgery only on TV. Never is he allowed to do real surgery, except on animals. Never does he meet Soviet students, especially no Russian girls. You must open up your systems."

"But we are helping Nepal by training doctors."

"How can you say you are helping Nepal? You and the Americans just play games and use us. I have another cousin brother who works at the customs office on the Indian border. Two months ago big trucks came to the border with big wooden boxes addressed to the Soviet ambassador. When the inspector demanded that the boxes be opened, this second cousin brother heard their argument."

"But a customs inspector can't open boxes addressed to an ambassador. That breaks diplomatic privilege."

"This is Nepal. Our customs people have the privilege of Gurkha soldiers! When Gurkhas suspect trouble, they do what's necessary. We will stand up to you. We will stand up to the Americans. Those boxes were opened, regardless of your diplomatic privilege. They were full of enormous electronic instruments, parts for big antennas, expensive equipment. We found you were sneaking in special equipment to listen to our telephone conversations. I have a third cousin brother. He is a secretary in the American Embassy records department. He too was at my uncle's funeral, and we all talked. He said the Americans know we caught you with this equipment. He says all the Americans are laughing. The Americans say the equipment is to listen to telephone conversations, maybe even conversations within the royal palace! You do not allow Nepalis to talk privately even in royal bedrooms!"

At Khandbari Bazaar, we walk past the police checkpost. Special trekking permits are required beyond here. The sentry calls, "Halt!" I halt. This Russian is going to look very suspicious trying to walk past a checkpost at night with his flashlight off. This Russian is going to have to show his American passport. This big-mouthed Russian might not even make it out of the police jail and back to Tumlingtar to catch the plane six days from now – let alone along the trail ahead to Shakshila.

The Brahmin calls to the sentry, "It's OK. It's Ram, the schoolteacher, walking with a traveler. We're talking."

We walk through Khandbari Bazaar. A small restaurant appears to have ready Nepali rice with soupy lentils, *dal bhat*. Ram says good-bye. I step inside and set my pack against the whitewashed earthen wall. A hand-hewn wooden bench sits in front of a store-bought table in the middle of the room. Others here are still talking but not yet eating. Only when conversation is finished and they're almost ready to depart do Nepalis eat. Then, with their food finished, they leave. But for me, with almost 2,000 feet and six miles yet to climb tonight to Bhotebas, this restaurant may be my last chance for a prepared meal. Can I make Shakshila by the day after tomorrow?

Chapter Nineteen

Two days later, as evening shadows climb the valley and the snowy peaks north of the Arun River glow in the setting sun, I walk the stone-cobbled trail into Shakshila. Doorway after doorway is empty, the village deserted. Only the chickens are home. The hollow percussion of my footfalls mingles with their cackles. Even the pigs are gone. As I enter the section of two-story stone houses, my steps resonate even louder.

Pebbles roll and clatter under my feet. I feel like an invader here. What's happened to the children and pigs, their giggles and grunts? Shakshila also looks different. Eight months ago I didn't enter from the south. What I re-member as a regular layout of paths now seems a maze. Where exactly in the village am I? I stop in bewilderment. The rattle of pebbles under my feet ceases. Then I hear voices humming – off to the right and down the slope. A child's head pops up from behind a stone wall. I follow the cobblestones in the direction of the hum beyond the child.

As I round the corner, a shout comes up toward me; behind a vanguard of pigs surge hundreds of people. Beyond them, waiting in an open square, must be a thousand more. Shakshila numbers at most six hundred; where have all these people come from? What is this open square where there used to be vil-lage? I catch phrases passing from villager to villager. "It's father of Jesse!" "It's father of Jesse!" "Where is Jesse?" Moving toward my reception committee, I spot Myang in the second row. His smile spreads from ear to ear. He breaks through the croud, comes up, head bowed, palms pressed forward and together, grabs my hands, and touches them to his head. "Where is Jesse, Jesse's father?"

"Jesse is in Kathmandu with his mother," I reply. "I am alone. I've come to talk with you and the people here."

Myang grips my wrist, pulling me through the crowd to a small flat terrace before a temple – strong, high walls of hewn stones, and a tin roof, here in Shakshila where all other roofs are woven bamboo. The metal glistens in the evening light, drawing the valley's evening warmth to this place.

"Where did this temple come from? It wasn't here eight months ago."

"This is our new temple, father of Jesse. We built it. The king's government gave us 80,000 rupees. More than school, water system, or health post, a temple was what our village needed. So, with that government money we built it."

Coming through the crowd is the lama, one of the men in the village who often came to sit by our fire to get sweet tea from Pasang. Two boys, priest's assistants, are with him.

"Welcome to our celebration, father of Jesse," he says. "We are waiting for you. Come sit inside the temple."

"What? Waiting for me?"

"Yes, we first decided to have this celebration a month from now, after the cement arrived to build drain gutters. Then the temple will be truly finished. But my brother, the lama who studies astrological books, two weeks ago he studied his books and said we must celebrate today and tomorrow. He said a great guest was scheduled to come today. We did not know who the guest would be. Thank you, father of Jesse, for coming."

I look across the packed courtyard at the corners of the temple. Open dirt ditches wait for their cement. The lama expects me to follow him inside, but instead I move to a pile of leftover rocks. Inside, the temple will be smoky from yak-butter lamps, and there will be more than fifty people in what looks to be a sixteen-by-sixteen-foot room. Adjusting two flat stone slabs, I make a seat, then adjust two more stones and prop my pack against them to serve as a backrest. This celebration will take hours. If I'm to be the chief guest, I'd best settle in.

The head lama and Myang greeting the author as he enters Shakshila

Two weeks ago when the lama's brother switched the date, I hadn't even bought my air ticket from Kathmandu to Tumlingtar. In fact it was exactly two weeks ago while on the medical expedition that I stopped the talking and decided to come here. How could people with primitive astrological books know that someone would come – and predict the date?

I sit down. People step back, exposing a packed-earth stage. Beyond it towers the temple, a twenty-by-twenty-by-twenty-foot cube built of massive gray rocks, carefully cut. No mortar, just precision, holds together two-foot-thick walls. Down and out from the main roof flares another roof, making a porch on all four sides. What unschooled architect designed this gracefully balanced building? Certainly no resident of this village ever before designed a temple. There are no other such structures in the valley. No paper, no engineering schooling – only lines etched in the mind and trust from other villagers provided the shape and authority for this design.

These people trust their knowledge the same way I trust mine – secure knowledge brings comfort. But I feel frightened for them, for soon they will lose that trust. They will see the material wealth of the outside, and wanting that, will forget the inner wealth they now have. Their world, which has held together here for centuries, will come unglued. These people will start believing that "educated" trust is better. They could learn to trust the telephone, a call from me saying I'll be there in two weeks. Would that be more reliable than the word of the lama? Not this time: Had I called from Kathmandu, not knowing the airplane schedule, expecting to walk more slowly, I would have timed my arrival here two days from now.

DANCING BEGINS ON THE EARTH-PACKED STAGE. FIRST THE WOMEN FORM a row, standing awkwardly and shyly. The crowd chants, and the women shuffle with the cadence. Then one by one the men drift into another row behind, joining the rhythmic movement and clearly making suggestive remarks. I am uncomfortable because the people knew I was coming. I am even more uncomfortable because of how the men *and* the women treat the women. Their Loomi language, a variant of Tibetan and Nepali, is a clashing of strange guttural sounds to me. (Only when talking with me directly do the people speak Nepali.) The people here are bolder, more sexually open than in southern Nepal, with its strong Hindu orientation. Racy advances are clearly being made by the men shuffling behind the women – and everyone is

Myang's wife blowing up the fire for morning tea

laughing. Behind me a girl of maybe nine turns and hugs her mother's legs, as uncomfortable as I am.

A young woman wearing a pink blouse dances in the line and blushes; she might be fifteen, maybe sixteen. Her earlobes are crimson. She rubs one hot ear on one shoulder, then tilts her head and rubs the other. Both lines continue their shuffling. The crowd chants, and the lines pick up the pace of the dance.

A man in the men's row slides down his line and stands directly behind a girl in a green blouse. He calls out something. The crowd snickers. The green blouse lass looks at the ground and blushes too. Is she the younger sister of the one in pink? The shape of their mouths, she could be. The crowd snickers some more. My stomach is tight. I hate this. Why do men pick on women so? Why do women let them?

The man calls again . . . and the girl in green bolts. She rushes forward toward the crowd. The man charges after her. Cheers come from the crowd. Both lines stop their shuffle dancing. The crowd is so dense it arrests her flight and from its midst she is spun around and thrown back out onto the stage. The man catches her by the arms. Her body hangs before him handcuffed by his grip on her wrists, head bowed to the ground, limp.

"Take her! Take her!"

Suddenly she stiffens, straightening in his arms, stands and faces the man. What is she about to do? I've never seen an unmarried woman in this part of the world so bold. Will she fight? Fire is in his eyes. Mettle is in her stance. She steps back, but catching a foot on a rock in the dirt, she flips out from his reach, tries to recover, and falls to the ground – arms out, legs apart, spread-eagled on her back. Forward he lunges.

Bodies around me rise, surging with warmth, the air suddenly hot. Doesn't this girl have a brother or father who will protect her? Anywhere else in Nepal, some man would have come forward. Maybe not; there is something about groups of people who are doing wrong – regardless of education, regardless of position – that incapacitates individuals, even the well-intentioned. To stand out with bravery, to buck the common sin takes character, strength. This woman, alone against the group, has both. The victim standing alone, brave. After it's over we call them martyrs, but while it is happening, who steps forward? The temperature around me must have increased five degrees. We laugh with discomfort while they cry inside.

"Do it! Do it!"

The man is falling down on her. He lands. But he is moving forward too fast. Was it the heat of his assault? Was it a push from behind? With his fall, he slides forward on top of her. His stomach stops over her face.

She bites (and bites hard). Up he howls, hands grabbing his stomach through his thin shirt. He's off, legs flailing, running into the crowd, holding his gut.

Fifteen minutes later, villagers still hold each other, weak from the joy of hysteria as they tell and retell the story. Another legend has begun. In time, the dancing returns. It looks as if it will last all night.

I leave the party at eleven. Inside the temple the cadence of chanting and prayers continues: "Om Mane Padme Hum Padme Hum Om Mane Padme Hum." (O jewel in the heart of the lotus.) On the hewn-plank floor of Myang's house about fifty yards away, I unroll my sleeping bag and embrace oblivion. When I awake at five the next morning, the dancing and chanting still hum on. The sound of the zipper as I open my sleeping bag awakens Myang's wife, lying in her bedroll on the other side of the room. She kindles the fire from its embers and brings me a large glass of hot, sweet tea. Myang is not around; he's been with the party all night.

I move to the front porch to watch morning come to the village. The light is gray, cold, and still. I squat on the front porch, back braced against the wall, and watch women perform their routines, children start their chores, and men stagger home. Myang's wife keeps my teacup hot. At six-thirty, warmth and sun break over the ridge.

That day I ask around for ground bear skulls. I have a long talk with Lendoop, who seems sad. It is dangerous to kill ground bears, he says; no skulls are available. He talks about how aggressive they are, how big they can get. "We only kill tree bears," he says. All day I talk to various people. Even tree bear skulls are not available during daylight. The villagers don't understand the international (CITES) treaty for endangered animals and my explanation of my scientific collecting permits. But they do understand nightfall, and the news of my interest is out. People bring me their guardians from grain storehouses; the vermin will have to get to know new skulls. The next morning at seven-thirty, I leave Shakshila with two more tree bear skulls I've picked from those offered, similar in size and in the cusp wear on their molars. I'll have to come back next year for the ground bear skull we so badly need.

During the first few miles of the hike out I plan my route: knowing when I must be in Tumlingtar; planning my travel to reach certain villages when day will be breaking or ending, to see the actions of people's lives; knowing the places on the trail with special trees and private views for an hour's rest during the day; knowing I like to walk two hours each night after dark and one hour or more each morning before the new day rises to this earth. And, as I work out my schedule, I always allow a free hour to be with the wind that flows through the top of each pass. There are sixteen hours to work with each day and setting aside five for contemplation still leaves eleven for walking.

The mind travels farther and faster than the feet in walking hour after hour, a hundred feet up, hundreds of feet down. And while the feet move the mind searches. There are unexpected links in our global ecosystem, unexpected and inexplicable. What is the relationship between an American man and a Nepali village now? What are the pressures on bears in the Barun Valley – because of that man, because of other men? Musk deer pods now sell for $50 each in the Khandbari market because of a $500 value in Hong Kong; and so too, at the same prices on the same markets, sell the gall bladders of tree bear and ground bear as stimulants for sexual potency. Threatened by forces that drive the ego and libido of tired men, the supply is in the Barun forests. The market is in the concrete jungle.

But we cannot point fingers across the oceans and say the problem of harvesting wilderness products for sale is a characteristic of the tropics – for growing in shade at the roots of hardwood trees in the mountains of the eastern United States is the ginseng root, in demand as one of life's elixirs in the same markets of the Far East. My neighbors back home in the West Virginia hills also sell for these same markets. They sell ginseng legally, and they illegally sell the gall bladders of American black bears that their dogs chase down. We criticize the sale of tiger bones and rhino horns in the East while ignoring the roles we play in the West. In West Virginia too the futures of bears and plant roots too are driven by forces thousands of miles away. The pressures that strain our ecosystem are now a planetary interlinked system, communicating unpredictably, compromising once-strong relationships unexpectedly. The threads of life tie us all together and we must learn to see more clearly the patterns we weave into this fabric.

Fifty hours, two passes, and seventy miles later I arrive in Tumlingtar; it is four hours before my flight. I drink six glasses of hot sweet tea in the thatched tea hut and watch the caroms game. The shopkeeper fries up some bread. As it sizzles, the Twin Otter drops out of the clouds, buzzes the field to disperse the goats, and bounces to a stop. With both my hands full, I walk out across the grass, through the bamboo booth that is Security, and climb on board. The hot bread, sprinkled with brown bazaar sugar, is better than the airplane candy.

Chapter Twenty

Six days after I had left, I arrive back in Kathmandu. Jennifer and Jesse sit in the hotel garden, talking. Approaching their table, I overhear Jennifer say, "Today Papa should leave Shakshila. Remember the village where all the people used to look at you?" They look up in surprise as I sit down; no astrologer told them of my travel plans.

Jennifer has her own story to tell, one that's upset her and pours out of her. Our paperwork for adopting a Nepali orphan cleared weeks faster than expected. Two days earlier, Jennifer had gotten the news that the orphanage assigned us a three-month-old girl. Suddenly, new emotions wash through me; I'm no longer sure I want a second child. I feel trapped by another good thing.

"After receiving the phone call, I took Jesse to see her, Dan'l. The matron is wonderful – she loves each baby. She does a wonderful job with the resources she has, but those are so limited and she needs so much more. I couldn't believe that a large closet serves as their nursery. Everything was very clean. At one end, a window without curtains lets in light. We entered that small room. There were two rows of maybe a dozen baskets lined up on a shelf against the wall. Each basket held a baby. Imagine a walk-in closet with baskets of babies on the shelves instead of clothes. And not a single baby was crying or even making a noise. It was really spooky."

"It's probably warmer in a space that size in winter, Jennifer."

"As I walked into that room, Dan'l, I knew something was wrong. Jesse was holding tightly to me – he felt something too. We looked around, then Mrs. Shrestha, the orphanage administrator, pointed out our baby.

"She's a lovely girl, but I don't want her. With my first sight of this baby I knew she wasn't mine. She was like a picture on the wall, not a baby in our family. She felt so far away. Reaching to pick her up was like reaching across a chasm. I'm sure she could grow to be part of our family, but right now we're reaching to the other side of the world and taking something that isn't ours."

What's going on? Is Jennifer really having a sixth-sense rejection of that baby? Or is this her way of telling herself (or me) she doesn't want to adopt after all? Whatever the reason, if she's not sure she wants to go ahead, I'm not going to insist.

"We'll not take that girl," I say. "I'll go over right now and tell them our request is canceled."

"You can't do that, Dan'l. They've gone to a lot of effort to arrange everything, and so fast. That baby's been assigned to us. She has to have parents! We're her parents now. You're her father."

"Well, I don't care. What am I to do? You say she isn't ours, and next you say we have to take her."

"It's worse than that. There is another girl in another basket. Walking into the nursery, my heart went out to that other little girl even as I picked up my own. This other one two baskets away. She felt right."

"What?"

"Yes, and I asked about her. Mrs. Shrestha said she was already taken, that she has another sponsor."

"Maybe we can have that changed? If you like one baby more than another, I'll go talk to them."

"You can't operate like that, Dan'l. These are babies! It's not like exchanging clothes at the store. The other little girl belongs to someone else. You don't just take someone's baby."

"OK. OK. But if you don't feel right about this, we're not going through with it. I'll go over right now to talk to them."

At the orphanage, Mrs. Shrestha was eager to show me our girl, proud to have processed the papers in just one month. In our contacts, all the staff had shown concern for the orphans and for the ethics of adoption. How do I now tell them "no"? First I talk about how many other people want a child. Then I say that Jennifer and I are unsure about adoption; maybe we still want another of our own.

Mrs. Shrestha does not hear these arguments. After half an hour of talking past each other, she and I go to the nursery. The baskets line the shelf just as Jennifer said – a lot of babies, it seems to me, and all quiet. I step immediately to one basket just inside the door. In it lies a girl, awake. I run the back of my finger across her cheek. A smile flicks up, lips pulled tight like tape across her face. I look into her eyes, and she looks back. Her smile passes. Everything about her face is tight – cheeks, lips, eyes. There's a tension, a discipline about it. Then I notice how thin and weak her body is. Undernourished? Maybe even malnourished. She's been fighting to hold on. She has no hair. I like this girl. There's that smile again. Are those dimples? I reach to pick her up while Mrs. Shrestha talks with the matron.

"Your girl is over here." Mrs. Shrestha interrupts my thoughts. She points to two baskets beyond this one.

My face flushes as I turn from the first basket. I pick up the new baby. She's bigger, stronger than the first girl, better nourished. Her skin is looser on her face. She gives a strong kick, smiles, kicks again – is that her trick? She's really sweet. But Jennifer is right: This baby does not feel right.

But how can I reject this child? I cradle her in my arms. Time and love will bring her close. She kicks again, then smiles. She has been well cared for. They do a good job here.

I ask Mrs. Shrestha, "What do you know about this girl? How was she orphaned? What's her story?"

Mrs. Shrestha gets the file, then reads: "Girl baby. Born September fifth; caste Maharjan. Mother age thirty-two, died from hemorrhaging during childbirth at the maternity hospital. Father, who has no relative or other children, turned baby over to hospital saying, 'If I take care of the baby my fields will die. If I care for my fields the baby will die.' The baby arrived here considerably weak and underweight. She needs special care; that's why we think you might be the right parents."

Mrs. Shrestha looks at the plump baby I'm holding, shuffles through the several other papers in the file, skimming each one, looking for more information. She looks at the baby. She looks back at her papers. She calls for the matron. Then she goes into the other room where the matron is. Another woman comes in. The three women talk excitedly in the next room, but in low voices. They come into the nursery, look at my little girl, then quickly through the other baskets. I can't catch what they are saying. In my arms, our baby starts to cry. I rock her back and forth and walk around the room a bit. But she continues to cry. In a few minutes, Mrs. Shrestha comes back into the room holding two files and walks to the first basket, to the little girl with the tight skin and lips. She's distressed. The other two women stand close to her, talking softly. The baby in my arms is crying even louder now. I hear nothing of what they are saying until our little one stops to gasp for air.

"It must be. It has to be," the matron says.

"Yes," says Mrs. Shrestha. "But how did it happen?" She turns to face me. The matron takes my baby in her arms, and the little girl quiets immediately. Throughout this time, all the other babies in the room have remained quiet.

Mrs. Shrestha speaks. "We made a mistake, I think a bad mistake. That one is not your child. Your child is this one." She points to the first basket.

I look into that first basket. Is she the same that Jennifer was attracted to? The baby there looks too weak to smile, but still she does. She looks up at me. Yes, those are dimples – and she has a wonderful disciplined smile. She feels just right. I look at the women and then I understand. Gilbert and Sullivan, *H.M.S. Pinafore,* the same thing: They mixed up the babies!

"Please wait twenty minutes. I must get Jennifer." I race to the hotel on my motorcycle, the deep thumping pistons of that old BMW now whining as I coax seconds off the trip and snake through the crowds of Kathmandu. The motorcycle on which the family began, on which Jennifer and I courted fourteen years before. I collect Jennifer and Jesse and weave back through the narrow ancient streets to the orphanage, Jesse sitting astride the gas tank, hands holding the handlebars.

Mrs. Shrestha tells us the story. "The first girl we showed you belongs to a Nepali businessman. A month and a half ago, he was riding on a bus from his village with his wife and three children, coming to see relatives in Kathmandu for the holidays. On a steep turn, the brakes failed and the bus went out over the cliff. His wife and three children all died. He was one of the few who survived. He was lonely. He walked through villages looking for a child to adopt, looking for someone to call his family. He found this girl three weeks ago, who for some reason also had no family. Now she is his. He left her here with us while he arranges for a woman servant to care for her."

One of the orphanage women picks up the baby from the first basket. "This other girl is yours. We think the mix-up happened when the hospital people came to the orphanage last week to immunize all the babies. They were all out of their baskets; they were all crying with the needles. In any case, this little Maharjan girl whose mother died during her birth, she is your daughter." The woman places the tiny tight-lipped girl in Jennifer's arms. Again, the baby smiles. As Jennifer holds our new child close, a tear from her face falls onto the little brown cheek.

Now a four-person family arrays itself on the big black motorcycle; Jesse's again astride the gas tank, holding on to the handlebars. Sitting sidesaddle behind me, Jennifer cradles her daughter in her lap, little Tara, protected by her new mother's arms. We're due for dinner with friends in an hour and a half. Before that we must track down diapers, bottles, and formula in the bazaar. A couple of Jesse's T-shirts will serve as Tara's new baby gowns.

It is Thanksgiving Day.

Chapter Twenty-One

I've gone as far with this mystery as I can. I'm not finding the ground bear skulls that we need on my own. Before we return to the United States I need to set in motion assistance to help us get the skulls. It shouldn't be impossible – after all, ground bears are what the scientific literature describes. I decide to ask my graduate school friend, Shah Dev, who also happens to be king of Nepal and a keen outdoorsman.

As I wait in the antechamber, I wonder: Will Shah Dev be this time warm, a friend, or will he be aloof, a king and reincarnated god? The door opens; the principal private secretary to His Majesty enters beaming. He motions energetically for me to follow. As I walk behind him, I ponder how impossible must be his job. A kingdom of people seeks to bring its petitions, to enter a new age. A monarch seeks to assert his will, to represent the old age, the continuity that is Nepal. This is the man who must please both. As we pass another room, I spot the minister of finance sitting in an armchair, reviewing his papers for his audience in twenty minutes. On guard at the door of His Majesty's formal study, the aide-de-camp in green fatigues stands proud. He smiles in recognition and with a polished movement swings open the door. Nodding to him, I walk into the Royal Study.

His Majesty Birendra Bir Bikram Shah Dev, age thirty-nine, stands with feet astride on a snow leopard skin in the center of the room, hands clasped behind his back, grinning broadly as I walk toward him. Reaching out, he pumps my hand with a warm handshake.

Forty straight-back chairs line three walls. Set in from the fourth wall is His Majesty's desk, with a high-backed black leather chair. In front of the desk, grouped around the leopard skin, are three armchairs and a coffee table. This large chamber feels smaller than it looks because of Shah Dev's warmth. The formality of the room and his position disappear as two old school friends settle into the armchairs. Shah Dev continues to grin, sizing me up. I grin back, doing the same. He's lost weight and he's trimmed his moustache.

Neither of us talks, adjusting to the reality of the other's presence, switching from roles into being friends again. Shah Dev reaches back to his desk for his tiny pipe in its stitched leather casing and the blue tin of tobacco, custom blended and shipped to the Himalaya from the shores of the Zuyder Zee. He scrapes the pipe bowl with that little stainless steel tool even commoners use, flips the tool around, and packs in his tobacco. (He bought his first such tool one fall afternoon when we stepped in out of the rain at Leavitt and Pierce's, the tobacconist's just off Harvard Square.) Pipe now going, Shah Dev looks intently at me, left hand hanging over the arm of the chair, left leg crossed over his right. Quietly, I return his stare and grin back.

Kings choose the topic of conversation. "So, Dan, what have you been doing?"

"We followed your suggestion, Shah Dev, to search the Barun Valley. You said in all Nepal no place is as wild as the Barun."

"What did you find?"

"We found villagers reporting two bears in the jungle. Both are black. One is large, very aggressive, and lives on the ground. Five villagers have difficulty carrying a dead one. This ground-living bear seems to be what science calls the Asiatic black bear. I'm sure you know it; you must have shot some. But villagers also report another bear, for us new and mysterious. It is smaller, shy, and lives in trees. Two villagers can carry a dead one. The villagers call the big ground-based bear *bhui balu* and the little tree-living bear *rukh balu*. Upon further investigation we found evidence supporting the villagers' claims. A little bear does live in trees and makes unusual nests. We found five nests, a trail of footprints, and three skulls. As far as we can tell *rukh balu* is unknown to science; it's never been scientifically described and might therefore be scientifically new."

"What do you mean, unknown? *Rukh balu* is not unknown. I have heard of *rukh balu. Rukh balu* is found in several places in Nepal." Shah Dev leans forward, looking at me quizzically.

"You mean Nepalis generally speak of *rukh balu* and *bhui balu? Rukh balu* is common?"

"Not every Nepali, but those who know about bears. Or Nepalis living near the jungle – they know of *rukh balu."*

"Shah Dev, this Nepali knowledge is not scientific knowledge. Science says there are four bears in the Himalaya: sloth bear, *Melursus ursinus;* red bear, *Ursus arctos isabellianus;* blue bear, *Ursus arctos pruinosis;* and Asiatic black bear, *Selanarctos thibetanus.* Clearly, the sloth bear, red bear, and blue bear are not tree bears. Science reports that the Asiatic black bear is the only bear to exist in the high eastern Himalaya. Where Nepalis report *bhui balu* and *rukh balu,* Western science reports one bear – and no scientific description of any of these bears fits with what villagers describe as the tree bear."

Shah Dev's eyes sparkle. He leans farther forward. "Let me be clear about this. Are you saying science does not know about something Nepali villagers know about?"

"Yes."

Shah Dev hasn't worked his pipe since the story began. Reaching for the phone, he dials his brother, Prince Gyanendra, who is knowledgeable in wildlife and conservation matters. The older brother speaks quickly, hangs up and pushes the phone back to the center of his desk. I expect the prince is already on his way to the palace.

"What does this mean?" the king asks after several long moments of looking at the ceiling in silence.

"It means we need more evidence. When we examined our first skull at the Smithsonian alongside the *Selanarctos* skulls in their collection we found that our skull was smaller and more delicate. But the skull of one specimen doesn't prove anything except maybe that Barun bears are simply small. We need skulls from both types of bears. If two skulls collected from the same jungle are different, that will prove there are two different bears."

"Those skulls will be easy to collect. First we shall arrange the necessary permits for endangered species; then I shall tell my hunters to go shoot both bears for science."

"I already have the permits."

Shah Dev settles back in his chair, remembers his pipe, scrapes the bowl clean, fills it, and again lights up. I remain quiet. His Majesty is thinking. Smoke curls upward. Over the years I have known him, as people keep coming to him with personal needs, Shah Dev has consistently demonstrated a recognition of the national interest. He is well aware that seemingly little things can link to unexpected bigger things. It is so hard to guess ahead of time what those will be.

"We must be very careful," he says. "If we do anything too quickly, we can overlook something important. And if you are making a mistake, it should be clear that it is your mistake, not ours."

He is right of course. Science is science because it is careful – and in his efforts to be a wise monarch Shah Dev is also careful.

A side door opens. In walks Prince Gyanendra Bir Bikram Shah. I rise and step toward him. Walking past me, he bows before his brother and, still bowing, walks forward. His Majesty remains seated for this second key person in the kingdom. Older brother offers younger his hand, obeisance is performed. This deference must happen each day when they meet for the first time. Then the prince straightens and greets me with regal dignity. He is always poised, always firm of spine, always polished in speech.

Sitting down again, I lean forward, elbows on knees, alert. I know the king brought the prince here because he knows the prince thrives on catching mistakes. The prince is going to be out to catch any flaw in my thinking.

"Dan, tell your story to my brother."

"Your Royal Highness, His Majesty and I were discussing a discovery of Bob Fleming, myself, and our families in the Barun Valley. Over the last two years we've conducted wildlife observations there and found that villagers claim there are two bears in the jungle, *bhui balu* and *rukh balu*. *Bhui balu* seems to fit scientific descriptions of *Selanarctos thibetanus*, the Asiatic black bear, but *rukh balu* seems unknown to science, for there is no scientific description of a different small, shy Himalayan bear, one that lives in trees. This bear known to Nepali villagers is unknown to the world. So far we have collected three *rukh balu* skulls, one set of paws, and intriguing field data on nest making. All confirm villagers' reports and indicate a different bear. Now we need *bhui balu* data from the same habitat, especially skulls, to compare with accumulating tree bear data."

The prince breaks in. "Let me understand. You say no scientific distinction is currently made between *bhui balu* and *rukh balu*. However in Nepal people consider these to be different animals. Are you saying science does not?"

"Yes."

"So what do you propose? How do we test what you assert?"

"Two issues need separation, Your Royal Highness. The first is the *rukh balu/bhui balu* question. Are these two different bears, and if so, how are they different? Second, is one of these bears the yeti?"

"Wait," His Majesty interrupts. "You did not mention that. What is the yeti information?"

"As Your Majesty knows, there are two types of yeti evidence. One is what villagers report; no doubt you have heard such. Basically nothing can be proved with these stories. The other evidence has substance, but only two reports are generally credible, two sets of photographs taken of yeti footprints. The most famous is by Shipton in 1951. You must have seen that – a track almost thirteen inches long, very clear with noticeable large toes that look like human toes. The second sighting, photographs, and plaster casts, made by Cronin and McNeely, were from a yeti that walked past their tent in 1972."

I pull out photographs from the file folders I have with me. "Your Majesty, please examine this *rukh balu* print. When my brother-in-law and I found this, we thought we had found the yeti. However, as you can see, the photographs show the prints of bear nails. Although the nail prints prove it to be a bear, the print shape is not what we expect from *Selanarctos thibetanus*. The absence of a 'thumb' print in the normal track is the reason experts have dismissed the Asiatic black bear as the maker of the yeti tracks. Cronin and McNeely's yeti prints are very similar to these *rukh balu* tracks, except that their photographs show no nail marks. However, since their tracks were made in softer snow, it is possible the nail marks didn't show. Also, they reported to Bob Fleming that when they tracked their animal into the forest, it, like the *rukh balu* we trailed, used submerged rhododendron branches to walk on.

"The Shipton sighting is more difficult, because their evidence is only two photographs, a close-up and a long-distance shot – and in taking their close-up, presumably they selected the most mysterious, human-looking print in the trail. But there is more evidence in these photographs than was first thought. Professor John Napier, a distinguished British curator of primatology, obtained the original negative of the Shipton photograph and discovered that the lower section of that negative had been edited out when the famous picture was published. With this new evidence we see half of a second print having what could be nail marks. More importantly, Your Royal Highness, Napier shows how the yeti print could have been made by an animal setting hind paws into its front paw prints. Napier did not know of *rukh balu*. Adding now what we know of *rukh balu,* Napier's overprinting thesis becomes even more convincing."

"OK, your point about yeti is understood. However, you said there are two issues: bear and yeti. Now tell us about the bear."

"Well, the issue is how *rukh balu* and *bhui balu* differ. Three explanations can be offered. First, the difference may be gender based: the ground bear is the male, the tree bear is the female. A second explanation might be that the tree bear is a juvenile ground bear. This I discount because villagers see tree bears with cubs. The third explanation is what villagers maintain, that the two bears are different. Why not test whether the villagers are right?"

"One interesting aspect we could use your help on. Your Majesty might already own a live tree bear in your Royal Zoo. I examined this bear through the cage. It is the right size. Its front paws appear to have the thumblike claw. By itself, the zoo bear will prove nothing, but it is of interest. Could Your Majesty arrange to have the animal tranquilized and let me examine it?"

The king touches a buzzer behind his desk. Before the buzzing stops, a door opens. Instantly, the aide-de-camp is one step inside the door and standing at attention.

"Tell my private secretary to come in. Tell General Shushil I want to see him, Narendra too. Tell Bishou to come."

The king, the prince, and I now move into a conversational holding pattern. His Royal Highness starts it off. "You recently were in the villages?"

"Yes, I made a quick trip to the Barun to seek more bear skulls. While there I saw a new temple Your Majesty's government built for the villagers. They appreciated it very much. . . ."

"Which Barun villages?" asks His Royal Highness.

"The ones where the Barun and the Arun Rivers meet. This is an interesting place. . . ." I stop; neither brother is listening. People are entering, filling the chairs along the wall. As they enter, each bows at the waist, palms of hands pressed together above the forehead, and walks forward this way to a chair. Consternation is obvious on everyone's face. Except for the principal private secretary, who is smiling, each seems to be wondering: Why was I summoned? What is going on? They remain silent while we wait for one last arrival. Then His Majesty looks at his staff and says, "This is my friend, Dan. I have known him for many years. He has some interesting discoveries. Please, your report, Dan. But only about bears."

I explain about the tree bear and the ground bear — that although Nepali villagers know of both, Western science knows only of the latter. "If there are two bears, if villagers are right, then this will be an important discovery for Nepal. I have asked His Majesty for help."

"Yes, I am interested and want the answer to this question. You are to help Dan in any way needed. He wants to study the bear in the zoo. He wants to do further research in the Barun Valley next year. I promised the help of palace hunters. Dan is careful and will not violate any ecological principles; also he has international permits. Please make arrangements as needed. Dan, this will be enough, I think."

Everyone stands up, clearly preparing to leave. I rise too and stand while they depart. His Majesty looks at me, hands clasped behind his back.

"Your Majesty, thank you. It is always wonderful to see you. Thank you for your support."

Shah Dev holds my hand, not letting go; his head rolls back while he rocks his weight onto his back foot; a smile breaks, then opens to that warm grin. "Dan, it is going to be fun to watch you handle this. I'm sure, knowing you, there will be more surprises. You must do a good job with this — from what I know, and take this as a suggestion, the wilderness of the Barun is more important than the bear. What we do in the Barun also affects conservation in adjoining areas — such as the Everest area and the proposed Arun Valley hydro project. Let me draw your attention to these broader issues, not just the bears." He gives my hand a final gentle squeeze, then releases it with a formal handshake. "Good luck."

Chapter Twenty-Two

At 7:15 the next morning, Bob Fleming, three-year-old Jesse, and I rendevous at the gate of the Kathmandu Zoo. Seven government officials are there already waiting in morning fog. Most know nothing about why they are here; they are simply following orders from the palace. I explain to the director of the zoo that we want to study the black bear. The director requests that his tranquilizer blowpipe to be brought. For half an hour we drink tea and wait. The gun arrives. Nepal's chief ecologist suggests using a different tranquilizing drug. We wait an hour more and drink more tea. Finally, a dart is injected. The bear falls asleep, is weighed, her footprints cast in plaster of paris. We are packing up our instruments as the zoo opens its gates at ten.

The female bear weights 52 kilos (119 pounds), cusp wear indicates she's middle aged; she has something of a thumblike claw – it's unclear how it would look splayed out in the snow. All in all, she's a promising tree bear suspect.

Through the morning, one man has been particularly energetic. It was his idea to order hot tea, his idea to cast the footprint in soft malleable cow dung to form a smooth mold for the plaster. This man is a relative of the king, Bishou Bikram Shah, deputy private secretary to His Majesty.

A few evenings later, most of us who were at the zoo, plus a couple of others, gather at the secretary's house: Hemanta Mishra, chief ecologist for the Department of National Parks; Tirtha Bahadur Shrestha, Nepal's leading botanist; Rabi Bista, a hotshot forester; Kazi, a naturalist whose time in the field exceeds that of any Nepali scientist. After Bishou has supplied everyone with beer and the conversation has rambled sufficiently, I turn the talk to yetis. "What do Nepali villagers think the yeti is? Not what do you scientists think, but what do villagers think?"

"Dan, Nepal needs the yeti. The yeti is our international mascot the way the bald eagle is America's." Hemanta understands better than any Nepali environmentalist how the West views Nepal. "Nepal is a land of big mountains; Mount Everest, the tall snows – they help this otherwise small country be well known. But for the West, Nepal is a land of mysteries hiding in those tall mountains. Westerners come here to explore, to discover. The biggest mystery is the yeti. What is it? Where is it? Westerners talk about the yeti mystery more than any other animal of Nepal. The yeti keeps Nepal's aura of mystery burning. If Nepal answered the question of yeti, for the Westerner Nepal would have lost a lot of her magic. When I go fund raising to get support for Nepal's tigers, rhinos, or jungles, yeti is my closest ally. I don't even bring up its name – it is already in everyone's mind. It is elusive and rare; people quickly accept that other animals in Nepal must also be elusive and rare."

From his corner of one sofa, Tirtha Shrestha breaks in: "Yes, but Dan'l's question is not whether or not Nepal needs the yeti. Dan'l's question is what do Nepalis think of the yeti?"

"Yes, he asked what Nepali villagers think yeti is," says Rabi from the other end of the sofa. "In my experience it depends which villagers, which caste, or which ethnic group you talk to. First, what is yeti? In the Nepali language we didn't even have a word for it until maybe ten years ago. *Yeti* is a Sherpa word, and because we Nepalis don't so respect the Sherpa ethnic group, we didn't bring the word into our language directly. We noticed how important yeti was to Westerners, that they talked about it, as Mishraji here said, so we brought *yeti* into our language from English because we respect Westerners more. Dan, if you ask a Nepali what yeti is, you'll get a different answer depending on whom you ask. Some Nepalis may not even know the word."

Tirtha, polite, does not interrupt, but waits until Rabi pauses. He does not allow his territory to be invaded. "While helping write the fourteen volumes *From Mechi to Mahakali* describing everything in Nepal, I talked with many people, and I agree with Rabi; different Nepalis think differently about the yeti. But one thing is true of all Nepalis. For all Nepalis the jungles contain *bun manchi,* some jungle wild man. Is *bun manchi* the same as yeti? I think the answer is no. I have asked hundreds of Nepalis for descriptions of *bun manchi* and yeti and always descriptions differ. The only thing consistent is the idea of 'Jungle Man.'"

"The idea is very strong," Bishou acknowledges. "In fact sometimes I believe in *bun manchi* myself. But when asking about descriptions of *bun manchi* we get nothing. Never have I talked to a villager who has seen *bun manchi,* villagers see only damage to crops or flocks. In my work for His Majesty's hunts I supervise the best village shikari hunters. Really good shikaris do not believe. They say *bun manchi* is spirit."

"Maybe *bun manchi* is like our Hindu gods," Rabi suggests. "We cannot describe our gods in English because the way you have put your English language together you do not have words to understand the idea. A Hindu god is not like your English God, whom you think of as a spirit. Hindu gods are spirit and also they are real and they are in places. That is why we have idols. Yet Hindu gods are not idols. Hindu gods are more tangible than Western gods. We think of them as historically real like you believe your Jesus a real person, but the history in which our gods are real is not human history, is not part of a single time line like you trace to your Jesus. There are other real histories. This is the problem. You cannot accept how there can be different realities in English.

"Your English language, your ideas are too small. I need more beer! Talking philosophy is too difficult. I didn't say it right, but I am right. This is the problem. In English you cannot accept how there can be different realities." Rabi fills his tankard from an open liter bottle on the coffee table.

"No, I understand," I reply to Rabi in Nepali. "You cannot easily express such ideas in English. The Nepali language, like all Sanskrit-based languages, has more room to deal with a nonphysical reality for life. English can talk about nonphysical realities, but we do so as though we're trying to produce a product. It is parallel to the way Westerners try to meditate – they do have some success I suppose – but they attempt this through absolute linear progression like the assembly line of Western factories. In English trying to explore the nonphysical is like trying to fly with a body that has short wings – it takes a lot of energy. The soaring exploration that is possible in other cultural and linguistic systems is not possible in English.

"When I come to Nepal and start using the Nepali language, my feelings change. Maybe we can compare English to a sports car: it runs tight and fast and covers a lot of ground. But the Nepali language is like a Nepali bus; more can climb on board than can get into the sports car. The bus moves more slowly, but it has more room for other people and whatever animals or baggage they bring along, room for every idea. People who speak only English never know how spiritually limited, forward-driving, narrow product-oriented their lives and attitudes are."

Rabi claps. I feel foolish and stop talking. "Good, Dan, very good." Hemanta and Bishou laugh. Embarrassed, my face hot, my scientist friends smirking, thinking me a sophist, using flimsy allegory, once again my method sloppy.

Tirtha has politely waited. Poised for a moment of silence, he resumes, "What I am trying to say is that all Nepalis agree there is *bun manchi* but what they describe from one place to another is totally different. As a botanist I don't understand the mind, but this is what I think *bun manchi* is in the mind of Nepalis."

Tirtha bends forward from his corner of the sofa and looks into my eyes. "Yeti and *bun manchi* dignify the Nepali villager. Our caste system is built upon each person having a lower caste. For a villager in a mud house on the hillside, struggling for status with richer people with bigger fields below, having the yeti raises such a man's otherwise low status. Having *bun manchi* be a man, a wild jungle man, but still a man, in a caste society makes the bottom castes not on the bottom."

He continues. "Who are these poor people? These are low-caste people who have land near the jungle, land being cleared. Such poor villagers want to be considered part of civilization, not part of jungle. *Bun manchi* makes them more civilized than this jungle person they talk about."

"Very good, doctor sahib," Hemanta has listened intently while Tirtha focused his speech on me. "Very good; and maybe such poorest villagers on the jungle's edge also find *bun manchi* convenient to explain why their fields so often are eaten up. *Bun manchi* gives them excuse for being poor."

"Ah, Hemantaji, you keep coming up with the economic explanation," I say, looking around at the others. "Maybe Hemanta is wildlife's chief economist as well as chief ecologist!"

Bishou roared. "Very good, very good. Wildlife's chief economist."

"A good thing, too," I add, "for Hemanta has raised a lot of money and saved a lot of Nepali wildlife."

"Also, I think, Dan, there is another point about villagers needing *bun manchi,*" Tirtha continues, still leaning forward looking at me. "I have already said yetis make villagers appear more cultured, less animal-like; they raise a villager's caste. But part of being cultured and not being an animal means having mythology, having stories that explain who we are. I give you an example. You Americans have built a mythology about Russians; you need Russians whom you characterize as 'bears' to make yourselves appear as the cultured people, as 'not bears.' This mythology is purely American. The Russians have their own mythology about America. Part of any culture is having mythologies. In America you believe your Russian bear mythology so strongly, you spend billions of dollars to defend it. Maybe there is truth about Russians being dangerous bears, maybe not. Maybe only their claws are dangerous and not their hearts. What is clear is that this is your mythology and how passionately you believe it. Mythologies are not fairy tales – all scientific Americans believe in some mythologies. Scientific Americans die for their mythologies."

Tirtha is now expansive. "So, too, Nepali villagers have mythologies to explain who they are – maybe this is the role of *bun manchi* mythology. *Bun manchi* adds depth to local culture. It defines who people are and who they are not. If I as a scientist convince villagers there is no *bun manchi,* and they believe me, I take part of their self-identity from them. Is yeti real? Is it really the tree bear? Whatever you Westerners decide will not affect us very much. The yeti as animal is your question, for you to decide."

Bishou sets down his beer. "Good, Tirthaji. Russian bears and tree bears. Let us go to other room. I have some special meats. Let's eat. You must guess what meats they are."

"Give us a hint, Raja. Which jungle did these meats come from?" I ask.

"That is your mystery, Dan. All I will say is that there is no bear meat on my table. Please come." As Bishou talks, Bojaya, his wife, lovely and skilled at cooking the exotic things of the jungle, opens the doors and leads us into the dining room. A long table is spread with bowls of food. There are two types of yogurt and a platter piled high with garnished rice. I count five meat dishes. Two are fowl; one I bet is partridge; the other, I have no idea what it can be. Two are red meat; the greenish gray has to be wild boar; the other, sambur stag? Where in the royal provinces, protecting which royal land, has Bishou recently been? Is that fifth the tiny barking deer?

In the midst of all of Nepal's many problems, as human population pressure cuts away at habitat, the country's wildlife conservation programs have been remarkably successful. This table and all recent field data show that in the areas under management, there is almost uniformly a surplus of wild animals. Significant reserves have been set aside; more than 7 percent of the kingdom's land is now protected. Except for still great need in protecting and expanding the forests of Nepal outside the formalized preserves, most of the conservation pieces of this country are in place. We must get the last critical piece of land, the Barun Valley, preserved. We need to get hard scientific data on its biological wealth, create improvements in how conservation benefits the local people so that their cooperation (and well-being) is secured, and have the tree bear–ground bear question settled, too.

Chapter Twenty-Three

November 18, 1984. After nearly two years, I've returned to Makalu Jungli Hotel. Tin lids, now rusted, stick up through twigs and dirt by the old camp fire scar, junk we thought we'd properly disposed of. By the jungle's edge a sliver of plastic that once wrapped pepperoni gilds a new shoot of bamboo, litter someone from our group thought would never be noticed. This would be clean jungle except for our trash. I smile ruefully. Today is Sunday, and I remember the vehemence of the prophets: Ezekiel, "Is it not enough for you to drink the clear water? Must you also churn up the mud with your feet?" Or Jeremiah, "I brought you into a fruitful land . . . but you defiled it and made the home I gave you loathsome."

In contrast to our visit, the only signs of the shepherds who have camped here since then with their flocks is the meadow itself. Local people who did not have the freedom brought by a lifestyle of consumption have left their mark by keeping this glade free of bamboo and brush for generations. I move around our old campsite like an animal checking its cornerpost markings. We should have carried out all that we brought in. Does our species possess an ancient need to make its mark: Note you who come after that I was here? Or is it laziness? Those who live in simplicity (and the simple livers seldom voluntarily choose that style) are the ones who don't consume. Living within an economy of consumption imprints onto the environment both at the acquisition and disposal ends. Despite the best efforts of the best intentioned to camouflage (packing out what you packed in, recycling and reusing), if you don't truly live simply, the problem builds. Eventually there will be a final solution. Will it be retaliatory or redemptive? Will it come for our generation or for the next?

Ecosystem boundaries are changing. It used to be that a large watershed pretty well defined an ecosystem. A watershed collected the water, gathered in the radiant sun, created the air currents, and rimmed an earthen pocket that its life forms called home. Purely biological bears seldom went over the mountain because at an appropriate scale a drainage defined their home ranges. Now ecosystem boundaries are economic – and our economy, even the economy of Shakshila, is a trinket in the global market.

WE – THE MEMBERS OF THIS EXPEDITION – SET UP CAMP BY OPENING gear that we've brought from the city, and some of us have brought from the other side of the world. That done, Lendoop leads John and Derek Craighead, Bob Fleming, Tirtha Shrestha, and Kazi up the slope to explore the jungle. Pasang stays by his fire, preparing supper. For the last time I cross-check all supplies against lists to make sure we have what we need for the next month, before our contact is cut with the villages. Then the porters leave. Strange: Our contact will be cut with the local villages, but through radios, contact is not cut with Kathmandu and the world.

With three hours still before supper, I push through the barrier of stinging nettles on the edge of camp and start after the others. Dave (Jennifer's older brother) has come along to take pictures and make traps. He joins me as I push through the stinging nettles. We walk up the steep slope, and I look around for other scars of our last visit. What lasts? Bark heals fast in this cloud forest, but a few trees show the old blazes that once guided us back to camp. The mud slicks worn by our travel two years ago are overgrown now with grass and brush, but with our new pursuit will soon wear back open. The undergrowth is denser than it was during February.

After an hour of fast climbing we catch up to the others. Reopening the trail, Lendoop leads John and Derek Craighead. A palace hunter carrying one of His Majesty's glistening .30-06s follows, royal bear protection. Bob and Kazi walk more quietly and somewhat apart, discussing the birds they hear.

Derek Craighead on an overlook in the mid–Barun Valley

Lendoop glances right and left as he swings his kukri, following precisely our trail of twenty-one months before. I wonder what signs he's using. I suspect he's playing the woodsman's game with himself. As his kukri slashes and the undergrowth falls, my eyes usually glimpse a cut twig or two, a cut made by Myang or Nuru two years before.

Beneath these growing plants are dead and decaying plants. My measurements from our last expedition have already been confirmed on the trek in. The detritis on the Barun valley slopes is up to one meter deep, the greatest ever reported for the Himalaya. Rich, pristine, subtropical forest in the Himalaya has yet to be properly studied. Here in the Barun we see that without people removing the litter for fire fuel and bushes for animal fodder, steep Himalayan slopes are capable of holding vast amounts of decaying biomass, acting as an enormous sponge for moisture, creating a rich, stabilizing nutrient base.

At 9,000 feet, we rest while Bob and John search under an oak for scratches on bark and broken acorns, signs of bears feeding. Smiling at me as we wait, Lendoop points up the slope. He and I walk up the thirty yards. He slips out of the fork of a sapling a square corner from a faded candy bar wrapper that Nick and I placed there as a trail indicator two years before. The paper now is bleached the color of tree bark.

As our group climbs higher, Bob hears the white-gorgetted flycatcher. Three quick notes, and Bob recognizes a voice he has heard only four times before. Eight hundred thirty-five bird species are recorded for Nepal – more than in the United States and Canada combined. Bob has seen virtualy all of those – his modesty prevents him from telling me the precise number – and knows more than two thousand of their bird calls. A week earlier, while trekking through the lower jungle, in the middle of a conversation, Bob stopped, hearing the spotted wren babbler. It called once. Three years before in Sikkim, Bob had heard the bird call twice, and from that he learned its call. When he heard the wren babbler this time, he took off through the undergrowth, Kazi upon his heels. Working in from two sides, helped by another call, back in the underbrush, they found their bird and confirmed a new species for Nepal.

Two hours later we reach 10,000 feet. It is a good afternoon. The Craigheads are seeing a cross-section of this jungle. We are fortunate to have this father and son team. John and his brother, Frank, are probably the world's leading bear zoologists. The brothers pioneered the use of radio collars for tracking wild animals in the 1960s. John developed the rigorous methodology for using satellites to map wildlife habitat in the 1970s, and now in the 1980s, John and Derek are demonstrating how it is possible to describe ecosystem parameters through satellite-based remote sensing and computer modeling – and all of this high technology is confirmed by meticulous ground-based field-work. After the group catches its breath, they head down for supper. I wait behind, sitting under a big birch that rises through the canopy like a giant smokestack, savoring being back in this jungle. After the humans disappear, the birds change their singing. The other jungle sounds become more regular.

Our exploration of these jungles mixes hard science and hearsay. Sometimes, it seems, we know a lot. Other times, understanding this environment, deciphering the yeti signs, feels as if we are losing even that which we once knew. It is reminiscent of the mapping of Africa in the fifteenth century when, as ships started to sail the African coast, not only rough coastlines but also cities, lakes, and rivers were drawn inside the unknown continent. Then the need came for greater precision. Coastlines were not just sketched but measured and accurately drawn. Hearsay was no longer accepted. African maps by the sixteenth century had precise coastlines, but reflected nothing of the people and places inland. The added study gave Africa an accurate frame but took away the picture inside. Hard biology is giving us an accurate frame for life, but by disallowing the complementarity filled in by the mysterious. Biology is losing the intimacy even a child revels in. It is only the study of life; it must never be confused with the definition of life. Our purpose on this expedition is scientific – to test hearsay against facts – but we must not lose that which we otherwise know.

Twenty minutes pass, then a twig snaps behind me. I turn slowly. Has a curious mountain chamois approached? No, it is Lendoop, squatting amid the bamboo. I had not known he stayed. Did he snap that twig as a gentle reminder of the time? Is he eager to get down to Pasang's luxury cooking? For a village hunter, coming into the field with Western scientists offers opulence equivalent to an extended stay at the Ritz-Carlton. But even if it is good food he wants, let's not hurry away. This is our first time alone together this trip. Out of my backpack I pull the snapshot of his family, taken on the porch of his hut a year ago. There squats the pretty ten-year-old daughter and her little brother. To the villagers, photos are almost magical; the shots Bob and I brought are the only color photographs of themselves they've seen.

Lendoop quietly studies the picture in his hands. Then, just as quietly, his massive shoulders start to heave up and down. Lendoop is weeping. I wait, letting tincture of time attend his pain. After some minutes, he stops, and the story comes.

"Three months ago my daughter went that day with three other girls to graze the goats above the Barun River. One girl, being thirsty, scrambled down across the rocks to the river to drink. My daughter went with her, for the river is very fast there, sahib. As the first girl leaned and scooped water, my daughter held her dress.

"Suddenly one of the girls slipped – the two girls watching above couldn't tell whether it was my daughter or the other. Rocks there are always wet with spray. Both girls slid off the rock into the white foam. This was on those rocks half a mile above where the Barun flows into the Arun. Their heads didn't pop up once in the tumbling white teeth of the water. Neither my girl nor the other was seen again.

"After a week my wife learned from women she met on the trail that a body lay on the riverbank a day's walk downstream – just before the gorge between Num and Hedangna villages. All night I walked to that place. On the bank I found those bones, mostly bones really, the flesh eaten by jackals, and yes, I thought them to be my daughter's. Sahib, with a blessing and a gift to the gods, I sent her body back into the Arun's current.

"But that caused me many problems. Across the Arun from our village Shakshila is Shibrung. There, one week before I found these bones, a thirteen-year-old boy finished going through everyone's fields, finding ears of corn the harvesters missed, and collected these together. Looking to make some rupees, he loaded sixty pounds of this corn in a basket and went off carrying it to the market in Khandbari, four days' walk away.

"After two weeks of absence, his father, now most distraught, set off down the trail to search for his son. On the trail above the gorge between Num and Hedangna villages, the father found the boy's empty basket behind some bushes. He asked around. No one had seen the boy. But they told him of the bones I had sent into the river the week before. The father notified the police and accused me. The police came to Shakshila and arrested me for murder and theft of corn. In chains I was taken to Khandbari. Thirteen days in jail; finally I was cleared. But now I owe 3,700 rupees for legal fees and fees to the judge – this is three years' income from my fields. Then, sahib, two weeks after coming home, my cow slipped and fell off a cliff. I borrowed another 1,000 rupees from the moneylender to buy a calf cow to keep my family in milk. I also sold my gun."

I sit silently. For Lendoop, the spiral of Third World indebtedness has begun. Lendoop, six months earlier one of the wealthier men of Shakshila village, could now be indentured for life. Without his gun, he must turn to trapping jungle animals to make money on the side. Two months of high wages as a hunter on our expedition will not cut his debt even in half – but it might save him.

Lendoop holds the photograph. He looks deeply at his daughter. After a few minutes he and I rise together and lope the slope down to camp like Nepali boys at play. The scientists have eaten and are in their tents or else sitting under trees writing notes. Pasang has saved us some supper. I join him and the camp staff around the cookfire for our first night back in Makalu Jungli Hotel.

Tirtha searching for plants (photo by David Ide)

Chapter Twenty-Four

November 23, 1984. My watch alarm chirps from inside my boot, its shaft turned toward my ear so the sound wakens only me. Dave sleeps on. It's five o'clock, an hour and a half before daylight, but I want to start before the others.

Today our team plans to climb to the southern Barun Valley ridge. For me this will be like ascending to hallowed ground. Two years earlier, Nick and I tried three times, and Jennifer and Nick tried once, to reach this ridge through wet, waist-deep snow. Each time we failed. We never looked across the valley to "binocular walk" the warm south-facing slopes, searching for "the something." Instead, in day after day of hard legwork we walked cold north-facing slopes. We found those important tracks, discovered those nests, heard those stories of skulls. "The something" became the tree bear. This morning with the snow gone I'm going to try again to climb this ridge. The climb should be easy. I want to be alone.

I lie in my sleeping bag for a few minutes, listening to Pasang quietly bringing up the fire, heating water. What will I find up above? The jungle is so dense. After two years, I still don't understand how its habitats interrelate. It is arrogant — but fun — to think that you can understand how ecosystems interrelate; the appropriate mind-set perhaps is awe. Satellite radiographic images plus high-altitude photographs have shown us how the valley runs, where deciduous trees become coniferous, where the conifers become alpine meadows. But photographs and satellite images don't give a "feel" for the Barun.

Last week, while we were in the lower jungle, I climbed to a lower crest of this same ridge. The jungle there was so dense even on the ridge crest that I couldn't see across to the other side. If I'd had a kukri, I could have cut a window in the bamboo. Instead, thrashing up the ridge, finally I found an oak. From a fork near its top, I looked northward and got my first view into the mysterious Mangrwa Valley, whose drainage starts at a pass at the Tibetan border. Lendoop reports big meadows at the head of the Mangrwa and a torrential waterfall that comes out of a cliff.

Today my trail will follow the one Nick, Jennifer, and I used two years ago. Climbing alone is my way of climbing with those earlier partners who, though not on this expedition, are still part of the team. Climbing alone I'll see and hear more wildlife.

I listen to the last calls of a spotted scops owl as it bids farewell to the night. Then I unzip the sleeping bag. Cold air rushing in, cut from my downy womb, I suddenly come alive. The cold brings a Calvinistic satisfaction that I'm about to snatch the most out of the coming day. Dressing quickly, I step out of the tent into the pre-morning darkness and head for the campfire. Pasang and one helper sit close by it, water heating in the pot. Aware that in the nighttime I prefer hot milk and honey, he offers me that now rather than tea, but I refuse. I want to grab every second from this day. "Pasang, I'll skip the drink; it takes too long. The others will soon be up and wanting their breakfast. I need time. I'd better get started."

Pasang hands me five oranges, a packet of biscuits, a stack of chapatis made the evening before. I smear peanut butter and orange marmalade on the chapatis, rolling them up and stuffing them into a plastic bag. Apologizing to Pasang again for not taking his honey milk, I bid farewell. Pushing through the nettles on the edge of the clearing, I'm warmed by the image of Pasang beside his fire. He always smiles and tries so hard, searching for the little things to make the lives of others happy, the mug of hot honey milk instead of tea. Surely there should be time in my life for a warm drink and fellowship. As I climb up the trail by flashlight, my mind stays with the two squatting by the cookfire, waiting for more sahibs to awaken so they can do their job amid the smoke. They wait for their moment of usefulness, with their hands opened toward the warm flames, both smiling. When camp is light and the food warm, Pasang's son, Tashi, will leave his sleeping bag and join them. He who rises last has the job of being in charge.

The morning starts to grow around me, illuminating the black spaces between the trees. As the sky grows gray with dawn, the blackness rises, compressing, retreating, into the treetops. The rising sun kindles day, distance becomes a dimension. Now I see the world continuously extending beyond the beam of my light. I see the next step, the next turn. Now less attentive to each step, I no longer spot fallen bamboo, and I start to stumble, catching my feet on roots. From the wet decaying vegetation that lies like a gigantic sponge on the jungle floor, my pants become muddy and soaked.

After two hours' climbing, Lendoop's freshly cleared out trail ends. I continue up through thin bamboo, climbing fast. Three hours out of camp I crest the same spot on the ridge where we had seen the "yeti" tracks. There, snow free, are the rhododendron branches on which "the something" walked, using them like snowshoes. Farther up behind the shade of a ridge, old snow still covers the land, and I see tracks made yesterday by a serow. This short-haired, donkey-sized goat antelope with white stockings is rare in most Himalayan valleys, but not in the Barun. The habitat is still secure here. The animal's trail angles off toward a clearing below. A couple of hundred feet higher, I cross tracks of the lesser panda, a tiny red-and-white-faced cousin of the giant panda, known from the eastern (Chinese) side of the Himalaya. It's unusual to see panda signs so high this late in the year. Was one pushing its range, looking for fresh bamboo shoots in this snow?

Higher still, I come across tracks of a musk deer. Pressure from poaching remains on this animal despite the best efforts of the government. Maybe the way to save it is, as Nepali biologist Sanat Dhungel proposes, to trap and farm the animal. Saturate the fragrance market, bring down the price, and make the illicit harvesting unprofitable while creating a local industry of musk deer farming for local people. This is certainly ideal musk deer habitat. Throughout this forest hangs one of its favorite foods, the hanging lichen *usnea*. A hundred yards farther, the musk deer tracks are joined by those of a leopard. Both prey and predator's tracks are clear, as if they were made yesterday evening while the snow was hardening. The trail we travel takes a sharp left turn. I stop and watch the tracks. After a short distance they cut left into a bamboo thicket. Did the deer know the leopard was following and therefore seek refuge? There's no sign in the snow that either was running. Whatever may have happened in that bamboo, the action is long since over.

Tracks in snow provide a zoology guidebook to a habitat's wildlife. But reading them entails a lot more guesswork than reading tracks in the soft sand of a riverbank. Snow type, wind, lower atmospheric pressure, canopy overhead, angle of sun, ambient temperature, these and other variables immediately start shaping what's left for the eye to behold. As I catch my breath and study the variation before me in the tracks, I wonder what the rest of Shipton's tracks looked like that day in the snow. He claimed to have picked "the best one in the shade." What would an experienced tracker like Lendoop have made of Shipton's tracks? Tracks change so fast and so much at high altitude, but once-living things don't. Biological relics endure at altitude. The cold high climate is devoid of moisture, bacteria, and fungi, nature's agents of decay. (On really dry mountaintops, such as California's White Mountains, dead pine tree trunks have not rotted after more than two thousand years.)

I check my altimeter: 13,600 feet. I should be nearing the top, maybe just beyond this thicket of bamboo-laced rhododendron. The trail seems to angle off to the left, taking a more level route. But I'll take the direct route. I start up the steep slope, stepping on the resilient rhododendron branches; it's like climbing in a three-dimensional spider's web.

My body isn't used to this kind of stretching. As I pull on one thin branch, it bends toward me. As I push on the branch beneath my feet to take a step, it bends down and away. The branch at my waist is firm and doesn't give way until I bend over it and step on it. Balancing the elasticities, slowly I climb higher. Cold wind falls down off the ridge, through the bamboo and rhododendron, chilling my sweat-soaked shirt. People pay at amusement parks for this sort of thrill.

After two hours, through the branches I see blue sky, the top of the ridge. I collapse in a clearing and look around. Here, on the back side of the ridge, is a shepherd's trail. Villagers bring their flocks here in summer for high-altitude grazing. This back, south-facing side of the ridge that I've reached holds pleasant meadow walking. Had I followed the level trail to the left into the bamboo thicket with the musk deer and leopard, I would have rounded the ridge and found this trail two hours ago. Rather than my rhododendron spider's web, I could have walked these meadows like a shepherd following his sheep.

Tired, still sweating, I lie back in the meadow to rest. Warm sun loosens my muscles and my sense of time. I doze. Voices coming up from the meadow below awaken me. Around the ridge, having followed the trail, Lendoop and the others appear. I roll over and watch them. It might take them half an hour to ascend the long grassy meadow.

As they walk, a wall of clouds rolls up the valley, coming fast, maybe at ten miles an hour, driven by rising hot air off the Indian plains. Great whipped-cream-like white puffs soon enfold me, swirling cold, moist below and above, reducing visibility to ten feet. Then the clouds part and through a fluff-rimmed telescopic hole I see, a mile away, a landscape of green trees and rugged cliffs.

When Lendoop reaches me, we joke about my stupidity – he spotted where I left the trail. Lendoop grabs my shoulder for a brief wrestle; then we fall back into the grass to wait for the others.

That evening with our group assembled in camp on the ridge, I talk with Tirtha Shrestha. Although my notebooks are filled with data, I press him for a description of how the zones of the Barun stack upon one another. The key to understanding biological change in the mountains is remembering that the average annual drop in temperature is one degree Fahrenheit for every 250 vertical feet gained. Tirtha explains how decreasing temperature creates an array of habitats, which is what makes the Barun so special.

"The lower part of this valley is remarkable, unexpected, a phenomenally low valley floor for the center of the Himalaya, only 3,000 feet. Here in the Barun the subtropical forest is characterized by *Castanopsis* trees, which you call chestnuts, and *Schima* trees, which are in the tea family. Because of such low altitude, botanically the floor of the Barun is subtropics, but even some tropical species are found. In the rest of Nepal this subtropical lower Himalayan region is almost completely settled and certainly is cut. Here in the Barun is the last pure remnant, the last place I know of where pristine subtropical jungle exists without people."

"What's so special about the subtropics versus the tropics?" I ask.

"Subtropical ecology is not as diverse in number of species as is tropical. There is keen interest today in species diversity. To protect genetic resources that emphasis is appropriate, but for the needs of humans, subtropical ecology certainly historically has been more important and is now also more endangered habitat. Look around the world. In many places tropical ecology *still remains*. Though being viciously attacked, there are large tropical forests

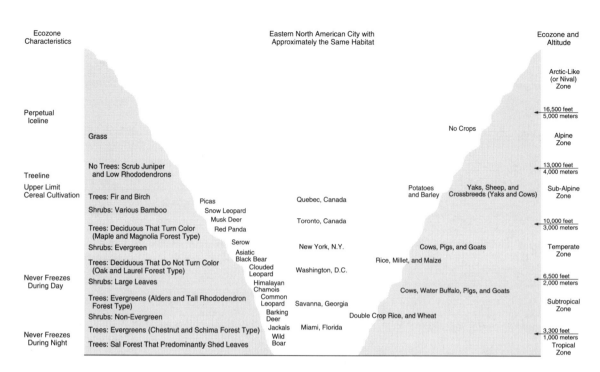

Sketch of Barun Slope Ecozones

not yet cut down. It is important to stop their loss. But pristine subtropical habitat has been almost completely destroyed – so much so we do not even mourn its loss. This destruction was not just recent; for millennia the human species has focused on the subtropics – it was here that our great civilizations developed on all continents. The ecological cradle for our species is what we've now used up – and is where most of the world's poor people today live.

"Farther from the equator, in temperate and colder ecozones, human history that uses industry has come. This is where most resources now are, as they once used to be in the subtropics. It is also where houses and clothes are needed, things poor people like Nepali villagers cannot afford. But can this industrial epoch of civilization with its high consumptive needs endure like the ancient civilizations? Will we generate enough wealth through this development to transform historic inequities earlier civilizations were not able to reform? Of course, you cannot analyze the human species just on biological needs, and certainly climatic happenstance is not determinative. But subtropical and warm temperate are just about perfect human habitat, and people grow well there. You call this the 'sun belt,' I think.

"The important point I am trying to make is that, after millennia of human habitation in these places, the pristine subtropical habitat has been almost totally extinguished, although, as the Chinese and Indian civilizations show, people can still successfully live in the changed biome. Here in Asia we have the longest running demonstrations of the now popular term *sustainable development*. But I'm mixing ideas."

"Yes, what about the Barun?"

"First, you must understand some more dynamics of biology. Why are so many species in warmer habitats? One reason is biochemical. Warmth encourages biochemical reactions to flourish. This stimulates genetic activity, opportunities for genetic adaption; therefore you see more genetic diversity in the tropics. Second, warm climates have more consistent temperatures, a form of habitat stability, allowing species to evolve for precise niches, or for what we now call biodiversity. Third, cold weather, especially freezing temperatures, greatly limits habitat diversity. The econiches cannot be so precise. Species must learn to adapt to a fluctuating environment. I've heard you use the term *bioresilience*, and that is the biological strength that replaces biodiversity as ecozones exhibit greater temperature variation.

"Now consider the Barun. As climates move away from the equator, as habitat moves up the mountain slope, in the course of a year the range of annual climate change increases. Species must become more robust to respond. Subtropical species are hardier than tropical species, temperate species hardier than subtropical, and so forth through alpine and nival or arctic.

"There are further biological reasons why the Barun is exciting beyond being a sanctuary of otherwise lost subtropical habitat. Most interesting to me is the compression here of a wide range of biological zones. This is the only place left in Nepal where the eye can ascend a mountain slope in an unbroken sweep and see in that sweep habitat from subtropics to arctic. Indeed few such places exist anywhere on earth that span seventy degrees of biological latitude – all in outward appearance as before people really took over, although in fact people have been here for a long time. It is like viewing North America from Florida to the North Pole, except here that distance is covered in only seventeen miles.

"Consider the diversity of habitats in this space. Above the subtropical is the warm temperate zone, where broad-leafed trees hold their color year round. As in the tropics, in the warm temperate zone the trees remain green. *Schima* and *Castanopsis* are still found, but also now rhododendrons, oaks, laurels, and figs. But whereas the trees themselves remain green, the understory is no longer evergreen year round; some bushes turn brown in the fall and drop their leaves.

"Our Makalu Jungli Hotel camp at 7,400 feet is above this warm temperate zone. It is like your cities of Washington, D.C., and Philadelphia. This pure temperate zone in the Barun is from 6,500 to 8,200 feet. The dominant trees are deciduous, new species, easily distinguished now in November as they change color and leaves fall, maples, cherry, and for me a new family, *Tetracentron*. The *Tetracentron* here in the Barun are of gigantic proportions – probably the largest in the world. Only a few years ago, the Japanese discovered these trees in the Himalaya. Fossil *Tetracentron* is known in Japan. Finding the tree in Asia proved in another way to the Japanese that their country was indeed land that broke from Asia many millennia ago.

"Just now I stated how neglected the subtropics are. Temperate regions are also ignored today in the conservation press. I don't understand it because that's where the Western conservationists live. If you want to understand really dynamic biology, investigate temperate regions. For example, trees that cope with freezing have interesting, specialized vascular systems. They also change the colors of their leaves. With each season such species experiment with the processes of adapting to an environment that is daily and seasonally fluctuating in temperature and nutrient cycles. Just as tropical species are evolving genetic capacity, so too in these fluctuating regions those life forms are evolving bioresilience.

"Above the temperate, the cool temperate zone appears. Here in the Barun it is between 8,200 and 9,500 feet, totally deciduous, with magnolias, maples, birches, and sorbus being the dominant canopy species. The undergrowth changes from deciduous to evergreen shrubs, especially a lot of bamboo. Bamboo is very common and makes walking difficult."

John Craighead comes up as we talk. "Here, I found something else in the bamboo – try these shoots for dessert." John hands over a shoot the size of my thumb. I crunch into it. Red pandas have good taste.

Our talk turns to animals, their food options in different ecozones. Tirtha gets up, turns, smiles and says gently, "Now I must organize today's plants."

An hour later, I roll out my sleeping bag and get ready for bed. On this same ridge twelve years ago a "yeti" walked past Cronin and McNeely's tent as they camped in the snow by the side of a small ridgetop pond. Our site is almost identical, a few miles lower on the same ridge. I don't want to be sleeping inside a tent while a yeti walks by outside. "I've got a warm sleeping bag and I like to look at the stars," I tell the others while tying shut my pack and setting close at hand a powerful hand spotlight. Firmly, with a steady wind, the night settles in cold over the high Barun ridge. I lie in my sleeping bag and look up at the shining Himalayan night.

Maybe the yeti came by Cronin and McNeely's tent not because it was curious about their camp, but because it was headed to that pond. Ponds on top of Himalayan ridges? Where does the water come from? I hadn't thought about that before, but ridges are the only places, really, you find ponds in the Himalaya. Springs are often on ridgetops too – but ponds are not lower down. I've always wondered about the yeti's food up high; I've never thought about its water supply. You'd expect the springs lower down where they could be fed by the mountain reservoir above. Why?

It must be because of the soils. The Himalaya are sedimentary, horizontal layers stacked on top of each other. The rain falls. The snow melts. Whatever its source, water seeps down to a rock layer, and flows along that barrier until it comes out down the ridge. So when water falls on mountains with sedimentary ridges, it can get caught by a rock shield and never really leave the ridgetop, seeping out up high. In the flat places on the ridges ponds will form. As I look out into the clear night sky, I wonder about these high ponds, little pocketfuls of water held up near the sky. The once-marine rocks under ocean floors that compose these mountains have lifted themselves up from below sea level and now make large drops of water again up in the sky. A raindrop, a pond drop, there are so many dimensions, changes in scale, involved in understanding how our planetary systems work. The stars sparkle up in the heavens above my ridgetop.

Chapter Twenty-Five

My alarm chirps again at 5:00 A.M. A light dusting of snow blankets the ground; a cold wind flows over it. No breakfast fire is going yet. No one else is stirring. Sitting up, snow-dusted sleeping bag still drawn tight around my shoulders, hood over my head, I sweep the ground in the dark of morning with my powerful flashlight, searching for footprints. Not even mice prints show around the food packs.

Like a caesarean operation, the unzipping of my sleeping bag places my trembling body in a harsh new environment. The world is cold and hostile as it rushes over me. This is why people sleep in tents. With the wind tugging at my opened bag, the warm contents – socks that were drying, the extra hat, the water bottle – spew onto the snow. Grabbing for the scattering articles, I reach fast into the bag and pull from the bottom my still-warm and pliable boots, then hurry to the Craigheads' tent to wake Derek.

At 5:20, Derek and I leave camp behind. No scientific reason exists for this sortie into the darkness; we're not looking for any animals. Yesterday afternoon, sitting on that ridgetop above the rhododendrons, when the clouds opened I looked the several miles across the Barun Valley into the massive brown face of Makalu, the fifth-highest mountain in the world.

With that parting of the clouds I had a vision of what it would be like to participate in a sunrise on the east face of Makalu – to see this mighty mountain grow into life out of the darkness of night, to see its blackness rise into red brown. Makalu has seen, I calculate as we walk, 13,650,000 sunrises. Derek and I are heading up to join her for this her most recent.

We first unzip then shed parkas as we climb the ridge. The sky grows light fast at this altitude. At 15,000 feet we're higher than anything in America's lower forty-eight states. Makalu's summit is still 12,000 feet higher. As we climb, light grows behind earth's third highest, Kangchenjunga, off to the east in Sikkim. When the sun hits us here at this altitude it will be twice as strong, with four times as much ultraviolet radiation, as the sun sailors feel. When the first beam hits Makalu's summit, the magic begins. We have crested the ridge, and now we wait, our cameras set up on tripods. Six miles across the valley the light strikes the summit, then like a yellow window blind rolls down Makalu's face, yellow on brown rock and white snow, and, as it comes on down lower, yellow on the white birch trunk seven feet in front of me, and finally, warm light on my cold back.

Derek pulls out jerky made from the elk he shot the season before at home in Montana. My pocket adds dried apricots. We share breakfast. The time passes with richness. At nine o'clock John, Dave, Tirtha, and Kazi join us and take their early morning pictures.

At ten o'clock we survey the south-facing slope. Binoculars walk back and forth, stopping on all exposed rocks, seeking the flick of an ear or an abnormal color to the rock. The morning sun has been warming that south slope for over three hours. Animals should be starting to move.

"Hey, look at that cave!" Derek is pointing up-valley.

I move over beside him. Yes, it's so obvious. Why didn't I see that cave half an hour ago, when I worked that slope with my binocs?

"What a cave!" John now studies it too. "Let's go to that cave. Look, that stream's not twenty yards away from the entrance; a cave with running water. See that grassy ledge for sunning? See that meadow in the valley below? All sorts of animals will feed in that. Look, there's bamboo up higher for fresh shoots. Damn, what a cave. Too bad we don't have a way of getting over there. Dan, how long would it take to hike it?"

"Hiking from here, maybe a couple of days; round trip, maybe even a week. No trails between here and there, maybe cliffs as well. I'm sure tempted, though, to switch all efforts toward getting there. What do you think? That's the heart of the Barun Valley. Whatever animals are in this valley, that cave is their last redoubt. As people encroach, that's where the wild stuff will retreat to. If we want to find what's here, that cave is where we should be."

"Wait a minute, Dan," John says. "Your tone once again sounds as though you're thinking yeti. I came here to study bears. You and I have been over all this before. The yeti simply cannot exist – and I can prove it scientifically. With the grizzly bear we've shown it takes a minimum population of more than a couple dozen individuals for biological viability. A species cannot survive if there is just one or two. If the numbers drop below the minimum viable, the species dies out. If you're interested in the yeti, read our data on the grizzly. You're not just looking for one animal, you're looking for a population. And for a population, you need sufficient habitat to support those numbers.

"Below us, around that cave – that looks like good bear habitat. This valley is the first real wilderness we've seen here in Nepal. In the U.S. it takes a lot of wilderness for bears to live. What's interesting to me, and why I came here to Nepal – beyond the mystery of whether the tree bear is a new species – is to see why and how these bears are able to live with habitat so reduced and so penetrated by human uses. The valley around that cave is the first of what I'd call significant bear habitat."

An hour later we start descending, wanting to reach Makalu Jungli Hotel, 6,000 feet below, by dark. There are traps to check, baited for bears with good, smelly meat that's beginning to decay. A good stink, John Craighead says, is the best way to snare a bear. There's a lot still to do on the plant and bird survey. Makalu Jungli Hotel is our base for this expedition. But all day as we descend I wonder about that cave. What's it like? Is there any way to get to it? Helicopter? Should we plan it as a base for the next expedition?

After supper I go to the cookfire. Lendoop and Myang are talking about the big festival that will come to the Barun in two months. The Barun waters are believed to be exceptionally pure. Three to five thousand Hindu pilgrims will come from the south for spiritual cleansing, especially Brahmin and Newari castes from the big bazaars, Chainpur, Dhankuta, and Khandbari. How will Lendoop, with all his debts, I wonder, get money to spend at the festival?

"Sahib, all the people who come are not pilgrims," Lendoop explains. "Myang is part of a second group, the entrepreneurs. They sell *chang* (barley beer), or *rakshi* (rice or millet whiskey), corn cakes, or lamp oil. Other local people get pots and offer a meal of cooked rice and lentils. Myang sells the couple of earthen jugs of *chang* that his wife makes. But as this quickly is bought, or he drinks it, then Myang has fun."

"Sahib, it is harder now to make money," Myang breaks in. "Professional sellers travel from festival to festival and take our business. The cloth sellers especially cheat us; they are not like shopkeepers in Khandbari, who must make you happy at each sale so that others from your village use their shop. These peddlers know just how much of what type of cloth to bring and set their prices by guessing how many rupees each villager can pay. Good cloth of strong colors sits outside to draw customers. They show these but sell from larger bolts of thin not so good cloth."

"These foreign merchants from India work together," Lendoop adds. "Next to the cloth seller a tailor always sets up; they are fast-stitching low-caste people who carry in hand-powered sewing machines on their backs. They never go back over a seam twice. Seventy cents it cost last year to sew a shirt."

"With the cloth merchants come also trinket merchants," says Myang, "also, peddlers from India; they sell shiny beads, soap, cigarettes, candles, combs, mirrors. They cannot speak Nepali, but their tin trunks always are full. When I was a boy only pilgrims came to our festival from India."

As they talk, I gather that another group is growing in size: the party-goers. The attraction of sacred waters is diminishing as other waters run strong. "Maybe this year I won't sell *chang*," Myang tells me. "My wife will do that. She'll make the money, and I'll have a free place to refill. Last year more than two thousand people got drunk."

The scene must be standard. Impromptu dancing begins. Men, married and unmarried, outnumber, five to one, the unmarried teenage girls who are permitted to attend. Fed as much alcohol as they want by the men, the girls dance close to each other in a gentle, drunken chorus line, their finest silver coins sewn to the rims of their hats. Hungry men like Myang circle the chorus, watching, making jokes, trying to draw attention.

"He has hopes for this year," Lendoop laughs. "The good girls get drunk. The best girls get presents too. As evening comes, men join the chorus line, invited by the women. They dance all night. The music makes everyone feel lonely. Chanting, one singer leads a line, the chorus joins with repetition. As night comes, some couples break from the line, slipping into the bushes." Lendoop laughs again. Myang and Pasang laugh too.

"Sahib," Pasang joins in, laughing, "the more attractive girls walk very slowly past the trinket sellers as they head toward the dark."

Myang's expression suddenly changes in the firelight. He turns to me and asks point blank: "Sahib, you think me wrong. You're not laughing with Pasang and Lendoop. I think you think me wrong."

I'm at a loss for words. My face flushes and I wonder whether in that light they can see the red color that will tell them more than any answer my mind now scrambles to put together. "Well, I was thinking about your wife. What does she feel like? Does she wish you would not go?"

Silence. Everyone is silent, Myang, Lendoop, Pasang, Tashi. I wish I had not spoken the truth for it hurts perhaps too much and cannot cross the assumptions behind cultural lines.

Myang, though, breaks the silence. "Sahib, each of us is a person. Each of us has our own pleasures, which maybe we take perhaps too much of. Maybe my wife is not happy. Maybe also she has things she takes too much of."

"I'm sorry, Myang. I spoke too strongly."

"No, sahib. I did not speak strongly enough." I sense real anger now behind Myang's words. In his village circle he is used to being obeyed. "I think you do not understand. We all, everyone in the world, has things they take too much of. That means you too. You sahib folk take too much money. You ask whether I think about my wife. Have you thought what we feel when we see you take so much good food, good clothes, and pay us so little?"

"Yes I have, Myang . . . and it makes me feel embarrassed." I am silent. The cookfire flickers. Time passes as we listen to Pasang's teapot bubble.

Pasang leans forward, lifts the lid and ladles hot sweet tea into nicked white enamel mugs. Each of us, at a loss for words, sips, sucking loudly. Once again we share the communion rite of the Indian subcontinent, together drinking the only common denominator of food shared by this ancient land's hundreds of millions from the megarich to the absolute poor. The fire flickers, its unifying flame bridging our diversity. With the white enamel chalices we have again become friends.

After some minutes Pasang's son Tashi (essentially self-taught, a pharmacist, a painter, a superb interviewer, one of the most broadly talented people I know and the one who organizes the field staff on my expeditions) breaks the silence and gently moves us into less risky territory. "Lendoop, some people say the caves here in the Barun are really doorways that lead to Shambala, to a valley of special enlightenment. They say if you find one of those caves, you do not need to seek after pretty girls – the happiness of one night lasts forever."

"Sahib, I too have heard of such caves. One of these caves is Khembalung, three days' walk from here in the Apsuwa Valley."

"Lendoop, have you ever entered one of these caves? Or have you ever known anyone who has found enlightenment from going into one?"

"Sahib, I have entered many caves, holy caves and caves where animals live. Every cave I have entered has not been interesting. They are dark, smelly. But I think this is because I did not come to these caves with the right mind. A lama from our village went off to meditate in the Khembalung cave many years ago, and he disappeared while inside the cave. One day people came there to see him, and he was gone. Only his metal bowl and a sleeping blanket were there. That lama has never come back. Maybe, we think, he entered the enlightenment through that cave."

"Lendoop, have you ever known other times when people entered such magical caves?"

Myang answers now. "Yes, my brother had a friend who watched his yaks in the meadows of the Mangrwa Valley. This is a very wild valley, sahib, with a big waterfall. One day my brother's friend fell asleep, and the yaks wandered away. Suddenly sharp, loud screams awakened the man. He sat up and was afraid. He looked above him to a cliff where he could see a cave, and there seemed to be smoke coming from a fire in front. It was not very far away. There by the fire were a *shockpa* and a man. The two were wrestling. First, the man would look like a *shockpa,* then more screaming and the change would happen again. Suddenly, the *shockpa* was thrown into the cave, and the man ran in after him. The door to the cave closed, and the cliff ledge was just a cliff."

"Did your brother's friend go look more closely?"

"Yes, he was very afraid. He went right away though, but first he lit a big flaming torch to protect him from the *shockpa.*"

"A fire torch in the daylight?"

"Yes, *shockpa* are afraid of the power of light. He lit the torch and climbed up to the ledge."

"What did he find?"

"Just blood on the ledge. Fresh blood in three small pools. The door to the cave could not be seen."

The story is chilling, even here at this fire where my companions have imperceptibly all crowded in a little closer. The night feels big and very black behind. I turn to Lendoop. "Lendoop, do you know of any big caves up the valley?"

"Yes, but sahib, I do not know this cave in the Mangrwa Valley. I have talked to the man Myang describes, but I do not know his cave. The only big cave I know is one pilgrims go to below Makalu Base Camp. There is a snow leopard in the cliff that guards the route."

"I've heard of that one. You do not know any others?"

"No, sahib."

"Are there any trails going up the valley from here? Did you see that big cave this morning? How can we get to that?"

"I saw the cave. It is strange. Never before have I seen that opening. Somehow the door of that cave opened today, but it was not there before. That is what Myang was saying, sahib. Doors open to caves. You saw it today. No, sahib, there is no way up the Barun Valley to your cave from here. Too many cliffs stop your travel. Even I can't go. And maybe if you went back, even tomorrow, you would see the cave door closed, just rock."

"You mean you just have not found the trail, Lendoop."

"Nobody has found such a trail, sahib. I think a trail that way would be very difficult. The only way is to cross in high, farther up the ridge you were on today. It would take maybe four days with porters."

Chapter Twenty-Six

November 25, 1984. Tirtha and I sit beneath a large maple. Nearby, his four plant presses are open, waiting for the clusters of leaves held in his two bulging knapsacks. Lendoop sits between the two packs, taking the twigs out one by one, unfolding the six to eight leaves on each twig, meticulously stacking the specimens in little piles, holding the piles down with pebbles.

Our expedition starts to trek out of this jungle in two days. These are the last plants Tirtha will collect. To take their scientific place in Nepal's Royal Herbarium, each specimen must be spread out between newspaper pages and pressed flat in one of his presses. It is routine work that Tirtha has done many times. As we talk, his fingers sort, flatten, and order the leaves, unconscious of their movements and using no wasted motion. To finish pressing the leaves before us will take the rest of today and all of tomorrow. We have a lot of time to sit under this maple and talk.

Tirtha starts by asking, "Daniel, you often mention your hypothesis of bioresilience. I think I understand it, but it is a new way of looking at biology. Could you explain a little more how you developed this?"

"Tirtha, you know I am not a biologist. Many of the assertions seem incomplete."

"Daniel, you're not good at apologies. What do you mean by bioresilience?"

Tirtha shakes out some remaining leaves from his field pack. As the leaves flutter to the ground Lendoop puts them according to type into his little stacks.

"Well, Tirtha, when I walk around the jungle there appears to me to be another way of looking at the strength I see in the life there than just by measuring it through biodiversity and ecological relationships. The biologically diverse forests of the tropics are alive. They are bursting with great numbers of species. But I know from observation that, despite their diversity, theirs is not a robust system. Tropical life forms are delicate. When their life support systems change, they die. When something dies it is quickly attacked and its once-living tissue is used by other forms of life. Life there is very intricate, but there is little depth. The shallow depth of the topsoil symbolizes to me the thin line that life itself lives on. The soil of tropical rain forests is a thin matrix across the ground out of which grows a luxuriance of life. A chain saw in cutting down an acre of trees may eradicate forever numbers of species. Few seeds are dormant in the soil. The nutrient biomass of soil is weak. Rains falling on this cleared ground may wash away that thin soil and that place's potentiality for life. The tropics are diverse in species – but delicately so."

"What you are saying is that tropical ecology despite its diversity is not resilient," Tirtha breaks in as he unfolds the pages of a newspaper, getting it ready to receive his leaves.

"Precisely. Further north, where seasons come and go, where life must learn to live with cold, fewer species exist – but they are more resilient. They have the capacity to respond to change in their environment, to adapt to an environment that goes through seasons, that experiences long periods unlike the long periods that went before, be these changes of temperature or moisture. There are life reserves in these less biologically diverse zones. Everything is not living in exuberant abundance. When death comes, decay takes place more slowly. Organic depth builds – as does the soil.

"For me the potentiality of life can be understood through examining the soil. Is it deep, does it hold nutrients, water, and seeds? If the soil holds reserves, life is more likely to grow back when the life above is lost. But in resilient ecosystems the likelihood of losing the life above is also not so high; roots burrow down into the soil building a foundation. If cut, if burnt, the biome above is likely capable of regeneration."

This long-winded talk must have been boring to Lendoop, who knows we are soon leaving. He is full of questions. "Sahib, why on this trip do you not kill any animals? This jungle is full of much good meat. Why have you only been interested in bears and plants? Why, when you eat meat brought from Kathmandu, do you not also kill animals in the jungle? Fresh meat here is better than Kathmandu meat."

"Shikari, we like jungle meat – chamois is sweet. But for us now to hunt jungle animals would scare away the bears. It is the bears we came to find."

"Then, why, sahib, do you allow Kazi to shoot birds? Firing his gun five, maybe eight, times each day at little jungle birds scares more bears than the big gun the royal palace hunter carries fired once or twice." Tirtha smiles widely with Lendoop's question, almost laughing.

"You are right, my hunter friend, it doesn't make sense. Maybe Kazi scared the bears and that is why we have not found more."

"I think you sahibs do not want to shoot. I think you think shooting is not good. It is your religion? Is your caste too high to allow you to kill?"

Tirtha really does laugh now. "Lendoop, it is not Western religion, but it is a matter like religion. Westerners are afraid the wild places of the world are being lost. They are afraid that the wild animals will be killed and that the trees will be cut down. Their fear has become like a religious belief. They call it conservation. They want to save these wild places and the wild things there."

"But, Tirtha sahib, such thinking I do not understand. There are so many wild jungles and so many wild animals in the world."

"Not true, shikari," I interrupt. "Here, this Barun Valley is one of the last such wild valleys in all Nepal. There are also a few other wild valleys in China, India, and Bhutan, but lacking government protection these are disappearing. You know that the Barun has been here forever and you think it will remain also forever. You are a man and know about how many more years you have. But by the time you do die as an old man, unless we act this year, the wildness of the Barun Valley will have died before you. This Barun will not last forever."

Lendoop ignores me. He looks at Tirtha. "But, doctor sahib, I do not understand. Why do the Westerners worry so about wild things? Deer there are many of. Bears damage people's crops, and little birds do nothing. Why do Westerners worry about these animals that take care of themselves, that grow by themselves, when there exist people, real people, without water, in villages without homes, thousands of villages, villages without food? Why do Westerners not worry about these, the real people?"

"Some things do not make sense – especially once they are separated into different departments for government action," says Tirtha. "Westerners, like the officials of His Majesty's government, are concerned about many things, but they can act only in the department in which they work. Westerners I have known seem to specialize in this way. Few Westerners and certainly not their institutions are like you, the villagers of Shakshila, who do both farming and music or community jobs and building houses. With development, people stop being involved in many things; they specialize in their work. Some take action to help people. Others help themselves. Others act for animals."

Lendoop is uncomfortable. He probably thinks he has spoken too strongly and that Tirtha or I am offended. He gets up from the root on which he has been sitting and walks over to Pasang's campfire for a cup of tea, squats beside it, talking, and doesn't return. I would like to leave too, but I had better not. Tirtha might misinterpret my leaving and think I was offended by how he spoke of the West. The silence that we now share is awkward.

"Tirtha, may I get you some tea?"

"Yes, Dan'l, thanks." I walk slowly to the fire. It gives me a chance to make a quick joke with Lendoop about taking the leaves of tea plants over to the botanist sahib so that he can study these also. I return with two mugs. Tirtha and I drink silently together. My anxiety loosens; a pressure inside me seems to drop.

"This conservation business, Tirtha, as we were trying to explain to Lendoop, is puzzling. There is so much going on in America that doesn't make sense. Americans are aware of a big environmental problem, but the actions they take are little solutions. And despite such good intentions, for the environmental problems such little solutions will not build one on the other to make a big difference. The little solutions taken by Americans do more for our American conscience than they do for the collective problem."

"What do you mean?" asks Tirtha, placing his knee on a now full, two-foot-thick, plant press. He pulls on the straps, getting them as tight as possible, adding two more straps crossing the other way, and pulls each of them tight.

"Let me give you an example, Tirtha. Westerners believe litter is a major environmental problem. Picking up litter is one of the few things almost any

American group, schoolchildren, even groups of business executives, can be motivated to take on. Cleanliness. The group does it for an afternoon and feels it has helped the environment. But picking up litter is not an environmental act — it is an aesthetic act. Litter neither deletes resources nor really contaminates other resources. Litter control is an overly simplified solution to a much more complicated lifestyle problem, consumption and resource utilization. This problem Americans are avoiding, hoping that time and technology will save them. Maybe seeing the litter subconsciously reminds us of overconsumption and that is why it is easy to mobilize cleanup action. Maybe if we left the litter, it would haunt us into doing something about the root problem."

"I understand," Tirtha replies. "If the problem is complex, if the real solution is demanding, people change the problem and avoid the solutions. They hear about junk being left high on Mount Everest by expeditions; they press to clean up this garbage. But here in Nepal garbage is not the conservation problem either. Our environmental problems also come from bigger things — cutting down trees, building roads where they should not be, building wider roads than they need to be, building fields on slopes that are too steep, and perhaps most importantly having too many people."

"Tirtha, that is all true. But isn't the problem deeper, one of human aspirations? People, all people, want a better life. To have a better life, the way modern society teaches us to look at it, means each person has to take and own more. Cutting down a forest to get more fields makes some sense for Nepal, where there's malnutrition in every village. Another field might make real differences in the quality of life for one family. But when aspirations grow so that the government policy, as in American national forests, is to cut down more trees just to keep down the market price of timber, does that make sense? Keeping lumber inexpensive keeps house costs down, and building new houses is central to a growing economy, which keeps politicians reelected. Isn't the impetus for an ever-growing economy the real reason we have the ever-growing world conservation problem?"

"How do you solve this?" Tirtha asks. "We cannot change people from wanting more. Pressing to reduce consumption, to talk about a change of lifestyle, is not an implementable solution. The 1960s in America showed that even the best-intentioned people are only willing to live simple lifestyles for short periods. The Communist failures have shown that you cannot expect people to work for the common good. People are selfish. They have families to take care of; they put these ahead of society. American TV has established the American dream of personal pleasure for the whole world – and Americans must live now with a world nipping at their material-based heels. How do you solve this problem?" Tirtha is taking apart his second plant press, opening page after page, making sure mold has not started to grow on plants already collected. When he finds a page a little moist, he sets that in the sun to air for an hour or two.

"You know, Daniel, speaking as a Third World conservationist, one who often attends world congresses on environmental issues, it is getting tiring listening to the U.S. lecture the world on the environment. It is as though you see environment protection as your contribution and you're saying environment destruction is our fault."

I break in. "You're saying: Stop lecturing us about protecting the rain forest and reducing our population growth. Before you lecture us more, clean up your own contributions."

"No, Daniel, I'm not saying that – those points are true but that's really conservation politics. As a scientist I'm concerned about two specific U.S. processes that affect plants: loss of U.S. freshwater resources and loss of U.S. topsoil. Your poor agricultural practices (which you think are so good) are squandering these vital resources. Soil and water are gifts from God. The U.S. has the world's greatest food producing capacity – just as the tropical countries care for the rain forests that produce so much of our oxygen. The U.S. has a global responsibility to care for its water and soil resources; it is not really yours.

"One of your jobs is to use what you have been given. You have a responsibility to produce food for all of us. You are flourishing with civilization because you grew on subtropical resources which we exhausted over millennia to develop the basis for your civilization and ours. You are standing on our shoulders; you are not self-made, and of course we are standing on yours. Your water and your soil are not yours – just like the rain forests producing oxygen are not exclusively the possession of the tropics."

I break in again. "You're saying we all are linked in a world ecosystem that is more than natural resources, that includes accumulated knowledge, right? Each country owns a share of world resources. Each region has contributed its resources at different periods of history and in different ways. History and ecology come together to show our mutual dependencies, what we gain from each other – a planet of peoples, plants, and animals."

"Yes, we in the Third World cannot impose our desires as the West can through the strings of financial institutions. But increasingly I hope that the truths of science, and more importantly the truths of equity, will teach us all to be pragmatic. We are all dependent on each other."

"I suggest that we stop pressing plants, Tirtha, and take a walk in these woods that we will soon leave." The two of us walk by Pasang's fire, refill our white enamel mugs, and step into the forest, quietly drinking, listening, watching.

A WEEK LATER, DECEMBER 2, WE SIT OUTSIDE THE BARUN JUNGLE, AT THE confluence of the Barun and Arun Rivers. The chopper is due tomorrow. We have been buying bear skulls from the local villagers and have now collected fourteen skulls. All but one are old, brown and dirty, rather different from the Smithsonian's. Most have sat for years in villagers' granaries to scare off rats and mice.

"Well, John, what does a bear expert think?"

"Let's arrange them first into some kind of order. Some you see are tiny, others large; some are old, others young." John takes half an hour, arranges them according to size and examines them carefully. Then, using tooth wear and skull sutures as the calendar, he lays them out according to presumed age.

"Well, John?"

"I'm not a bear taxonomist. But, to me, all fourteen skulls look as though they are from the same species. I see only size and age distinguishing these skulls. Nothing here suggests these represent two different species."

"Maybe these fourteen bears are all tree bears, Dad," Derek suggests.

"How likely is that, Derek?" I ask. "First, villagers claim the big skulls here are ground bears. Do you believe what villagers say about there being two different bears or do you not? Further, what are the chances of fourteen tree bears and not one ground bear? Odds are against that unless they have a trapping technique that only works on one. If villagers are right about there being two types of bear, probably both are here."

But Derek's mind is searching for ideas. "What are the explanations you see, Dad?"

"Given what we have here, keeping an open mind that maybe there are real differences in the bears that don't show in the skulls, I see only one likely explanation: the tree bear is a juvenile ground bear."

I remember the stories the villagers tell. "Does that fit any known pattern, John? In some animals, such as the butterfly, there are major biological differences between juveniles and adults; the caterpillar is totally different from the butterfly. But among bears, do any other juvenile and adult bears differ in behavior as much as the tree bear and ground bear reportedly do? Among humans, adults and children differ enormously. Is such a behavior difference reasonable for bears?"

"All bears I know behave and eat essentially the same from juveniles to adults. That's because adult mammals teach their young. It'll be quite a discovery if in a nonhuman species there is such a difference – and man developed his differences only in the epoch we call civilization."

"John, what's so surprising about this bear being like people? After all, it has a humanlike footprint, uses snowshoes; people have called it a snowman for years."

"Hell, Dan, you never let up. Let's break camp."

"John, let's come back and find that cave."

Chapter Twenty-Seven

Tirtha's question about what I mean about bioresilience is important. As I have worked in the woods for four decades I have come to see that there is a missing dimension in current descriptive frameworks. Biological systems possess a great strength that is not being currently measured. Something is hidden there behind our current definitions.

In the beginning, the work of biology was to systematize the abundance of life. The year was 1753, the name Linnaeus; and thus began the great epoch of speciation. Out of a Babel of folk names Linnaeus gave living things a taxonomic arrangement: kingdom, family, order, genus, and species. Out of that system grew the quest of science to discover more species, to give names and to place in taxonomic order the tree of life. Earth was a resplendent garden and each living thing had its place.

The more biologists searched, the more they found. For example, the birds of Europe numbered 650 species. Across the oceans, the birds of North America numbered 700 species; the whole world, 8,600 species. But it seems the wealth among species increases as the sizes of organisms decreases. As scientists looked more closely at the little flyers, they found that the beetles of the United States and Canada numbered 24,000 species; the beetles of the entire world over 290,000 species. The rain forests, the great biological trove, were then described. Here species swarmed by the millions. Each had its own tight niche. The first discoveries were ground-based – and the numbers of species seemed more than the sands on the beach. Then biologists climbed into the treetops; tens of thousands more species were found and seemed to exceed the stars in the heavens. Each species was different. This wealth was called *biodiversity*. Many believed that this richness was the most important feature of our biological inheritance.

As years passed, some biologists probed the new field of relationships between species. How do we all, each little mite, each giant panda, each tropical fig tree, depend upon each other? Folk knowledge, poetry, religion, each speaks of our being part of a vast and interdependent system. Biology had at first concentrated on distinguishing life by its separateness, and dissecting the workings of each organism.

By the mid-twentieth century, biologists began to describe how relationships between species and with the environment are important, and they began to document that. This dimension of biological wealth they called *ecology*, the study of biological relationships. The categories of order now were ecosystem, community, family group, organism. Within each of these levels it was relationships that were looked for. As research mounted, this natural world and its biological wealth came to be understood as living within a vast web of dependencies. No species was an island. Each was connected to others through intricate linkages of physical and, in some cases, nonphysical connections. Each species, be it mite, panda, or fig, was part of larger communities of dependence. These communities worked within ecosystems – and functioning ecosystems created an interdependent balance on the planet. We live together.

But even understanding the diversity and the interdependence between life-forms was not enough. Life is always changing – and in our modern era life appears to be changing especially quickly. Neither biodiversity numbers nor ecological studies comfortably reflect the biological capacity of an individual species or communities or ecosystems to accommodate change. Indeed both biodiversity and ecological studies appear to suggest that the biology of the tropics may be more durable than the biology in the Himalaya. It is suggested that greater complexity builds greater biological durability – which when viewed from the perspective of resilience is not the case. Some simple systems may be able to take more stress than complex systems for in the latter when one component disappears the system may no longer function. A monoculture of grass may, for example, be able to survive environmental change more effectively than a pristine, complex rain forest.

There is another biological dimension: life's differing capacities to adapt. This needs to be probed. I call this dimension of biological wealth bioresilience. Bioresilience explores the ability among species to change, to adapt. Darwin recognized the role of change, suggesting that this adaptation built the separate branches of the biological tree of life – but biology has never developed a practice of measuring this or recognized change as a dimension of biological strength.

Each species exhibits varying capacities to adapt – and collectively there are differing adaptive potentials at the family and ecosystem levels. An orchid may not be nearly so resilient as a geranium, the latter blooming profusely under conditions that would kill the orchid. All the combined species of warblers eat the same variety of food as a single species of crow. The ecosystem of almost any town park (with relatively few species) endures great variability in pollution, precipitation, and use by the human population use which would devastate a greater number of species than an equivalent area of biologically rich rain forest and force it to dramatically reduce the species diversity. These illustrations point to a biological potential in species and systems that now we are not measuring. Some species, some ecosystems are simply more resilient than others.

Homo sapiens, the most resilient among all species, demonstrates well this capacity. Throughout its several-million-year history the human has pushed outward its habitat limits. First it added fire. It left the warm tropics and pleasant subtropics to enter temperate lands and added clothes. Similarly it added methods of passing along knowledge from one member to another and was ultimately able first to move into the hard-to-live-in tropics and then as knowledge increased to depart from its subtropical and temperate shores and explore new lands. As it added technology, it was able to accelerate the speed by which it moved to these new lands. And finally it brought these components together so that people could break out from natural boundaries and explore new limits to our envelope of life: deserts, cities, the oceans, and recently the summits of the highest of mountains, and finally space.

The need for a systematic understanding of bioresilience grows as the stresses on our world increase. We are putting the planet through enormous

changes. Human population numbers are growing and communities are extracting ever more from the land. Technology accelerates the potential and the reality for more efficient utilization of those resources. With these changes the extinction of species is proceeding around the world at a rate probably unparalleled in recent biological history. But despite these changes, the resilient among species will not die. When confronted with change the resilient will adapt to new niches. The capacity for resilience pushes favored species outward, as they find new ways to cope. This aspect of life has been analyzed by economists and anthropologists. It increasingly needs to be an analytical dimension of biology.

Resilient species have the potential to use biological bridges to survive periods of change. When the massive changes came at the end of the dinosaur era, the dinosaurs and other species had no bridges to carry them across. In the current world it is up to us to help prevent catastrophe, to help preserve a natural balance and the species in this balance. In some instances this may mean setting aside special reserves of protected land; places where change does not come; islands of biological history, protected as the world moves on. In other instances it may mean changing the way change itself is happening. Perhaps we can slow down the pace, or modify and mollify the way change is making room for the less resilient so they do not get trampled by our progress. As in the image of Noah's flood, we need an ark; we will all be the richer if we all survive, and such may be a bridge to help us.

The types of change now happening can be broadly separated into predation, nutrient changes (especially food and water), and habitat fluctuation (temperature, precipitation, and forcible habitat loss). In reaction to these changes, one individual organism or a collection of organisms can respond through defense – that is, protection from the change (adding a barrier or insulation, or creating a storage mechanism); adjustment/mutation – that is, changing its nature to accommodate the outside change (reducing consumption, changing metabolism, changing physically, utilization of tools, or altering reproduction); or migration – that is, removing itself from the change (temporarily or permanently).

Some species have greater capacity to change (for instance, they can learn or they can organize); some have greater depth by which to accommodate change (for instance, they have higher levels of biological development); and some simply are hardier organisms that can take a variety of food, climatic, and predatory fluctuation (typically they live in environments with great natural variability in temperature and/or precipitation). These more robust species can best cope with change. They are the most resilient.

But resilience is only one dimension of biology – and biology should not be viewed unidimensionally through any of its axes. Together biodiversity, ecological relationship, and resilience to change provide height, breadth, and depth, multiple windows out of which to see biological wealth. And there are other dimensions, too, such as the linkages to chemistry, physics, psychology, and geology. Each relationship, like each species, has others sitting beside it – and others sitting beside them on out in ways we do not yet understand. Movements by one radiate through the system.

The tropics bring to the planet a home for biological diversity. The northern and southern climes nurture the vigor of biological resilience. It is the interactions among all these that create the vibrancy of nature. Taken together this richness creates an even richer (and more accurate) understanding of life and our place within other lives, the magnificent dimensionality of diversity, dependency, and resilience.

Lendoop in front of the Saldima Valley waterfall

Chapter Twenty-Eight

October 1985. Last year the possibility of the discovery of a new bear excited Kathmandu. My brother-in-law David scurried through Teku Bazaar, buying metal from ironmongers, supervising bear-trap construction by grimy lads in the back of machine shops. Bishou, Tirtha, and I padded down the hallways of His Majesty's government removing bureaucratic obstacles. Bishou spoke as a deputy private secretary of His Majesty. Tirtha spoke as Nepal's most distinguished natural scientist, one of the elite Royal Academicians. I was the vanguard of international enthusiasm. John and Derek Craighead came from the States, adding scientific credibility. Narayan Prasad and other key helpers worked in the background. The wheels of government turned, and public interest focused on the tree bear. Was Nepal about to present a new scientific species?

Our research didn't provide proof of a new bear. The bear might not be a new species, but it could be a mascot for a more important and bigger project – to create a new national park for Nepal, to preserve the habitat of tree bears. Furthermore, we have more recently learned that the poaching of bears for their gall bladders may profoundly threaten their existence. The need now is to save their habitat.

After two days of walking the corridors I feel movement; something seems about to happen. Like a wisp of a stream high in the mountains, this now rising flow feels as though it will soon be joined, growing into a force strong enough to wash away the bureaucratic paperweights and corrupt deadweights who are allowing and sometimes profiteering off of the poaching of bear.

"We must plan carefully," says Tirtha, "to make every step easy for others to take so we can be successful in our new conservation objective." Bishou, Tirtha, and I meet over afternoon tea. Two weeks from now, nine international participants will arrive expecting to take part in a field symposium worthy of ten days from their busy schedules.

Tirtha continues. "Changes are happening in Nepal. People used to speak of village development as key to Nepal's future. And so, throwing our energy into development, we became dependent on foreign aid and driven by foreign-designed projects. But the real issue that has now come forward is not development. It is control. Foreign assistance has grown to become a new form of First World control. Now our thoughtful leaders call for development that is both sustainable and that we can control. We should use the coming meeting to focus discussion not around conservation, another Western idea, but on the issue here that will generate the broad support, sustainable development."

"Tirtha, I promised the international visitors a trip into the Makalu-Barun jungles. They want to see this amazing phenomenon they have been told about, pristine jungles in the high mountains. Can we include distinguished Nepalis too on such a trip? Will ministers and vice chancellors attend a working symposium in the jungle?"

"Nepal has never had a conference like that. Going to the jungle might excite them. Most of our leaders are bored here in Kathmandu offices. Hardships are no problem. Nepalis know how to live simply; in fact they enjoy hardship so long as there are others of suitable rank. It depends on how the invitation is issued. Some invitations are hard to refuse."

Bishou is both forever pragmatic and royally oriented. "We need to make it clear that His Majesty approves of the idea. The key is the Queen's birthday party tonight. Everyone will be there. This afternoon before the party, let us invite to our meeting General Sushil, His Majesty's uncle; Chancellor Bangdel of the Royal Nepal Academy; Vice Chairman Sainju of the National Planning Commission. It is an unusual combination and the news will get out; everyone will be curious. Instantly our jungle meeting will become the popular gossip around the room tonight, and others will want to join."

The following morning Tirtha and I gather for breakfast at Bishou's house. Bishou is still excited about his late-night meeting with Prince Gyanendra after the birthday party. He talks as he serves highly spiced scrambled quail eggs and rich sweet tea. "Last evening before H.R.H. left for Thailand, he had many questions. I spoke strongly about our work. H.R.H. gives permission to continue organizing and to use the King Mahendra Trust. Therefore, I sent a telex to the chief district officer and also called the Royal Flight Wing and reserved helicopters. Dan, your job is to handle all logistical support, staffing, and the international delegation."

Tirtha is worried. "Last night at the party too many questions were left unanswered. Some wanted to know more about the new park we propose. Before we can invite others, we need to clarify the concept."

Bishou breaks in. "We must keep the theory simple. Why is this new park needed? That is the first question."

Tirtha answers, "The Barun Valley is the only place left in Nepal where people can see what once old Nepal was like. Not only does pristine, subtropical habitat still remain here, but also temperate, alpine, and arctic. Creating this park will be like taking the seeds from a crop that is being harvested and placing them in safekeeping: bears, musk deer, crimson-horned pheasants, tetracentron trees – thousands of Nepal's seeds. If we do not preserve the Barun, it will be like eating one's last grass seed."

Bishou has been listening. "That is why we want the new Barun National park, but how is our park going to be funded? Nepal cannot afford more national parks, even if they are seeds for our future."

I answer, "Bishou raja, that is partly why you must tell people to come to our meeting. We need their suggestions to develop a new way to manage this national park. New principles are now known about how to get local people to take leadership, how money that was once spent on warden salaries can instead help these local people develop."

"OK, Dan," Bishou answers. "But if we start talking that way a lot of people are going to want to be invited. We're going to make a lot of enemies if we don't include such people and give them a forum at which they can ask their questions. How much money do you have, Dan'l?"

"I've already committed more money to this than I have. I came with only $15,000. Last night I calculated that this meeting and the survey of the boundaries we propose to do will together cost $25,000. With the other people you now suggest, the costs will go up beyond $30,000. We also have to do further field research. But I can't promise now more than $15,000."

"But you have no choice," Bishou replies. "We have made many commitments. Officials here do not understand an American organization that cannot spend more money when it has taken on a job. Everybody is going to be very upset if we do not do something more."

Gently Tirtha pushes to the root of the money matter. "Dan'l, you've started something. Now suddenly the government of Nepal is ready to move. Are you and your Woodlands Mountain Institute going to make this project happen? You're talking now about a big idea, about building a national park, about a government making a commitment of perpetual protection, and you wonder about a commitment of $30,000? Are you the type that once you get things going you become frightened that it is too big and pull out? The dream is big and might get bigger still. You may have started with the mystery of yeti. But the yeti has a habitat which now you say you want to protect and is very much alive as the symbol of the wildness that all people seek. The question is one of responsibility and credibility. If you are not going to be true to the quest, you are playing games in Nepal with important people. If you are not serious, maybe today call your foreign friends and tell them not to come to Nepal."

Tirtha and Bishou are silent. I lift up my half-full teacup feeling its warmth, swirling off the bottom what I know must be still undissolved sugar. A long, thoughtful drink. I swallow more than sweet milk tea. The stream that began high in the mountains is growing strong. Caught in it is a small, small raft and I see rapids rising ahead. Their approaching sound is clear. But I can't bail out; I want to know what's at the end of this quest and must ride the momentum now flowing. Something could well be coming together now that may never again be possible.

I set down my cup. An image shines in my mind of two particularly skeptical trustees I'll have to face at the next Woodlands Mountain Institute board meeting. I smile. Chutzpah scares them. They do not understand how big things can be done by little people. A hillbilly organization is about to catapult itself into international conservation – because what we're taking on is not just a park but an idea. The trustees agreed to the principle at the last meeting. There's no way to bring them into today's decision. It's mine to make – and make now. Do I really feel I can raise that money? Looking at Tirtha, I say, "OK, I'll find the money. Keep going. What must we do?"

Bishou answers, "Good. Many people are now interested. Meetings must begin here in Kathmandu. That way everyone gets involved. Let us rent a ballroom of a hotel. We'll have a big reception, make a display, invite speakers, get newspapers, radio, and television. What do you think, Tirthaji, will two days of such meetings satisfy everyone's interest? We must serve good food as well as drinks – just tea and biscuits will not be enough to make the project look serious."

"Yes," Tirtha joins in. "Two evenings are enough. People do not like to come to all-day meetings – they prefer evening receptions. They want to be included in a new idea and meet international dignitaries. The important thing is to involve a wide cross-section of people, to create the feeling of broad support. We must give people the chance to ask questions and make suggestions. A group called the Annapurna Conservation Project made a good start by giving village people a chance to make suggestions. In our project we should provide this same chance to the Kathmandu government people as well as local people."

Mass meetings for a cross-section of Kathmandu intelligentsia . . . tea and biscuits not enough . . . a hotel ballroom . . . for two nights . . . newspaper, radio, television . . . the cost of this thing is going sky-high. Whose chutzpah will be caught in this meat grinder?

Bishou joins in again. "Those two evenings here in Kathmandu will be the beginning. The second night should end with a public commissioning, an endorsement, of the special meeting in the jungle. That way everyone will feel they have a part in going there but will understand there's not enough room on the helicopters. Then, the twenty people who go represent the whole group. See my idea? The larger group sends the smaller; this way we have a much broader political base. Then, after the smaller group comes back, their recommendations get the force of the larger. Therefore, at the end we must have another big reception, something grand so that even more important people come."

My mental cash register keeps ringing up their purchases: helicopters for twenty people, food, tents, and camp staff for five days . . . and a third grand reception. . . .

Bishou interrupts my calculations. "The Royal Cottage in the King's Forest, what do you think? It is big enough, only twenty minutes' drive from the city. A nice caterer will handle everything. Yes, I think the Royal Cottage is best. The King's Forest is appropriate for a conservation meeting, and many people will find it interesting." I keep thinking that down the line were talking big money. There are in the donor community the institutional donors that give away their money by paperwork – and then there is also another smaller group. Thank God for these folks who have the funds I don't have, the International Fund for Animal Welfare, Mike, Spencer, and Dr. Tom. These folks realize that to make real change you must support real risks.

Two weeks later, after the sendoff reception at the Blue Star Hotel, the thwack-thwacking of rotor blades makes conversation difficult inside one of the His Majesty's helicopters. After an hour we can see the Barun Valley below. Four minutes of flying takes us across the jungle from the Barun's confluence with the Arun to Makalu Jungli Hotel – four minutes to cover what was a three-day hike twenty-eight months before.

When I left the States to come on this trip, Jennifer and Nick were confident that the Barun weather would hold true. They sent me off with chastening warnings that, once landed with big shots from around the world, we would all be made captive, cut off by weeklong wet snow, dripping clouds that helicopters couldn't penetrate, held hostage in a valley they couldn't walk out of. But that was supposed to be a trip for fun and fund raising. Now we'll have a dozen senior government officials too. The Saldima meadows could become quite a hostage camp.

I look out of the windows; there's no snow below. As we come to the head of the Mangrwa Valley the meadow opens. The helicopter hovers, then lands. Pasang, Tashi, and Lendoop arrived two days before, having dragged here over mountain passes and through the jungle the two live goats and eight chickens that will be our meat for the coming days, plus a string of porters with food and supplies. They've already set up tents.

We start building a conference center. In the yak herder's hut in the meadow, the porters weave a conference table and benches out of bamboo from the jungle. A stone beach is made down by the stream to assist with each person's washing. We scout scenic nature walks in the jungle.

Several days later the helicopter cabin shakes again as that craft slows, hovers over the meadow, and settles to land. As the dignitaries step out onto the Saldima meadow, everyone turns to gaze at the gigantic waterfall thundering from a lofty cliff, dominating the valley. Some amazing reservoir nourishes that magnificent arc of water. But John Craighead has spotted something else beyond the waterfall.

"Dan'l, is that smoke coming up from behind that rock ridge? Who would be back there, up that high, building a fire?"

It is smoke. John is right; there seem to be thin wisps rising beyond the waterfall. Or is it mist from a lake beyond the cliff? John goes off and studies the NASA satellite image of the Barun. Amid the several radiographic images we recently acquired, he spots an extremely large, frozen depression, maybe a mile in diameter, set in what appears to be a rock cliff. Is this a lake or just a glacier? Around the flat frozen mark on the satellite image are great snowfields that must feed the lake that drains through the waterfall.

We settle into work. From around the world, twenty-one people, twelve Nepalis and nine Westerners, have come to plan a new national park. A field-based meeting such as this requires around-the-clock activities to keep everyone busy. These are people used to being busy with breakfast and evening meetings augmenting their tightly scheduled work days. Morning bird trips, evening campfires, snacks must be organized. The foreign and Nepali groups must be kept interacting, not letting them split into two parallel cultures.

The next morning, General Sushil Shumshere Jung Bahadur Rana, His Majesty's uncle, opens the first meeting. "As chairman of today's session, it is my pleasure to welcome all of you to the opening of this historic conference. How unusual to have so many distinguished people." The editor of the *National Geographic* snaps a photograph of the director of a major American foundation squeezed on the hand-hewn bench between Nepal's secretary of forests and the chancellor of the Royal Nepal Academy. The light from the flash immediately slips out the cracks in the walls of woven bamboo and again our conference chamber is lit only by pinstripes of sunlight slipping in.

General Sushil resumes. "How unusual to have so many distinguished people in such a humble setting. Our conference table was lashed together only yesterday by villagers who can't read and who have never seen a vehicle move on wheels. But they know what grasses to use to lash our table together and what branches to use to make the benches on which we sit. Our feet rest in the old dung of yaks. Let us remember these symbols as we talk lofty ideas and ideals. We are here to design a new national park – not just a new park but, indeed, a new design for national parks. This meeting marks the beginning of a new approach to national park planning. What more appropriate setting can there be, and how much more qualified a group can there be? Ladies and gentlemen, welcome."

The sense of being a team builds. Rank and status among members are dropped. Being in the wilderness is exciting. Everyone pitches in. A member of the royal family carries food to serve others. The leader of the National Planning Commission goes around camp picking up trash. His thoughtfulness for the welfare of others sets a standard all try to emulate. The momentum of this teamwork continues into the meetings. We're breaking new park-planning ground.

Any sense of urgency to discover the tree bear's identity is gone. Now we worry about the animal's habitat. The politicians outline what might work and how it will have to be presented. The scientists use a full day to tell us what must not be forgotten, what must be included. The bureaucrats wonder how to process the unfamiliar into acceptable proposals. Is this meeting official? Does it have authority? Must something now be done? The international experts try to articulate the hard questions, or share a perhaps-relevant experience. A couple of the foreign women ask questions everyone else is afraid to ask, such as whether adequate recognition has been given to the need for unique new types of training, or even more embarrassing, whether we who have power and money are willing to let go of it.

There are major outcomes. First, not only the Barun Valley, but four other valleys as well, will be recommended to be preserved. To three hundred square miles is added all the territory east of Everest, grand sweeping proposals, perhaps a thousand square miles. This decision positions nature conservation in a powerful bargaining stance with the one-billion-dollar World Bank hydroelectric project proposed for the same region. Conservation is now directly interacting with the largest development project in the whole Himalaya. Second, statements by His Majesty and His Royal Highness are being taken very seriously: Conservation is for people; Nepal's natural resources are to enrich Nepal's human condition. (Not all the international experts are pleased by this outcome; for them there is a legitimacy in conservation for its own sake.) Third, like the composition of this meeting, conservation is recognized as involving all governmental constituencies, not just the foresters and the wildlife people. Conservation is part of development, not something restricted and done behind the fences of national park boundaries. And finally and most importantly, villagers are to be part of both planning and implementation. Not only will they have the chance to decide what they want and how they want it delivered; they are to be given priority over outsiders in training to become the staff of the preserve.

Mountains are recognized not just as geographical points and as more than ridges linking outstanding points. The uplifting of earth's crust also lifts up eyes and ideas and, always, the human spirit. As our meetings proceed, a feeling of contentment runs throughout camp. Three bottles of Scotch are found in someone's duffel. Bishou announces that we're going to have a big bonfire and party this last night in camp. To prepare for that bonfire three old friends leave the Saldima meadow and walk down into the jungle to fetch dead and fallen trees.

John Craighead and Tirtha sit across from me on a fallen rhododendron trunk, *Rhododendron campelli*, a tree in Nepal named after a man from Scotland. I sit in the bowl of lichen-covered rock, feeling as excited as a first-grader on the opening day of school, seeking advice from my two scientist friends. "That a national park will result someday from our plans here, a park beginning from a searching for the tree bear many months ago – it all seems so unreal. But I guess progress doesn't happen logically. We've started the making of environmental history here, and doing something about the environment can begin anywhere. Is it real, what we've done? Will it be real when it's done?"

"We must wait, we must see," John says. "It sounds good here today. Designing a national park around ecosystem principles, a park where man is managed as just one more species in the ecosystem, all this is a much more realistic way of setting up a park than normally. It is better than the U.S. Cavalry riding in, securing the perimeter, keeping man out, and setting up Yellowstone National Park a hundred years ago."

Tirtha adds, "I think it will become a real, legal park. As John says, this preserve has been designed innovatively, but also correctly. We have involved the right people. Many surprises and much work are ahead, but the momentum and blessing have happened here with these meetings. The idea has boldness and the needed support. Many people will try to set it back, but we are stronger now than the one or two people who will raise objections in the future. I do not think the process will be stopped."

"Reality among parks comes in different types, Dan," John says. "And when I say reality I am not just talking about parks that are real wilderness and parks that pretend to be wilderness. There is a feeling of reality you get visiting parks. When a park is real, it feels bigger than the area itself. It captures a helluva feeling and compresses such wholeness into one place. A real park makes you feel like you're part of that ecosystem."

"John, you're sounding mighty Buddhist," I chuckle. "What do you think, Tirtha? Doesn't John's reality sound like finding the whole ocean in a single drop, except that now, the metaphor is the whole earth through a single park?"

"No, Dan. It is more complicated. Reality, if you seek the Buddhist explanation for this instance, is the relationship between wilderness and civilized humanity. All things exist as reflections of other things. So civilization is civilization because it is reflected as a state against the 'mirror' of wilderness. Wilderness by itself is a whole. Civilization by itself is a whole. When we look at one in reflection to the other, then and only then we see them both."

"OK, I'm sorry, I joked about reality. But I do have a specific question for you two about another reality, something practical, a reality you can answer scientifically: grasses and sedges. I recall reading somewhere that the way you tell whether or not a meadow is pristine is to examine the proportion of grasses to sedges. Does that work?"

"Why do you want to know that?" John asks.

"John, usually when Dan asks strange biological questions he is thinking again of his yeti," Tirtha answers. "Given the point just made in this conversation, he must have another idea of how to find out if that animal is real or just a perception of reality."

"Tirtha is right," I say. "But please explain."

Tirtha, the botanist, begins. "In a pristine meadow there are usually few sedges; there are also few wildflowers. Grasses are taller than sedges. So, if the meadow is not being grazed by domestic animals, the grasses, growing higher, block out the sunlight the sedges need to grow. In a truly pristine meadow you may find only 15 percent sedges. But if the meadow is heavily grazed, grasses are cut back, the hardier sedges dominate, and you may find only 15 percent grasses and you also find more wildflowers."

"But, regardless of grazing, you always find mostly sedges along a stream or in wet areas. Sedges adjust better to changing habitat," John adds.

"Sedges and grass, what's the difference?" I ask. "I thought it was all grass."

"True grass has round stems," John replies. "Sedges have triangular stems. They flower from one point only, whereas grass flowers from nodes all along the stem."

Tirtha goes on. "The grass/sedges issue is an interesting lesson in biological diversity, Dan. Many people believe a pristine ecosystem will hold the greatest number of species. Not necessarily true. Pristine systems often climax out; a dominant species takes over and reduces species diversity. Maximum biodiversity happens where habitats are changing, like on the interface between forest and meadow, or on the estuary interface between land and sea. There are lots of specialized niches on an interface. In an alpine meadow, for example, to get maximum diversity of species, man in moderation often helps. Wild-animal grazing in alpine meadows is not adequate. An alpine meadow where humans cyclically bring in domestic animals will have not only a rich mix of grasses and sedges, but an abundance of wildflowers – in this Himalayan habitat, especially primulas."

"How do grasses and sedges relate to your yeti?" John asks.

"Let's pick up these dead limbs and return to camp," I reply. Tirtha laughs, and we start dragging branches up the narrow, naturally cobbled trail that is used occasionally by shepherds and by smugglers headed the back way into and from Tibet. There is a lot of dead wood. It's going to be a big, wonderful bonfire.

SEVEN-THIRTY, OUR LAST MORNING IN CAMP. DAYLIGHT ARRIVED AN hour before, and life is already a lot busier than on any morning before. Inside tents people are stuffing clothes into duffels, rolling up sleeping bags. Breakfast is hurried. One of the American members who heads a foundation investing in biological resource issues and his wife slip off to take a last walk in the cloud forest. I lean back against a rock, writing up my notes from the meetings. Putting the pen down, I look at the Saldima waterfall thundering off the rock face. Long, wispy puffs are rising behind it into the sky. Is it smoke? I wish I'd had time to hike up to the lake or glacier John spotted on that satellite image. The area behind must be huge to generate such a constant discharge of water.

But the immediate question throughout camp is when – or indeed if – the helicopter will arrive. Kathmandu November mornings are heavy with fog; seldom does it lift there before eight, sometimes not until nine. The flight here takes an hour and ten minutes. The chopper could be here as early as nine to take us out. Bob Davis comes over as I finish making notes; he is the official scribe for the meetings. But it is not facts that are on his mind.

"Dan'l, have you timed the morning clouds? The last four days the sky has been clear from before dawn until about nine-thirty. Then that cloud rolls up-valley, socking in the entrance. I've just now come off the ridge up there. The cloud is formed and positioned down-valley, maybe at 6,000 feet, and it's rising to meet us. Dan'l, that helicopter not only has to get in here by nine-thirty, it has to come in three times. Even if it just lifts people out of this valley to a cloud-free ridge, each trip will take thirty minutes. If we're all going to get out today, that chopper needs to be here by eight. Do the arithmetic. Will the fog this morning in Kathmandu lift by seven?"

"Hot tea, sahib." Smiling, Pasang holds out two steaming mugs. Then he turns back toward the bamboo thatch hut he has made his camp kitchen. He, too, clearly is ready to leave. The pressure of cooking for so many dignitaries, with each one's own likes and dislikes, with so few resources, all brought in on porters' backs, must have been an enormous strain – one he's managed to carry unnoticed. People like Pasang are noticed only when they screw up.

As he leaves I ask, "Pasang, how many more days of food do you have for this group?"

"After today breakfast, sahib, I have three more meals, but sugar only two more times for tea."

Twenty-one dignitaries, plus three on the cook staff, plus twelve porters we kept in camp as backup in case of trouble – in all there are thirty-six people in camp. When planning, we brought what we calculated would last this group eight days (five days of meetings plus three days of reserve). Round-trip for re-supply is three days by a porter running. The thoughts race through my head as Bob and I sip our tea. As always, Pasang made my cup extra sweet. Others, I bet, have gone up to him quietly and asked for extra spoonfuls. That's why with thirty-six people, a sixty-pound load of sugar disappeared in five days.

Bishou comes over drinking his tea and looking down the valley at the top of the approaching cloud. "Dan, we are successful, I think. We made enough friends with these meetings; we will win. Our idea has now the soldiers it needs to carry it through the difficult years, the difficult times, ahead. The future is only hard work."

"Bishou, how can you be so sure? We haven't even submitted our report. We don't know whether friends of today will stick tomorrow when they return to their offices. A big and strong enemy could arise."

"Dan, yes, that question of which friends we can trust, we do not know, and we must work very hard. But look around this camp. Look who is here. Look at the Nepalis. Have you ever seen so many powerful Nepalis drawn together

Shepherd with prayer wheel

for such a simple task? Just by coming they have promised their support. Unless a new reason allows them to change this support, we have not only their commitment but their obligation."

Dan Vollum, a conservationist from the Pacific Northwest who is also an expert pilot, joins us. "Dan'l, that chopper better get here soon. Flying up-valley among those clouds will be like trying to navigate up the belly of a snake – curving walls ready for smashing into at every turn."

Bishou smiles as he looks down-valley. The top of the cloud is getting closer. "Mr. Vollum, don't worry. General Sushil is here. He is in charge of the Royal Flight Wing. The pilots will come even if the flight is up the belly of your snake."

I look over to where the tents had been standing. They are all down. What was this morning a nylon town has returned to meadow grass. The coming cloud is about to wrap the grass in its blanket. Maybe this morning the cloud will be a single puff that will roll over camp, rise, and give way to clear sky. Maybe the chopper can hop over this puff.

Bishou keeps talking. "With our project we have created something in conservation that not only saves the environment but also helps people. No project in Asia is doing sustainable development. Maybe if we work carefully, we . . ."

Out from the cloud comes the unmistakable thwack-thwack-thwack. The chopper's coming. The cloud also approaching up-valley is so close I can throw a rock into it, but directly overhead is a hole of blue sky. The pilot will have to drop straight down, like dropping into a well. We all look up.

But Dan Vollum points suddenly into the fog and shouts, "There it is! There it is!" A giant grin half-circles his face. Following his finger I see the big white seventeen-passenger mechanical bird, made in France, flying in the Himalaya. It's coming in just above ground level, swooping and banking, running up the valley under the cloud. It looks incongruous, swerving around big trees like a skier running a slalom course, hopping over the smaller ones like an attacking *Tyrannosaurus rex.*

One group will get out now. Our rations increase by a third. We've bought valuable time. But with the general gone, how hard will the pilot try to get back? Thirty-six people surge toward the helicopter, toting duffels. The double doors open. All the Nepalis step aside for General Sushil. He refuses to board. I go over to him, waving my arm toward the open door. "General, please."

The uncle of the king stands back, motions to others to get on board, smiles, and pulls me away from the thwacking of the rotor blades. The pilot looks expectantly toward his general. Brigadier Sushil motions the others on. The pilot closes the helicopter doors, returns to his seat, throttles up his turbines. The general turns to me. "Dan, I wait for two more flights. You are low on sugar, I think."

Chapter Twenty-Nine

October, 1986. From around the world, we have come to Shegar, Tibet, to the base of Mount Everest in the People's Republic of China. We are here to start an adjoining preserve to the one started the year before at the Saldima meadows meeting in Nepal. That park will be the size of the state of Rhode Island. The new preserve in Tibet will be the size of the state of Massachusetts – or Taiwan, as our Chinese colleagues like to point out.

Government officials are excited and cooperative about conserving nature through using the local people as its managers. Outsiders are skeptical of whether management will be effective without professionals. But modern China has successful demonstrations of giving control to the people. This will be the first major park in the world where there are no outside wardens, where the local people will work through their regular administrative systems to preserve the land and the wildlife. The idea of local people caring for wild resources is not new. It is, after all, how land was always cared for until professional managers and people who didn't live in the area got what they thought was a better idea.

This night's stop, the ancient caravanserai of Shegar, is a long, long way from the more commonly known remote points of the planet. Kathmandu, Nepal, and Lhasa, Tibet, are, from here, distant cities where villagers in

Shegar dream of going for cosmopolitan bustle. To get to Kathmandu, you take a right at the fork outside the gate; to get to Lhasa, you take a left. And then, for either city, you have two hard days' going by four-wheel drive. Until the Chinese completed the motor road, Shegar was even more isolated – across the centuries, a rest stop within a walled fortress where yak and pony caravans stopped. Then it was two weeks in each direction to Kathmandu and Lhasa, a journey made only by pilgrims, traders, and those on the run.

At the Shegar dining hall, supper is long since over. John Craighead, Tom Roush (a physician friend from New York), and I remain around the big circular table, one of perhaps twenty such tables in this cavernous chamber, built for the Chinese army when they feared attacks by the CIA-supported freedom fighters of the Dalai Lama during the global tensions of the 1960s and 1970s. All of us gain insights with time and experience. The Dalai Lama's enlightenment is proven by the fact that his message is one now of peace, a powerful message he now speaks to the world, not just to his once-isolated people.

"Daniel, this place is huge, wild, remote. What are you trying to do with this Everest area? The world here – it is like the moon, sort of, like heaven maybe – it may sound trite, but that Everest we saw today has got to be the biggest thing in the world, huge, wild." Tom is talking about the land through which we've just traveled. "When you're there you know you're there, but also you know you're a long, long way from anywhere." Tom is still unwinding from the shock of discovering himself an unintended castaway, when our four vehicles drove off after stopping for sunset photographs of Everest atop a 17,000-foot pass, leaving him behind on that pass in cold wind surrounded by falling night and possibly spindrift snow.

"What prompted you, Daniel, to start this project?" Tom is a man who follows his own interests, and right now he doesn't want to go to bed. A devotee of the night from New York City, he wants a story that will make tonight real for him. We've been sitting here frozen, talking biology for the past hour. That topic – or was it the bone-invading cold? – tired the others in our group, and they left for bed.

"Tom, I came here looking for the yeti. I believed it was somewhere. All I really had to go on was footprints."

John breaks in. "We've been over this before, Dan. Footprints are a lousy indicator of whether an animal exists, especially footprints in the snow. They can tell maybe how long before a hypothetical animal passed, maybe whether it was male or female, maybe how big it is – but they can't tell you whether or not a yeti exists. It is as we have discussed before, a matter of demographic parameters – fundamental biology. For a species to exist and survive, it must be in sufficient numbers to replicate itself over time. Even for a bona fide species, snow is a poor indicator.

First, snow melt changes shape – even more sometimes than the original shape of the animal's foot. At these southern latitudes and here at elevations, an hour of sun melts out a lot, and prints can still appear sharp. Second, the speed the animal is traveling determines what you see in the snow, a factor often overlooked. An animal running or going downhill can almost unrecognizably distort its normal track. Third and finally, snow conditions. A very thin crust – from windpack or melt-freeze often creates both print enlargement and especially enigmatic sharpness. From a scientific standpoint one print in snow is probably worthless."

"John is right," I say. "I've cooled a lot and learned a lot since I started looking for the yeti here in these snows. The most important thing I've learned is to remember the biases we all bring as observers. I keep thinking I know my own biases. They are more than psychological biases. Here in the Himalaya you don't function with all your senses. Extreme exertion results in low blood sugar and your judgment changes. Cold increases chances of hypothermia; observations are often rushed and certainly only partial. High elevations put the brain low on oxygen, so your brain simply doesn't work the way it normally does. These physical conditions, plus the extremely potent and unpredictable psychological ones, make even the scientifically intended observer inconsistent. They can also rekindle an imaginative boy's dream."

"I came here looking for a bear," says John. "This yeti stuff is just that – stuffing. But there is solid, interesting evidence concerning a bear. Despite our work we haven't yet answered that question about the bear. Even more important is its habitat – some of the most complex and spectacular on earth and some of the biologically most endangered in Asia. In the Northern Rockies, after decades of work, we're starting to understand how ecosystem pieces fit together. Here the questions and relationships are much more complex, larger, and the research will be much more difficult."

Tom refills his glass from a half-empty bottle of Bristol Cream sherry left behind by another member when she headed for bed. I try to feel warmer by talking. "In tangible terms, Tom, we are building two parks to preserve this spectacular region, but the motivating factor for me behind the parks is the yeti. The yeti is more than a physical mystery. Over the years the yeti has come to symbolize the unknowns of this planet. I came to this work believing a real yeti might exist. Like an answer to a math problem, it was a scientific postulate to be solved by a series of systematic steps. The assertion was either true or false, a problem to explain. Then the question changed. It's no longer a physical quest. Now, for me, as for most people of these mountains, the yeti is not an unknown but rather a string that ties together realities we know and realities we sense. It has moved beyond something concrete like mathematics and science."

"Extrasensory realities," John laughs softly. "The guy is half crazy, Tom. First we came out chasing bears. That I can understand. Now here I am back in the field a third time, and he's talking without embarrassment about this business, about how some supposedly real animal is not real but encapsulates that which is unreal and inside us, and – can you believe this – that which is real and outside us!"

"John, deep down inside, I think, most people want to believe in the yeti. Our most basic understanding of reality as humans resides not in rational proof but in that sense in ourselves of what we know is true. You or any person can hear facts, but still not believe. But then sometimes you hear just a fragment of an idea, and immediately you know it is more than an idea, it is truth. What makes this different? Our acceptance of truth comes from how things resonate inside ourselves. And, over the years, having had a lot of people bring up the yeti to me, I believe that inside almost all people is an urge that they want the yeti to exist because it speaks of our unknown past. Incredible as the idea now is of a biological missing link, to the gut it makes sense.

"I'll bet Tom here wants the yeti to exist. I bet at least once back in New York, when he was packing to come here, knowing he was going into Himalayan wilderness, the hope flashed through his mind: 'Maybe I will see the yeti on the trip.' If Tom has a typical human fantasy life maybe he even entertained a private vision: 'Maybe I'll be off some evening by myself, I'll step around a rock, and there will be the yeti, looking at me.' Maybe that is even what Tom was off alone doing at the top of that pass this evening, looking behind rocks."

Out of the darkness comes Tom's amused chuckle, sounding like "Hell." I look across. I can see only his silhouette, framed in the window against the starlit sky outside, body leaning back in his cold metal folding chair, hands fisted inside the pockets of his yellow and black down jacket, his shoulders hunched forward against the chill.

Then rumbling builds outside the walls. An old Chinese truck rattles into the compound. Its headlights sweep their beams in through the window over the big empty tables in this cold room. I first visited the room with Jennifer, Jesse, and Tara two years before, on my first trip across Tibet. This remains their project too. It is lonely working out here with them back there.

"We need a place on earth to hide the wild parts of ourselves," I continue, "a preserve big enough so there remains unknown, unexplored corners of the land – and of the mind. We need a place where, as our numbers crowd the planet, we can imagine mysteries roaming. With unknown land preserved, each generation can search again for the yeti – and discover the science of life interacting, which is ecology, and participate in the art of science violated, which is magic, and, as has been the case with me and my yeti search, discover more about themselves."

Tom says, "I'm not interested in that psychic stuff. I can take it or leave it. I want to know how you moved from tracking a bear – or yeti, whatever you want to call it – to creating these two gigantic national parks."

John answers, "Tom, searching for a bear, we found a special valley, a biologist's dream, and we said, let's do something about this. As Dan says, it is a place to hide the wild parts of ourselves, the bear we seek, and yes, even the yeti. Then we looked around, found another valley, had a meeting, got some support, looked some more, found another valley, got more people involved, looked over the ridges to see what we could see: mountains, rivers, a whole ecosystem here in Tibet. Then we looked by satellite, and found more valleys, another ecosystem. From around the world, by word of mouth, people kept coming to join with us. Now a team is at work, an amazing assortment of Nepalis, Chinese, and Americans. We are low on money, big on ideas and trust."

"John, I understand the physical side of the story. I want to hear about the operational process of putting it together. It is quite a jump from seeking an unknown bear to stimulating two governments to create national parks where none existed, especially when one of these parks is in a supposedly 'closed' country."

An hour and a half ago, the ever-present tea of China was hot in the cup I

Shepherd coming home to Shegar for the night

now sip. Now it runs like cold springwater down my throat, its temperature stronger than its flavor. Out of its cold, my mind sorts slowly how to answer Tom's question. Should I tell him more about the teamwork? About Jennifer, the kids, the many other private and public individuals involved from around the world? No, what Tom wants tonight is the dramatic and the romantic – after all, this is Shegar.

"Tom, the idea of two adjoining nature preserves on the north and south slopes of the Himalaya came to me on the top of a mountain in West Virginia in February 1985 during a snowstorm. It came like a vision. It had been snowing for three days; already two feet had fallen. I was upstairs in our home on Spruce Knob getting ready for bed. I was humming some tune – I always hum intensely when visions come. Somehow, the appropriateness of a large park on the Chinese side of Everest burst through to me, through that West Virginia snowstorm. By then the team in Nepal was already working on the park to preserve the Barun and the other valleys.

"In the fullness of that vision, Everest as a conservation center came into focus. What if the highest point on earth could set an example of people conserving their natural resources and improving their human ones? What if two countries, one democratic and the other Communist, could work side by side toward this goal with parallel nature preserves? Could international partners find a way of cooperating as colleagues and not as conservation colonialists? A 'good' lifestyle is usually believed to require wealth. What if a lifestyle model could be built with good health, water, education, trees, and wild animals in a context of poverty? These valleys of the Everest area are poor; two of these four counties here in Tibet where we're setting up the park are the only counties in Tibet where more than 30 percent of the population is below China's poverty line. Could this be a model of a sustainable future for some of the poorest people on our planet, people who can never aspire to a lifestyle of riches, a lifestyle of consumption?"

"Forget the theory, Daniel. What I want to know is what you did. You're an American. This place where we now sit is under Chinese control. The people here are Tibetan. In 1985, you had no relationship with China. To you and the others working in Nepal and living in America, this land was closed – and you were out of money, in fact in hock, and without an organization of significance." Tom pushes for his story.

"Tom, the theory is important. The idea was never mine. There was a rush in that snowstorm, like adrenaline, that came with this idea. But I knew right away it was an idea for the people of China and the people of Nepal, though the idea could be midwifed by people of any country. It was an idea especially possible here in the Himalaya, where maybe the people have not yet lost their openness. It's a truism, but no less true for that, that our Western consumption of resources, no matter how greedily we gorge our lifestyles, leaves us still fundamentally hungry inside. And it is also true, and apparent as you live with these people in these hills, that millions of people here in the Himalaya, regardless of specific religious insight – Hindus in Nepal, Buddhists in Tibet, animists in the back hills – do not hunger inside as we do."

"You're headed in the right direction, Dan," John breaks in. "The West needs to seek inner fulfillment based on a deeper appreciation of nature, rather than on a material greed that is not resource-sustainable."

Opened up, and onto an idea, I continue. "Basic inner satisfaction in life comes when we look inside, find our individual limits and accept these, building the cycles of nature into the trajectory of rising human aspirations – and retargeting the trajectory inward. It's the difference between a straight line and a round circle."

Tom isn't interested. "Daniel, you're not answering my question. What were the steps you took to implement the idea?"

"OK, here's the action. Three months after the storm I gave a scientific paper at an international conference in Kathmandu on national parks in the Himalaya. Attending that conference were key players from the Chinese nature preserve system."

"So, fired up by your vision, you just walked up to them and said, 'Let's get together and talk about a park around Mount Everest," Tom suggests.

"No, I almost did that, or as an alternative considered building the idea into my speech, but then it would have been official. Instead I waited until a cocktail party at Prince Gyanendra's home to which His Majesty came. When the time seemed right I walked over to the Chinese delegation, chatted for a while, and invited them to take a ride in the Royal Flight helicopter the next morning to see a park that was proposed for Nepal with the thought of considering one on their side of the border. No demands – I just asked them if they wanted a chopper ride out past Everest the next morning to see the new park."

"That let them make the idea theirs?"

"Yes, but they asked, 'How can you get clearance on the royal helicopter now, the night before?' I walked across the room, talked with a person, and returned ten minutes later and said, 'It's all set.'"

"So the key was connections."

"No. In setting up the Nepal park, friendships at many levels at first seemed key, but that camouflages the vital variable. From starting the work in China I learned that the key was building trust. Even in Nepal, as I thought about it, it was the same – building on trust, which in that case had been built over fifteen years. With the Chinese the chopper ride went well, though it cost me a bundle that I had to raise funds for later. But with that ride, the idea was opened. Two weeks later I routed my travel through Beijing on my way to the States and discussions began. The discussions were completely informal. Trust was building. Over the next year and a half I routed three more times through Beijing. In between, Dad, who was then living in Beijing, carried on discussions to keep the idea alive. Numerous linkages were made. With talk, everyone took ownership of the infant idea, as one by one all agreed it was good. We seemed to be working terribly slowly. For months and months there was only talk. But the process was no longer owned by just one person; a group momentum was building.

"Getting a project done is fundamentally mobilizing adequate will. Bureaucratic decisions ultimately boil down to personal decisions, personal guts, decisions of whether people are going to take risks. The Chinese kept saying, 'We must make preparations.' It sounded as though they were doing nothing. But in fact they were bringing together the authority, mustering the courage, and mastering the opposition. The Chinese understand that to get something done, strong leadership is not as important as creating consensus among all players."

John, who was a party to many of those discussions, remembers what happened. "Tom, we were supposedly doing nature conservation, yet we never saw much beyond the tea on the tables. As Americans we buy and sell in neutral environments – over the phone, by mail, quickly across a food counter. We have forgotten that a deal is what Dan says, a matter of trust. The idea of a massive park on the north slope of Everest intrigued the Chinese, but they didn't know who or what they could trust."

We've apparently answered that question to Tom's satisfaction – or he's given up. He switches topics. "OK, now let me ask you about what you wrote in your last letter about rediscovering Shangri-la. Is this sacred Buddhist valley another of your yeti quests – or is this real?"

"It's real, Tom. There is an actual valley, green with water in it, mountains around the rim, and in Tibetan sacred literature it speaks of such a legend and describes how to get there."

"Wait. You might get away with claiming you're searching for yetis you haven't found but you can't get away with claiming you've found the sacred valley of Shangri-la. All someone has to do is ask you to take them there, and unlike yetis, valleys do not run away."

"Wait, John. First understand the sacred legend. There are numerous references in Tibetan texts to Shambala, a hidden valley of enlightenment. The Tibetans believe Shambala is real because they possess something very real that came from Shambala. How could a real thing come from an imaginary place?"

"What's this real trophy?" John asks.

"John, hold it. Forget for a moment that you're a scientist and focus on the sacred legend. There are numerous references in the Kalachakra. Unlike other Buddhist or Hindu teachings, which seem to have evolved, the Kalachakra suddenly appeared in India about one thousand years ago, reportedly from a valley behind the Himalaya called Shambala. The sacred books of Tibetan Buddhism, the Tingyur and Kangyur, both tell of Shambala, as do writings by the Third Panchen Lama.

"But there is more reality here than a real text that suddenly came from somewhere. Lamas and ordinary people have allegedly gone to this valley and returned. It was real to them. There are actual reports that describe a physical place, a valley ruled by an enlightened king. The valley is walled off from the world by mountains perpetual with deep snow. High passes can be crossed only by the enlightened. It is blissful there. Crops never fail. People never get sick. No warfare . . ."

"Yeah, we know the legend, Daniel," Tom breaks in. "Their women all are gorgeous, never grow old. Death comes only if they leave the valley . . ."

"Not so. A beautiful old age is part of Shambala. In the legend, not the movie, people live to be about a hundred, not especially long; death comes, and with it, often, enlightenment."

"So, where is this place you've now found? How do we get there from Shegar?" Tom asks. "I guess we go out the driveway, take a right tomorrow morning?"

"First you must get to a hidden entrance valley. A number of hidden valleys reportedly have openings, sometimes crystal entryways, that lead to Shambala. One such valley, some sacred texts tell, is Khembalung Valley in Nepal. And I went into Khembalung by helicopter two weeks ago."

"You went into Khembalung, saw the beautiful girls, and came back to be with us?" John asks dryly.

"I went to Khembalung. It's south of the Barun. But I wasn't properly prepared through meditation. Understanding the Kalachakra is really a spiritual enlightenment process; a lama described it to me as the Circle of Living. Anyway, I don't understand it and wasn't ready. All I saw was fantastic pristine forests, sparkling streams, and snow-capped summits. I didn't see the crystal entrance."

"Uh-huh."

"There are some interesting Shambala explanations, John, ways that this could be a reality you would call scientific. One explanation might be that the people of Shambala are a religious order, perhaps a still-functioning secret religious order, committed servants to the world. Through their faith they have broken the chains that bind others to material wants and have focused their energies on centering into the deep meanings of life. But having gained enlightenment, and with the eternal way about to open before them, they don't stay in their hermitage. Rather, they step into the world of material wants to help other people and take up work as a secret order of servants.

"There's a second possible explanation: that Shambala has a historical basis in events perhaps a thousand years ago, when a civilization developed in a special valley, raised enough food, had a way of life that realized the pursuit of happiness. A real civilization flourished, then died for one reason or another. Out of this utopia that really happened some people left, took their story, and it is the Kalachakra.

"A third explanation is that the people of Shambala are all the figments of imaginative monks, cooped up in a dirty monastery, dreaming of what religious paradise must be."

John gets up from the table. "I came here to study bears, and now I am building parks. We've got meetings and travel tomorrow. I'm going to bed. One crazy idea I can handle, but not both the yeti and Shangri-la – we've got to keep things in perspective."

We all push back our chairs, flex stiff muscles, and head outside into the cold night and the centuries-old caravanserai courtyard. We walk past old trucks that now carry bamboo up from the jungles of Kyrong – the new pack animals of modern China.

"Well, whatever we're doing," John says as we walk, "we sure better be building a box big enough to keep pristine that yeti, miscellaneous hidden valleys, meditating/levitating monks, and whatever other hocus-pocus the world will someday want. There is too little wilderness left. This is too biologically damn important not to make sure it stays as pristine as possible. Maybe in some future unknown dimension, chewing on some sedge up here, some yak or somebody will get a real high. Damn, but it's cold. With half as much air at this altitude, darkness can ride mighty cold against your skin."

We walk through the courtyard. John and Tom go into the privvy. Its slippery concrete floor slopes funnel-like toward the spacious six holes, making business there precarious. I wait in this courtyard that has seen so many travelers for so many centuries. This world will now be protected because of what we're doing. The local Tibetan people will be stronger. I look up at the crystalline stars. Each sparkles out there alone. Yes, Jennifer would call this cold.

Chapter Thirty

February 11, 1989. We no longer live on the mountain but in town, in a house built by others and next to a school playground. Jesse is eight, Tara five. Their bedtime stories are over and both have gone to bed. Jennifer sits on the sofa, holding Luke, who is asleep in her arms and turned two today. Nick has come for the birthday and is settled into an armchair.

"Dan'l, six years ago this month we went into the Barun. Is there a tree bear? Is there a distinction between tree bears and ground bears? Is our bear the yeti?"

"Proof is impossible, Nick. I believe that most yeti footprints are probably from bears but we can't say whether there are in fact two distinct bears. The villagers' claim is unlikely."

Nick leans back. "So when we believed the villagers and not the scientists we were wrong."

"There's not enough evidence yet to draw that conclusion. More research is needed. However fourteen skulls can be placed into a sequence with all differences within normal variations taxonomically for *Selanarctos*. But taxonomy doesn't explain the dramatically different behavior we found."

"Could all skulls be just tree bear, not ground bear?" Nick asks.

"Maybe, but with fourteen skulls, the odds are that at least one should be a ground bear."

"But maybe the big ground bears are so vicious that villagers can't kill them. Or maybe even though the skulls don't differ, the bears do, like the Himalayan wren-babblers that look the same in all respects but are in fact different species."

Nick presses for a solution. "So, basically, Dan'l, you're accepting Craighead's hypothesis that the tree bear is a juvenile and the ground bear the adult? That the juvenile, as it matures, spends more time on the ground, becomes too heavy to climb trees; then, with disuse, the thumblike inner claw loses flexibility and assumes the normal *Selanarctos* position at the top of the foot?"

"Maybe. But the big problem with that theory is that there are too many tree bears and not enough ground bears to represent anything like a normal juvenile-adult population ratio. A population can't produce lots of juveniles unless it has lots of reproductively capable adults, and where are these? There isn't yet a scientific explanation that doesn't have a fundamental flaw. Six weeks ago in London, I spent a fantastic day in the British Museum, pulling out drawers of bear skulls. I was up on the seventh floor, with case after case of bear skulls around me, the greatest collection in the world . . ."

Jennifer laughs. "Sounds like one of life's great days, doesn't it, Nick? You find yourself with a free day in London, and you spend it in a musty room with hundreds of bear skulls, watching them appear and disappear as you open and close drawers."

"As I worked, another hypothesis came forward. More research is needed to prove it, and it challenges modern taxonomy, but it's the hypothesis that now makes the most sense to me. I got to wondering about Oldham's reference to that other tree bear, *arboreus*. Was *arboreus* a direct translation of *rukh balu?* I knew Oldham's original *arboreus* skull was there in the British Museum. I tracked it down, pulled it out of a drawer, where it's been sitting a hundred and twenty years, and held it in my hand. It reveals nothing. Pocock was right: *Arboreus* is another *Selanarctos* skull. To refresh my memory of what Pocock had said, I went down to the library and got his *Mammalia of British India*. He debunked *arboreus* as a direct subspecies on the basis of the skull, but he described two subspecies of *Selanarctos thibetanus* on the basis of differences in *coats* – which now are an unacceptable taxonomic criterion. According to Pocock, *Selanarctos thibetanus thibetanus,* from the eastern Himalaya, is smaller and has no undercoat. *Selanarctos thibetanus langier,* from the western Himalaya, has a thicker coat, and especially an undercoat."

"So," Nick breaks in, "you're saying Pocock discredited *arboreus* as a distinct subspecies, but he did allow that there are two types of *Selanarctos*, a big one and a little one."

"Right. Pocock said *arboreus* was in fact the eastern subspecies, *Selanarctos thibetanus thibetanus*. And there are two more things that are important for us: first Pocock described behavioral differences between his two subspecies, *langier* and *thibetanus*, and it is noteworthy that these are the same differences we found between the ground bear and the tree bear."

Nick leans forward eagerly. "So there might be a western and an eastern form of this species – this is what villagers are seeing – and maybe these differences are enough that as Pocock suggested they are different subspecies bear."

"Yes, and maybe taxonomically they are not even subspecies but just different forms. The taxonomical issue is different from the fact that there may be real differences."

"Well," says Jennifer, "all that is interesting, but we went to study yeti, not bears. This project got into bears and into creating national parks to protect bears, but it has yet to reach the yeti conclusions it started after. We know we found a bear on that ridge. Did we also find what others call the yeti?"

"Let's walk through the data one more time. The only alleged yeti artifact that has been studied is the Kumjung scalp. It's a molded portion of serow skin, and probably from a serow's rump, not even its head. So, eliminating that, after a hundred years, the only yeti evidence that is open for hard study remains footprints and stories."

"There *must* be more artifacts," says Jennifer.

"Not really. The hair and droppings collected by the three Slick expeditions were never subjected to scientific scrutiny. The same is true of McNeely's hairs and droppings from caves in the upper Barun; they are in storage someplace – he made reference to some trunks in his mother's garage. Village hunters have passed to me a few hairs, but there's just not enough there to work with. The only data for objective analysis remain footprints – and these are all footprints in melting snow, because snow starts to melt the instant after the footprint is made."

"Still just Shipton's and McNeely's footprints?" Nick asks.

"A lot of yeti footprints are alleged. I keep uncovering new ones. Folks go on trek, see a large print in the snow, come home with their 'yeti.' Every photograph I've seen seems to me to have a known animal explanation."

"So, six years after our staking family savings on the credibility of Shipton, McNeely, and Cronin, what are the explanations for their prints?" Jennifer presses her question with a wide grin.

"Cronin's yeti is a tree bear. Jeff McNeely got a chance eventually to get some of the things out of his trunks, and sent me photographs of both the print and the plaster cast. The trail matches the bipedal-like format. The size, shape, placement of the 'thumb' – all these features fit the tree bear. Also, the behavior they describe fits – nocturnally active, shy, solitary, uses rhododendron, and lives on exactly the same ridge where we found our tree bear evidence."

"What about the Shipton photograph?" Nick asks. "Is that also the tree bear?"

"The Shipton evidence is less certain chiefly because of what Shipton didn't bring back rather than because of the photographs and story he did bring back. Shipton couldn't have done a better job of building a hoax if he'd tried. I'm not implying that Shipton intended a hoax – all evidence points to the contrary – he and Ward were exceptionally honorable men in the old British tradition. Further, despite many opportunities in the years since their return they've been careful not to embellish their discovery. Yet they reported just enough to keep the mystery alive and brought back not enough ever to solve it."

"What do you mean?"

"Consider how shallow their data are. Two photographs: a close-up of a track and a half, and another shot of a trail going off in the snow – and when questioned about the trail years later, Ward says it's not the same trail as in their close-up. Here's the book, take a look." I pull Shipton's *Reconnaissance of Everest* off the shelf. "And the only explanation of these two photographs is this evocative and not very descriptive passage":

> It was on one of the glaciers of the Menlung basin, at a height of about 19,000 feet, that, late one afternoon, we came across those curious footprints in the snow the report of which has caused a certain amount of public interest in this country. We did not follow them further than was convenient, a mile or so, for we were carrying heavy loads at the time, and besides we had reached a particularly interesting stage in the exploration of the basin. I have in the past found many sets of these curious

footprints and have tried to follow them, but have always lost them on the moraine or rocks at the side of the glacier. These particular ones seemed to be very fresh, probably not more than 24 hours old. When Murray and Bourdillon followed us a few days later the tracks had been almost obliterated by melting. Sen Tensing, who had no doubt whatever that the creatures (for there had been at least two) that had made the tracks were 'Yetis' or wild men, told me that two years before, he and a number of old Sherpas had seen one of them at a distance of about 25 yards at Thyangbochi. He described it as half man and half beast, standing about Wve feet six inches with a tall pointed head, its body covered with reddish brown hair, but with a hairless face.[11]

"Is there nothing more? Hasn't Ward published further details?" Nick is incredulous.

"Yes, there's the caption under the picture":

> In general the tracks were distorted and obviously enlarged by melting; and where, as in this case, the snow overlying the glacier was thin, the imprint was very well preserved and the form of the foot could be seen in detail. When the tracks crossed a crevasse we could see how the creature, in jumping across, had dug its toes in to prevent itself from slipping back.

"No new facts have ever been added, although these have been presented in a variety of ways. People have sent me letters saying that Shipton, Ward, or other members of the expedition told them in personal communications other interesting tidbits such as 'all tracks were identical to the one photographed' or 'the length of the stride equaled my ice-axe length of thirty-seven inches' or 'in some prints not photographed there were five toe prints.' All these secondhand communications must be discounted. We must stick to published evidence. But let's go back to the telling of the story. Doesn't Shipton craft a beautiful tale? See how their few facts fill the mind with so much. First, the photograph, that splendid print. We see our wild ancestors in that footprint in the snow. Overlay onto that image then the drama of the description of that day in the high snows. And finally, the smooth change of database – the yeti is described as an animal, but the description is from another, secondhand source. Shipton's description is a scientific account. The description of the animal is folklore. A second photograph would have scientifically described the yeti much more than another Sherpa tale, but it is the tale that we have."

"So what does this show?" Like Prince Gyanendra, Jennifer presses the point, overriding romantic digressions.

"If they had taken two more photographs, the world would probably not have had this wonderful mystery for the past thirty years. Additional photos would almost certainly have settled whether this was a known or an unknown animal and if unknown, whether or not it was a primate. So much more could be shown with full photographs of both feet. So much more could be deduced from photos taken in those different snow conditions they referred to, especially photos of the toe prints dug in when the creature was jumping. And so much more could be deduced with another photo of the print (with that ice-axe head to show size) taken on a descending slope, because then I bet the print would have been shorter, and then we could probably answer for certain whether or not these were overprints.

"But the photographs I most regret not having – and in all the yeti discussion in the literature, the prints I've never seen discussed – are pictures of the other one or two yetis that apparently accompanied this one. Remember Shipton's 'the creatures (for there had been at least two)'? What did those other tracks look like? Were they the same size? The same shape? The same stride? Careful examination would show differences. And the toes: Were all prints of the toes like those bulbous toes on the print we have? Had such photos been taken, I'm convinced Shipton's yeti would be the same as Smythe's, another bear – whose identity, remember, was revealed because Smythe photographed many prints and not just the best one."

"So you agree with Napier and suggest a bear?" Nick asks.

"I recently went back and checked Napier's argument. It is interesting how the mind plays tricks. Napier never attributes his overprint theory to a bear. His proposal is in fact quite incredible: 'Something must have made the Shipton footprint. Like Mount Everest, it is there . . . I would say a composite, made by a naked foot treading in the track of a foot wearing a leather moccasin . . . The curious V-shaped kink behind the big toe, which has no apparent biological function, could be then explained in terms of a deep fold in the leather of the moccasin.'[12]

"Napier is right about it being an overprint, but I think he's wrong about it being a human composite. There are two reasons. First, it's improbable that

DANIEL TAYLOR-IDE

two people walking that route together, walking step after step in the anoxia of 19,000 feet, would do so with exactly the same stride, overprinting upon each other's tracks meticulously, the bare toes always beyond the 'moccasin' print. Second, Napier is a primatologist, not an anthropologist. He didn't know that villagers in that part of the Himalaya never wear soft-soled moccasins such that the bottom leather could develop 'a deep fold in the leather.' He's thinking about North American Indians. Traditional Himalayan footgear has rigid soles. Especially in 1951, before other footwear came in from outside these valleys, a local person would have worn either the hard-soled Tibetan felt boot or the rigid shoe of twisted grass rope. Both would leave a sharper indentation in the snow.

"There are five other things wrong with Napier's argument. First, the supposed 'heel strike' that others see at the back of the print is in fact caused by melting, because it matches a similar indentation on the side (not back) of the second print that is almost certainly caused by melting. So it's far more likely that these prints were made by a four-footed animal that brings its foot straight down rather than rolling into each step with a heel strike. Second, the print is concave where a hominoid foot should be convex; bipedal walking requires an arch to launch the toes in their pivotal role in each stride. Third, and very damaging to the claim that the maker is yeti, the top half print that Napier discovered on Shipton's original negative doesn't match the top half of the first print. Could an animal have a right and a left foot that look so different? Fourth, halfway up the print there appear at least three nail pads such as those made by a *Selanarctos* hind foot. That 'curious V-shaped kink behind the big toe' is such a possible nail mark, and nail marks, as I now know well, are bear signs. And fifth, overprint experiments with plaster casts on the captive bear at the Kathmandu zoo gave prints similar enough to Shipton's to satisfy me."

"Let me guess your conclusion," Nick breaks in. "It's the old Smythe explanation. The bear was walking up the Menlung Glacier, so the hind foot fell back; thus the thirteen-inch print. Had the overprint been measured walking downhill, it would have been maybe eight inches, the same size as the Tombazi or Cronin/McNeely prints. Shipton's yeti was a tree bear!"

"Bear, yes, but there are some other rather interesting clues in the Shipton account that taken together all strongly suggest a more complex bear explanation. Remember Shipton's words 'for there had been at least two.' The tracks were clearly confused. They couldn't tell how many they were following. The track and a half they photographed appear to be made by *Selanarctos*. When does more than one *Selanarctos* travel with another? More likely Shipton and Ward were following a mother bear with one or two cubs walking beside her. This isn't the first time multiple sets of bear prints have been mistaken for yeti. In 1954, Sherpas claimed mysterious footprints to be yeti, but Charles Evans examined them, saw nail marks, and pointed out that one set was substantially larger indicating a mother and a cub. I think this is the same. Furthermore, the season is right for such travel. If Shipton's yeti is a bear, the explanation must fit both the physical features of a bear's foot and known bear behavior."

"A mother and cubs, like the first group of three nests we found in the Barun bamboo," says Nick.

"Precisely. Shipton and Ward found a mother bear with cubs in the fall on the move for food."

"Or a female yeti with children," says Jennifer.

"True, but as the data can be plausibly explained by bears, why assume the much more unlikely?"

"Go on," she smiles. "But explain the absence of nail marks on the front when you acknowledge nail marks from the hind paw."

"The explanation is that, as Shipton says, 'the snow overlying the glacier was thin.' In thin snow nail marks don't show on the front; you see only indentations of toe pads. But nail marks show from the back paw in the middle of the print because *Selanarctos* carries more of its weight on its back legs, where its heavy rear end pushes deeper and shows those nail marks."

"But bears have five claws. Shipton's print has only four toe prints," Nick interjects.

"This is where another photograph would help. Remember, Shipton reported considerable snow melt. He picked the best print he could and all prints start to change the instant they're made. At 19,000 feet the changes are fast with sublimation, solid ice goes immediately to vapor. Prints change even when they aren't in direct sun. Between melting and sublimation, the big central toe on Shipton's print is, I think, a merged print made by two central pads that shifted together, a common happening when walking in snow. Isn't it more likely that two nail pads slipped than that a new unknown animal exists simply on the basis of a big toe print found in the snow?"

"Well, you may be right about Shipton's yeti," says Nick with a gloating smile, "but two years ago Anthony Wooldridge captured the yeti on camera, and the animal in that picture doesn't look at all bearlike. A picture of a real animal is a lot more certain than footprints in the snow."

Grinning, I run downstairs and bring up the 1986 volume of *The Interdisciplinary Journal of the International Society of Cryptozoology.* "Here, Nick, read this."

> At the point where a set of tracks led off across the slope behind and beyond a spindly shrub . . . was a large, erect shape perhaps up to 2 meters tall. . . . It was difficult to restrain my excitement as I came to the realization that the only animal I could think of which remotely resembled this one before me was the yeti. . . . It was standing with its legs apart, apparently looking down the slope, with its right shoulder turned toward me. The head was large and squarish, and the whole body appeared to be covered with dark hair, although the upper arm was a slightly lighter color. . . . I took a number of photographs. . . .[13]

"When Wooldridge made his discovery, I wrote and he sent a more complete report to me. I corresponded further with him, requesting photographs. I asked Tashi, who has gone with me on many field trips, to go to the same valley, which is several hundred miles south and west of the Barun, to check out several hypotheses I had. Tashi found that knowledgeable local hunters there made no claims about the existence of the yeti. Granted, Wooldridge's photographs look impressively like what we might expect the yeti to look like. However, we have to consider Wooldridge's physical state at the time he took the photographs. Without doubt, he was hypoxic from exertion and altitude; most probably he was also mildly hypothermic from travel as a runner in wet snow. Another big problem is this animal standing stark still for forty-five minutes – and by all reports, yetis are extremely shy. It's especially unlikely that a yeti would stand still in the open, in an avalanche chute, for that long. Further, to claim that this animal did so because it was dazed by a fall in an avalanche doesn't jibe with known behavior of mammals after being hurt; a mammal in shock will attempt to lower its head below its heart to improve blood circulation, often rubbing its head as well. So with nothing but a yeti-looking shape to suggest it, I guessed that this shape wasn't an animal at all, but a rock or a tree stump. I wrote to Wooldridge saying so, and he wrote back and then later published, following a return visit to the site, concurring that he'd mistaken a rock for a living creature."

Jesse washing plaster paw print casts made from the Kathmandu zoo tree bear – bottom composite overprint is similar to the Shipton print

"So, does the yeti have any evidence left to stand on?" Nick is sober.

"The great unknown of course are all the yeti reports coming out of Tibet. There is little doubt in my mind that all the Nepal and India yeti reports can be explained – and there basically is no place left for the yeti to live in Nepal and India now that we've explored the Barun. But in Tibet, yeti stories abound and there is a lot of open wild country still left. What so interests me is that I hear yeti stories from Tibetans who have never before met a Westerner. I hear these reports spontaneously and over almost all of Tibet, from Tibetans living in the west along the Tsangpo River and from Tibetans in the east living in the headwaters of the Mekong River a thousand kilometers away. They speak of *Dremu* who steals sheep, has human footprints, travels alone, ears flopped forward, lives high on mountain ridges, and can walk erect."

"With reports so consistent you still discard the yeti as real? Might not the yeti have retreated from Nepal with the population pressure there and now be living in Tibet?" Nick asks.

"Further inquiry from these reporters fills in details that start to point to a known animal, once again a bear but in Tibet not the black bear. Some of these Tibetan reporters I've talked to, unlike the reporters in India and Nepal, have actually seen *Dremu* and are not passing along someone else's story. They describe a large head compared to the body, long canine teeth, yellow hair around the face, a long snout in which the nose and mouth seem one, a mother that does not keep her young more than two seasons. If all these features were put together in one animal it would indeed be an abominable beast. The fact that the descriptions were so consistent, unlike the descriptions from Nepal, started me to think that maybe something was there. But then one day at the Lhasa zoo I looked through the bars of a cage and saw two of these animals in front of me. The *Dremu* is the super-rare, and never-studied, Himalayan blue bear, *Ursus arctos pruinosis.*

"And what was particularly interesting to me was that years before, in 1961 as a sixteen-year-old, I had asked the former king of Bhutan about the yeti – that king was unusually knowledgeable about Himalayan wildlife. He smiled and clearly had given the matter thought. His conclusion way back then – and remember that Bhutan and Tibet have historically been very close – was that the yeti was a blue bear. He was rather certain that if there were actual wild people out there that he as king would have other reasons to know about it."

"So you're saying that even in Tibet there really is no rational basis for us as humans to believe in some other wild kin out there wandering?" Nick quietly asks.

"Yes, I guess so. The yeti stands really on what it always has stood on, our inner desire that it be there – and if we have this feeling strong enough we look at scattered information and can interpret it to suggest that. Rationally, there is little left to support the idea. Remember Bernard Heuvelmans's *Gigantopithecus* hypothesis, the notion that a race of giants, a side branch of *Homo sapiens*, didn't die out between half a million and one million years ago, but survives as a remnant population in remote Himalayan valleys? Heuvelmans no longer adheres to that hypothesis, although other people cling to it despite the absence of any supporting data. Even the yeti footprints don't support the idea of *Gigantopithecus*."

"But you really cannot disprove the yeti at least," Jennifer chimes in. "It is just your word against somebody else's who wants to believe."

"One final refutation of the yeti is a little statistical exercise, a sort of mathematical proof that the yeti cannot exist."

"What?" Nick, the college math major, leans forward in his armchair. Too bad I hadn't uncovered this for him to work with when we were in the Barun, I think to myself.

"John Craighead pointed me toward the concept of minimum viable population biology, a field that is built on rigorous mathematics and careful field data from long-term observations of actual populations. The Craigheads have done precise analyses of how many grizzlies are required for a viable population. For a parallel species to the yeti, short of a hominoid, the grizzly is probably as good as any. The biologists working in this field have gone to great lengths to identify four variables that strongly affect population size: demographic stochasticity, environmental stochasticity, natural catastrophe, and genetic stochasticity. Over time these four variables whittle down a population's numbers. For a population to be viable over significant amounts of time, a surprisingly large number of individuals are required. One male and female just won't make a species grow when that species (an embattled *Gigantophithecus*, for example) is threatened by habitat destruction and predation. For a viable grizzly bear population, there must be at least thirty, maybe fifty, bears. This is a significant population."

"By extension, a viable yeti or *Gigantopithecus* population would require a community at least the size of the grizzly's. I say 'at least' because hominoids have fewer 'cubs' and spend more time raising them than the two years a mother grizzly does hers. Hence humans don't have the reproductive elasticity of bears, and, therefore, in all probability, hominoids require a greater minimum viable population than bears, perhaps twenty for a minimum. So it's highly romantic to think that two or three stalwart boy and girl yetis out there can be raising little yetis, keeping their race alive in the face of human encroachment. A handful of bears or yetis just can't survive in a hostile, restricted environment that forces them to remain in hiding.

"There's further support for minimum viable populations from the anthropologists studying the settlement of the South Pacific islands. They have demonstrated that a highly scattered population doesn't survive. A handful of people taking out in a canoe to settle a new island is unlikely to reproduce beyond a couple of generations. Larger concentrations are required, concentrations of again at least twenty individuals, and more likely double that number.

"To put it another way, once the population of an animal that has to exist in hiding gets so low that it's impossible to find, the population is probably so small that it's unable to sustain itself. Or, to put this in terms of the yeti search, since a population – not an individual – must exist, you are not looking for just one animal. You are looking for at least twenty. If after one hundred years of searching you haven't found even one animal when there must be at least twenty out there, it is, statistically speaking, probably not there."

"Ah, farewell my last fantasy: lost, romantic yeti survivors holding out in some secluded cave, noble savages lying in the grass making love to each other as their kind withers to extinction." Nick swirls the fading yeti vapors of our quest like the last drops of brandy in the bottom of a snifter.

"Yes, Nick, cold water hits hard. Remember the great cave Derek Craighead spotted in 1984 in the middle of the Barun Valley? So perfect – a large opening on a warm south-facing cliff, modest altitude of 8,000 feet, the last redoubt for yetis to retreat to, dense jungle, with no human village in any direction for five days' hard walk. Nearby were grassy glens where yetis could gambol in the sun. Remember my efforts to find a route to it that year and the next? The climate was ideal. It was protected by cliffs. Food was plentiful. If the yeti was anywhere, it was there in the Great Cave of the Middle Barun."

"Did you recently make it?"

"Sort of. Nearly two years ago we were in a helicopter surveying the boundaries for the new national park on the Nepal side. We were working the Ishwa Valley just south of the Barun. When we finished surveying the Ishwa, we headed over to the Barun. Our flight route took us across the ridge and meadow where Derek first spotted the cave. It was ten o'clock on a November morning – the same time of year, the same time of day as when he first saw it. The chopper was only twenty feet off the ground. I asked the pilot to hover, and there across in front of me was the Great Cave of the Middle Barun; big, inviting black entrance, mysterious.

"I pointed. The pilot saw it and flew the helicopter toward it. The clear stream flowing down nearby sparkled in the morning light as we swooped in toward that cliff. Then, as we hovered in front, the mystery was pierced. The cave disappeared before our eyes. The black entrance was a shadow cast by the cliff high above. The sun striking at a 10:00 A.M. angle on a November morning created the cave."

"Each yeti clue, I guess, disappears like that cave."

"It seems to."

Nick and Jennifer soon head to bed. I sit for a while in the living room, wondering. Does the yeti not exist? As an unknown wild animal, probably not; as an unknown wild hominoid, almost certainly not. But inside, I know that this is not the whole story. The biological facts don't fully answer the breadth of the unknowns opened. Biology is the study of life, but it is not life itself. There are other realms that also inform life.

Here I am sitting at the end of a century-long yeti quest with no new wild creature locked in a cage or on display in zoos throughout the world. But my journey has launched the creation of one of the largest "cages" on the globe, 8 million acres of contiguous wildness walled in by the world's highest mountains and the laws of two countries, a cage in which whatever does exist can still roam uncaught and unknown.

But inside I know the yeti does exist. It's just that I am not looking in the right way or in the right places. After having invested forty years of my life, having talked with hundreds of villagers, having corresponded with many Westerners who've made sightings, having bounced fourteen thousand miles across the Tibetan plateau by four-wheel drive, from north to south, from east to west, walked thousands more throughout the Himalaya, spent scores of hours in helicopters searching key Himalayan valleys, I know the yeti does exist. It is not, though, in the physical world.

During my journey I have seen parts of this other world, but not the fuller vision of the wholeness of life for which the yeti is a symbol. I must somehow combine that understanding with the rational, scientific understanding I'm gaining about how life interrelates.

Modern knowledge compartmentalizes understanding; biology has its answers, art has its insights, history has its truths. These are all separated. But the life we live is not compartmentalized. The mystery of the yeti can't be answered purely biologically, artistically, or historically. The explanations must be woven together in order to understand both the reality and the unreality of the symbol and the animal.

Chapter Thirty-One

In the rock face high above crouches the snow leopard, as it has for tens of thousands of years. To pilgrims who walk this trail, the leopard is the sacred guardian of the route to the cave of Lord Shiva up the Barun Valley. To Western geologists it is only a huge chemical stain in the cliff face. As I look up at the snow leopard in the cliff, I wonder whether my friend Rodney Jackson is right: Might the real animal's mating yowl, which reverberates through such valleys from January to March and which people have compared to the screech of an eagle or the wild whinny of a horse, be the mysterious call so often attributed to the yeti?

From my earlier fieldwork, I know real snow leopards do pass through the upper Barun, although they prefer drier land with cliffs frequented by blue sheep. But these high hills and gullies where pika, pheasant, and musk deer are found are also leopard habitat. Like tigers, snow leopards are solitary by choice from the time they leave their mother. Unlike tigers, usually there are at least two, maybe as many as half a dozen, in the same home range. Snow leopards signal their presence to one another with cumulative scratch marks, which they spray with scent at regular points on their route. Traveling at dawn and dusk, sometimes one snow leopard after the other comes down the same route, although never closer than a mile apart. They seldom come into actual physical contact with others of their kind except when mating. Snow leopards do pass through the Barun, especially up here at the head of the valley, although chiefly this wet jungle is habitat for the common leopard and the ultra-rare, tree-living, never-studied clouded leopard.

I've returned to the Barun to search one more time for the yeti. I really doubt it is an actual living creature. I have come again because I have more questions to ask, more ideas about wildness that I need to test. I've descended from Shipton's Pass at 14,000 feet on the southern ridge of the Barun, to Yangle Karka, a series of meadows below 12,000 feet. Most foreigners who've come to the Barun in the past thirty-five years have taken a left upon coming off the pass and gone westward up the valley toward the base camp of Makalu, seeking ice, glacier, and lofty summits. Only a few Japanese botanists and McNeely and Cronin turned east and went down into the trees and grass. The Yangle Karka region is, the shepherds say, the last good meadow of grass as you walk down-valley. Looking at its grass – or sedges – will tell me what lives here.

Every year during the monsoon, for more than two hundred years (and probably hundreds of years even before that), the herders who use this place cross Shipton's Pass into this valley to graze their water buffalos and sometimes a few sheep and goats. (Grazing for yaks is on pastures north and east of here, near Saldima.) The herders fear many things coming here. Like most Nepali people, they're social folk, preferring village life to solitude. They miss their neighbors and, even more, they miss their families. They're afraid that a snowfall might trap them in this valley. It's a two days' fast walk from home in Tashigaon. In coming they're afraid of getting lost or hurt: Help is too far away. The villagers come for one thing, grass – as much as their animals can carry home in their bellies and bodies. The villagers stay as far as possible from the edge of the jungle, afraid of wild animals and spirits that live there. On regular cycles for centuries they burn the upper Barun Valley slopes, cutting back the growth their animals won't eat, creating space to grow for the grasses their animals like.

In their affection for home and fear of the jungle lies my hope – the hope that an inner pristine Barun still exists where herders and shepherds, foreign climbers and tourists, seldom come. In a belt below the range of grazing and above the lower valley worked by hunters, I hope to find jungle, meadows, and animals where a human presence only extremely rarely passes through. Is there a place in the jungle that is still farther than the herders have yet had to go? Finding that will open to me another understanding of myself as a part of wildness. If such a place does exist in the Himalaya, it must be here in the middle Barun.

The herders who come here try to create a sense of home. Year after year they make thatch shelters and attempt to subdue alpine brush into meadow by their burning and grazing. Inevitably they change the original balance. One sign of that changed balance is the ratio of grasses and sedges. Jungle animals (musk deer, thar, serow, and chamois) don't alter the original balance even when large populations are present. Watchful for leopards and other carnivores, they feed within the protective cover of the jungle or high on rocky cliffs. Although they regularly pass through open meadows, wild animals don't stand for long periods out in the open masticating. Those that do so may grow fat for a while, but as with the fruits of most self-indulgence, they die early. A meadow that remains at least three-quarters grass, therefore, can pretty certainly be said to still bloom with wildness.

Domesticated animals are the ones that eat away and trample down the taller grasses, causing the sedges to take stronger root. Seasonal use by these animals does not significantly change the flora usually except in the mix of species. Establishing a village brings dramatic changes. When domesticated people sink roots, the trees come down.

Yangle Karka descends irregularly over the valley – not one meadow really but a series of grazing areas, cascading down the broad, glacially carved valley. In between grassy meadows are slopes of scrub rhododendrons and juniper. Wedged between rocks at one of the upper meadows I find specimens of the highest flowering plant in the world, the chickweed, *Stellera procumbens*, which grows in a tight cushion only inches across to protect itself against cold. Mountaineers climbing Makalu found this white flower with its five deeply divided petals growing as high as 21,000 feet. Those flowers are growing two vertical miles and five air miles from this cluster of rocks. On the eastern side of the lowest meadow I find *nigalo*, the thin bamboo that looks like overgrown kindergarten pencils. Its shoots are the highest naturally occurring red panda food. In the rhododendron beyond hangs *usnea*, the hairlike lichen favored by musk deer.

Grasses here account for no more than 50 percent of the cover. Yangle Karka is therefore heavily grazed. I must head down-valley, looking for other meadows. Rolling up the nylon tarp I sleep under, and stuffing my sleeping

A poacher headed into the Barun Valley (photo by David Ide)

bag into its sack, I say farewell to the large fir I slept next to last night. Its grain looks exceptionally straight, easy to split. It will be gone someday, maybe soon. *Abies spectabilis* is the only Himalayan tree that easily splits into boards with hand wedges and sledges that shepherds make from hard rhododendron limbs.

One summer the herders who come will cut down this tree, and will spend their days splitting it into door and window frames for their village. It may take a couple of years, it may take fifty, but this straight-grained tree will someday walk out of this valley on the backs of buffalo. At least, 10 percent of it will. The rest will be wasted by the inefficiencies of the hand cutting and splitting. Human use changes the balance of both grasses and trees. But traditional people are not ruthless. Sometimes it takes a long time for the balance to change; this fir and the herders have both watched Yangle Karka for many summer seasons.

Maybe the new Makalu-Barun National Park that has grown from our work will be successful – first the bears, then Saldima, then a Royal Task Force, then the implementation of new ideas within a government bureaucracy. Maybe, if we can truly get village participation, this tree and the other fir trees here will live. Part of the challenge will also be to prevent this from becoming such a well-run park that the local people become incapable of running it.

I start down the valley. The valley narrows, changing in shape from the glacially carved U-shape to the river-carved V-shape as the Barun descends, picks up speed, and cuts down through the valley floor. As I walk, my spirit expands outward into the space, filling it. The Chinese call this life energy *qi* (pronounced chee). Native Americans call it Medicine. It is a fire whose flames extend far beyond the inner source. It expands from the self to create the sphere of a being's extension. It becomes the interface of our interacting. These senses sometimes get hemmed in, unnoticed often even to the individual. Here in this openness they flow throughout the valley, making the whole place somewhat mine, somehow home.

I miss Jennifer and the kids. It was possible to visit the Barun six years ago with one two-year-old. But three children are too many to bring. They're back behind door frames made from other fir trees that are shipped across America instead of across passes. Why do we Westerners protest the cutting of tropical trees but not our own? The pristine Tongass National Forest is disappearing as rapidly as the Amazon. The remaining temperate rain forests are fewer in number and size than the tropical.

In the world outside the Barun, the world we call civilized, the debate about global environment continues, unresolved. Some say that environmental change is gradual, with regular gradients like the contour lines on a slope. They claim that we can make analogous small adjustments back and forth, restoring the environment where we've found degeneration. Others say that environmental change is not a slope we may slide down and then scale back up, but a series of almost irreversible steps. At each step, relationships stabilize until another critical amount of cumulative change impels another step, and with our rapidly expanding populations, usually downward. The truth probably lies somewhere in between. As on a mountain, sometimes the gradient is smooth and gentle, and we can move up and down quite easily. But sometimes we encounter a cliff, where just one more step will take us past the edge, with a catastrophic fall.

Many signs reveal such ecosystem change. In Nepal the presence of pheasants indicate that the jungle is pristine. If spiny babblers are found, the forest is in flux. If sparrows are present, you must be near a village. Each ecosystem has its indicators of eco-change. As I was leaving Kathmandu, Tirtha told me how leeches can be an indictor of atmospheric change – a redeeming purpose for those bloodthirsty worms. The sensitive chemistry of their moist skin indicates that acid rain now falls in Kathmandu Valley. Each day the exhaust from the new industrial life – a cement factory, a hundred brick factories, ten thousand cars, a hundred thousand motorcycles – has poisoned the air. When moisture now falls in Kathmandu, it brings proof that, despite the tremendous impact they have on our psyche, leeches are not very bioresilient and are no longer found in Kathmandu Valley.

This valley also demonstrates biology's sensitivity to change. Every 1,000 feet represents an average annual decrease of between three and four degrees Fahrenheit. As I descended the 2,000 feet from the top of Shipton's Pass to Yangle Karka, the alpine scrub changed almost imperceptibly: The plants only became thicker and taller. There seems to be a continuum. Now leaving Yangle Karka, suddenly, in a descent of 300 feet, some invisible biological threshold is crossed; real forest begins. Here enter whole new sets of life forms, plants as well as animals. All this is accommodated with a change of only one degree of annual average temperature. The number of biological species has easily doubled. Whereas above it was a land of occasional trees, bushes, sedges, and grasses, now there are dense trees, a new biological realm.

After walking east for five hours I encounter a new physical change as well: the Barun River. Behind me to the west, where it begins as a frigid drain to the twelve square miles of the Barun Glacier, the river can be waded if you can stand the bone-numbing pain. Here, though almost as cold, it has picked up water from the forest soil and side streams as well as speed. Cold water gushes strong and fast. The valley here makes a bend and at this point the river grows into a twenty-foot-wide torrent that bends from the south wall and turns toward the north, effectively blocking further descent. I find myself trapped between the river and the wall.

But if the Barun poses a barrier to me, to my descent farther into the valley, it has probably also stopped other people, especially herders. On the other side, therefore, might be truly pristine meadows of grass. The river here looks like its depth is above my waist with a bed of smooth, rolling, ball-bearing-like rocks. The footing is too risky to just wade across – and my muscles will cramp in that cold. I'm alone. Perhaps I won't be swept away like Lendoop's daughter, but this is no time for experiments. I could be rolled for quite a way in the current.

Although it is too fast and slippery to wade, if I tie myself with my rope, I can use the current to carry me across at the bend and the rope to keep me from being swept out of control. I take out a few items from the five-pound sack of emergency tools and tricks I always carry. The rest of the contents of my pack I double-wrap in plastic garbage bags, restowing in the pack, and lashing all openings tightly shut. Then I uncoil seventy-five feet of light nylon rope and loop it around a tree, with equal lengths on each side, knotting the two loose ends into a figure eight. I tie my pack securely to the middle of the rope up by the tree. After I cross, I'll loosen one end of the looped rope and pull over the pack.

Wearing only a T-shirt to cut the wind and running shoes to protect my feet, I fasten a nylon sling with a metal snaplink around my waist, wrap the double nylon ropes through the snaplink for friction, and step backward into the water. The glacier cold contracts my gonads into my pelvis. Three feet from shore the water takes my weight off my feet, and I lean back against the rope, feet wide apart and angled against the rocky bottom. I mustn't let my feet be swept out from under me. The force of the current carries me backward and downstream, but because the river is bending sharply, I'm pushed across in the space of thirty yards.

When I climb out onto the south bank, my legs feel like solid wooden pegs.

I sink to the grass, to the quiet space just above the ground out of the wind, absorbing heat from the earth and the subtropical sun. A griffon floats overhead, wings out flat, making slow, wide circles. This aggressive carrion bird is probably hoping I'm about to die. I flex my legs, trying to pump warm blood down the arteries, then lift them and move them slowly in bicycle-riding circles. I feel the wind on my legs. Now the chill moves to my chest. I need to put on my clothes.

Staggering to my feet, I untie the figure eight at the end of the rope, and pull on the line tied to the pack. As the pack slides off the other bank and hits the water, the current grabs it and charges with it downstream. The pack bobs like a cork as I pull fast on the line, reeling in yard after yard. Ten pulls, and I have it. I draw in the rest of the line, open the pack, and dress.

Soon, warm, my last candy bar eaten, I walk down-valley, heading toward the big oval patch where my satellite photo showed a change in vegetation. What will it be? Three hours later, at 9,500 feet, I come out of the forest into a meadow less than thirty yards across. Around it gradually rising in height stands a temperate forest of maples, magnolias, and birches, much like those near our camp at Makalu Jungli Hotel. But unlike the meadow at Makalu Jungli Hotel, which is only 2,100 feet lower and would naturally fill in with trees if it wasn't kept open by shepherds, the forest here is firmly held back by some natural method.

At this latitude in the Himalaya, meadows don't form naturally below 10,000 feet except as scar tissue from a forest fire, landslide, flood, or avalanche. But a forest fire here, amid one of the wettest of cloud forests, is inconceivable. Landslides don't occur on flat valley bottom; earth falling from the hills would leave its signature in huge piles. Neither was this meadow created by flooding. There's no evidence of backup debris. Furthermore, the meadow is on only one side of the river and tapers up against the side of the valley.

An avalanche remains the likely possibility; a gigantic deluge of ice each winter pounding down from that cliff above could wipe out everything and hold this space frozen until late in the spring, thus shortening the growing season by maybe even two months, long after the rest of the forest around has bloomed, cutting down saplings that might each year take root. Or maybe this meadow is caused by a ledge of rock layer just beneath the grass that prevents larger root systems from taking hold. But that possibility is out; quick digging shows the soil here is deep enough to support bushes and bamboo.

Alpine meadows north of Makalu

However it was formed, my hand lens shows grasses predominate in this meadow; sedges form only about 15 percent of the cover. Nor are there many flowers either. Here is a true natural garden in waves of grass. I'll stay a while. Maybe in this meadow I'll learn more about my place equidistant between the atoms and the stars. By listening inward and outward, expanding horizons toward both the very small and the very large, I can begin to understand the unknown.

A large oak stands away from the edge of the meadow against the hillside, limbs reaching high toward the Barun ridges. At its base I spread out my sleeping bag, unfold my nylon tarp, prop my back against its trunk, roll two rocks into place on either side, and wedge my sleeping pad between them. Now I have a comfortable seat with grand armrests, a side table for my teacup. But moving the rocks has made me aware of my intrusion. I am once again changing what was, just by my being here, always leaving footprints. When I walk beside the river tomorrow morning looking for animals' prints in the sand, I will leave more of mine. The tall grass, at least, bent by one passing of my feet, will rise again.

In the millennia before science introduced its method for ordering and testing, before science gave us results-based formulas for differentiating causality, there was another kind of human knowledge with a different integrity. Its functioning, our ordering of reality does not yet explain. Whatever its methods of working, I have seen its accuracy. The Brahmin schoolteacher walking home to Khandbari knew my thoughts as I knew his. The villagers of Shakshila knew I was coming two weeks before I arrived. Both Jennifer and I recognized our daughter despite mixed-up hard data. The man-eater somehow told Grandpa she was coming. Such understandings accept the interconnectedness between reality and nonphysical realities. These understandings know where links between living faith and living flesh are congruent.

In parts of the world such ancient acceptance of the wholeness of life is disregarded, even discounted, and hard-headed thinking has taken over. Reality can be accepted only to the limits that are so far defined. The great belief systems of earth that worshiped the strength that comes out of mystery lie fractured, perhaps irreversibly damaged by falsely accepted all-knowing. Do we walk in tunnel vision with technological blinders on using a telescope and thinking that we see distance and a microscope and thinking that we see deeply?

For Himalayan sages, the interconnectedness among the realms of reality remain valid. They speak of a sacred city, a hidden valley, secret understandings. These are symbols of our human voyage into the unknown – as a rocket ship is a symbol of our physical voyage into the unknown, or five interlinked Olympic circles are a symbol of our quest into the limits of the body. Using such symbols for our voyages, we understand better our place with reality and nonreality. Like different species of flowers together in a meadow, all these transcendent understandings create whatever is the blossoming of our life. The more voyages we make, the farther we take them, the more complete is our understanding of the segment of existence that we are allowed to get to know, our life.

Chapter Thirty-Two

As I settle into my new camp I spot in the brush beyond the oak a three-foot-tall plant with dark green leaves and a soft pink, lady's underwear–like flower, *Podophyllum emodii*, the Himalayan may apple. The altitude is low to find this plant, but this valley is wet. May apples are increasingly rare in Nepal. Village plant hunters stalk them, seeking the egg-shaped, purple, pulpy, heavily seeded fruit, sold as a cure for cancer by pharmaceutical companies. In their zeal for profit the hunters pull up the may apples by their roots.

Once medicinal plant hunters start combing the jungle, the balance of plants there changes. While seeking the valuable *Rauwolfia* that they can sell the hunters also take any other plants they can use for themselves. Thirty years of hunting have almost exterminated *Rauwolfia serpetina*, the red-flowered, coffeelike shrub whose root is a cure for hypertension. The pressure on may apples has just started. Clearly though, with the plant so visible here, plant hunters have not reached this valley.

At the edge of the meadow I find another plant whose future is similarly imperiled, *Nardostachys jatamansi*. A curious little plant, long, tightly furled leaves binding miniature "corn ears" on a stalk, its roots have a fragrant oil, also an apparent cancer cure. Once again, to harvest the roots hunters must pull up the whole plant.

The news is out that the forests of the world may cure diseases – one quarter of all medicines sold in the United States come from plant sources. As more plants with medicinal potential are discovered, the hunt intensifies. Local farmers, suffering from increasing pressure of population growth and now working marginal land rather than the more fertile soils on valley bottoms, eagerly seek alternative crops to harvest. Growing wheat or rice does not bring hard cash.

Meanwhile, conservation groups around the world continue to try to raise money to fund the search: save the rain forest, save the jungle – perhaps somewhere in that giant reservoir of genetic diversity there grows a cure for cancer. Aside from the questionable practice of playing on modern emotional fears about dying to raise money to save these forests, basing a conservation argument on using the forests of the world as pharmacopoeias is probably a counterproductive rationale.

First of all, when a plant with medicinal value is found, economic demand encourages people to scour the jungle and eradicate the plant. Such extermination is unnecessary since eventually, once the wild source is exhausted, pharmaceutical companies will synthesize the compound. Second, while the developed world may get a new drug, the people in underdeveloped countries who harvest it get only an economic boom to be followed by the inevitable bust when their hunting eradicates the plant. To date these peoples are not being taught to farm medicinal plants as sustainable cash crops. Third, to justify holding hundreds of millions of acres of pristine land for the sake of potential access to unknown plants with unproved disease-curing properties is the ultimate anthropocentric rationale for conservation.

The forests of the world should be preserved – but amid all the pressures on the world, it is important to frame the argument within a more balanced and integrated understanding of the reasons. We are dependent upon plants – they feed us and heal us. Our planet needs their diversity. Our planet needs protected watersheds. Our planet needs the oxygen these plants produce, and does not need the carbon dioxide they consume. Our planet needs the balance of life that all these offer. But most important, as our planet enters now the greatest era of ecosystem change since the epoch of the dinosaurs the transition that we are already in will be less catastrophic if as much biodiversity and bioresilience as possible can be sustained.

Our planet needs our planet. Our planet as a whole owns our planet. As the

Unnamed peak in the Makalu massif

commonality of the DNA in many species indicates (if not the quiet voice within our soul) the whole planet is inside each species just as all species are inside the planet. To lose the wildness of the planet is to lose part of ourselves.

Thinking about preserving wilderness out of a concern for cancer is useful, but in a different way from which it's been used so far. Human populations have, like a cancer, metastasized. Their dangerous growth is not so much in terms of numbers – we could achieve a balance with nature if we really tried – as in terms of escalating aspirations and resource consumption. The cure for this cancer lies partly in assisting impoverished peoples to develop sustainable utilization of their natural resources but even more in changing how we, the affluent, respond to the unreality of our lifestyles. Is it possible for us to stop wanting ever more? We are wealthy enough to afford to make changes. We are the ones with the opportunity to go into the lifestyle store and try other options to reduce our mortgaging of the future. We can test new priorities to find ones that fit. We can choose appropriate poverty now – or have our grand-children join the desperate in poverty later.

This argument is not black and white – just as the conflict between us (the enlightened) and drug companies (the villains) is not black and white. The pressure for harvesting wild plants did not start with the drug companies. All people have potentially exploitive uses they seek from the jungle: medicines, grass for grazing, or a place to go via jet fuel for vacations. It is a question of balance and honesty. We each live within hypocrisies between our actions and our beliefs.

Off beyond the soon-to-be-endangered *Nardostachys jatamansi* with its cancer-curing root is a jack-in-the-pulpit, *Arisaema constatum.* My childhood image of this plant was of a cobra, its emerald-green hood hovering over a red coral throat. Over the centuries Tibetans have descended to these jungles off the high plateau two days' walk to the north seeking this plant. Its tuber looks like a yam and cannot be eaten raw. A toxin in the roots makes the throat swell, and the eater chokes to death. The Tibetans, though, grate the tubers, wash the shredded flesh repeatedly to remove the soapy-tasting saponin from the pulp, and ferment the mash to separate out the poisonous toxin. Then they wash the mash again and spread it in a thin layer to dry. After that, they grind it into flour, and use it to make bread. Certainly, growing barley or wheat is an easier way to make flour. How did the Tibetans ever figure out such botanical chemistry? How many people experimented with eating, choking, maybe dying? And even more improbably, how did they ever discover that this flour was effective in curing piles?

Searching for medicinal plants is not wrong. Discovering ways in which species in our ecosystem can help each other heightens our understanding of our mutual interdependence. Modern life has created a rich mosaic of people, like the plants in a rain forest, so many of us with so many different skills and understandings, an interlinked system of people, apparently with the abilities to help each other. Although ever more diverse, are we adequately resilient?

Have we become so specialized that many of us bloom like tropical orchids, glorious in our special niches, but if our niche changes, our specific skills are no longer needed or are taken away, do we die? An orchid disappears here, a tree is lost there; such losses, though sad for lost beauty, are part of a changing planet – like the Taylor boys who grew up honing their jungle skills and then found that there were no jungles in which to use those skills. Do the species that remain hold the resilience to bounce on? Is each of us pushing ourselves to undergo new adaptive experiences? Are we interacting with the changing world, strengthening our diversity?

NIGHT FALLS AND I COLLECT FALLEN BRANCHES TO KINDLE A SMALL FIRE. I can't camp without a campfire, our most ancient possession, our center of warmth and source of fellowship. My fire-building method is to place two large sticks down parallel, then place crossways between them thin, tiny twigs that soon catch and throw their flames into the larger sticks. The campfire provides warm tentacles – a hearth of family when a man wanders alone making his home.

Looking up I can see stars burning overhead, large fires light-years away. The miracle of an eye, like the mind, permits travel over vast distances. The mind, though, also pierces inward into the night questions. Focusing outward, my eyes adapt from the intensity of the small fire before me to the vastness of the night around. I scan the night sky. What is hidden out there?

I rise and walk across the glen. Time passes. My eyes see more as I wait. As I survey the dark walls of the Barun Valley, my eyes stop. There, down-valley, partway up the ridge, a light shines. Or is it the new moon's reflection off a rock? I move around to see if the light changes with angle. The glow is not reflection. Tonight, it seems, I'm not the only person in the Barun Valley. Who is up on that slope? Dare I go find out?

I roll up my sleeping bag, fold up my tarp, lace my pack tightly shut, throw a rope over a tree branch, and hoist the pack six feet off the ground. I might be gone for longer than I plan – bears, pandas, a snow leopard, and especially mice might be interested. With small food items in one pants pocket, extra batteries for my flashlight in another, and a few bandages in a third, I head into the night.

The problem with night walking through jungle is planning the route. Taking the next step is easy; the flashlight shows the way that far. But it doesn't reveal the best route; obstacles ahead are unseen. Walking at night is a confrontation with an unknown future, not with an immediate, beam-filled present. Indeed, the focus the beam gives on the present is what makes night-time so scary because of what it leaves out.

The farther I walk, the more afraid I grow. What is making the light shine up on that slope? Villagers would surely stop lower in the forest. Certainly it is not herders. Plant hunters? Probably. Smugglers? Shot by that new idea, I stop. It would be really stupid to approach a smugglers' camp at night.

Might it be a yeti? Making a fire? That would mean the yeti is a hominoid, not bear, an animal like us. Like a scared kid, the ideas race through my mind. A fire would mean the yeti is an animal that gathers with its kin around a fire circle – eats cooked meat. Is it possible? Is human prehistory still active on this planet while above satellites circle?

I walk on, fearful now. There is not enough starlight. The sliver of the moon does not show much. My fingers cover my flashlight lens, opening a larger slit of light when I need to see more, narrowing to almost nothing when my steps are routine. It's unlikely that my light can be seen from up on the mountain slope. Covered by my hand, the beam never shines in that direction, the light too weak to reflect off leaves and draw notice. Beings sitting by that campfire would have their eyes adjusted to that light and not be scanning the night beyond. I walk on. The slope is steep, and recognizing my fears I laugh softly to myself. Walking at night, walking trying to be quiet, adds strain. Is that the reason I grow more afraid?

But now I also suddenly grow tired. Walking in the Himalaya is always steep, always hard; walking at night is especially hard. Reaching around rocks, over fallen branches, makes steps longer. Shorten the stride. Climbing a staircase two steps at a time is four times the work of one stair at a time. But my fatigue seems more than night walking. It is the weight of leaden legs that don't want to go. How far have I come? How far to go? My mind hammers out the questions impatient children ask. When will we get there? On a trip in the car these questions drive me to frustration. Now they make me sweat.

I face the fact. I'm scared. I want to turn back. I want to crawl into my sleeping bag and hide from whatever is up there on that slope. I head back to camp. The distance passes quickly. I haven't really walked that far. Half an hour later, before crawling into my sleeping bag, I notch three sticks, tie them in the center, and splay them out into a tripod. Carefully, I point a fourth stick through their fork directly toward the light, aiming like a rifle toward the spot on the slope where I must go in the morning.

Secure in the warmth of my sleeping bag, I wonder about that life up there warmed by that fire. What would I do if I met the yeti face to face? The first need must be to communicate no danger to a species that has built its survival on not communicating with *Homo sapiens*. The question of communication with the yeti is one of the most interesting unknowns about the creature, as the achievement of communication by hominoids is probably our most triumphant success. Half a million years ago our large human brain developed; we supposedly became wise, *sapiens*. But for hundreds of thousands of years, in our tools, in our hunting, in everything that we know about our species, there was no indication of the work of one being built upon the work of another. Suddenly, though, less than one hundred thousand years ago changes started. Tools, art, travel, houses, agriculture, and regular use of fire all came into the life of our species. Why did nothing happen for so long? Why did everything then start to take off? *Homo sapiens* made its most important discovery: language. With the ability to share knowledge wisdom developed. Our species developed the ability for human minds to work together, and perhaps more importantly, for human minds of one generation to pass along their discoveries to the next.

Memory, that which before was unique to one now became accessible to all. As memory grew our discoveries compounded. But at first this memory grew within our groups, within one language. We were separated. But as language skills compounded, as languages became translated and the wisdom of one group entered the memory of other groups, synergies grew between peoples. The pace of learning kept accelerating. Tools were developed for sharing: writing, printing, then broadcasting, and now computing. The speed of language ever accelerates — the distinctiveness between peoples keeps falling away as we become ever more linked.

The resilient among these ancient peoples developed ways of sharing their knowledge across generations. Language was passed not just from mouth to ear but from one generation across seven generations. Before such messages were sent they were sent by song and fable. The resilience of the Australian aborigine attests to this through their survival in the harsh outback, through the wisdom of their songlines. The harmony that the African Bushman has found amid the extreme severity of the Kalahari Desert also shows how wisdom can build to create resilient life efficiency.

If the yeti has survived undiscovered for so long, it could only have done so with a sophisticated ability to communicate – at least among its own kind if not also somehow understanding something of the communications of our kind so as to avoid us. If the yeti has learned to communicate, it cannot therefore be some sort of prehistoric hominoid, certainly not *Gigantopithecus*, which separated from *Homo sapiens* a million years ago, and probably not even Neanderthal or Cro-Magnon. A yeti that might be out there, to be successful in its hiding, must therefore be one of us. Something is clearly out there making that fire – so I tell myself, there is nothing to fear; it has to be one of us. Sharing the comfort of company in this valley, I fall asleep.

The next morning it takes only two hours to reach the ledge under the overhanging black rock, maybe 300 feet above the valley. A screen of trees and bushes grows in front, blocking direct view of the spot during daylight. The ledge itself is maybe six feet wide and twenty feet long, a shelf of up-sloping ground relatively free of bushes and grass. The ground is fertile soil that would grow bushes and grass if rain could reach back in. The earth is hard. Three old fire scars show that this is a periodic camp. In each are loose ashes.

But from one, smoke thinly spirals. The smell rises rich through my nostrils, evoking emotion-laden flashes of other times. Only humans make smoke. It's one of our species' universal signs, a sign, like footprints, of our passing, as children are a sign of our future. Here before me are signs of recent human passing. Is he or she – or are they – still here? A chill ripples over my skin.

I look around. I listen. I wait. Nothing. The embers at my feet send a farewell filigree tightly curling upward, a sign of unknown people just gone. Loosening in their spiral, the two wisps float apart, tiny and hairlike, they finally disappear in the air at the roof of the ledge. There are no bones here or other relics of human presence. Bones, though, don't really last; small animals seeking calcium chew them up. Footprints, too, get obliterated by wind and the passing over of others. But, strangely, ashes carry traces of our ancestors' fires. They can lie inert for millennia, holding their story of once providing warmth and maybe food. (It was carbon dating of ashes found two feet deep in the soil that told my friend, Alton Byers, that people have been burning and grazing the Barun for more than two centuries.)

Somewhere before in the Barun I have seen smoke curling upwards. That early morning three years ago, John Craighead and I were at Saldima looking up at the sky. We thought at first that the wisps were clouds, or mist from the hidden lake behind. But maybe it was smoke, not clouds. Was someone here? In the ash of the second fire scar is the answer: a fresh footprint with five toes. Kneeling down, my knees trembling, I feel alone, feel hunted, feel like a man pursued by a force that is out to get him. The ashen footprint my hands now touch is huge. It seems shaped like the print Shipton saw, only smaller. But footprints in ash have a different definition than those in snow, although the outer lines are sharp the inside is hard to discern. This certainly qualifies as a yeti footprint, a footprint not in the snow. But what is it really?

The yeti that is a wild animal I know to be a bear. I know that. But are there other yetis? Might these footprints be simply from a group of people who have cut themselves off from society, a voluntarily reclusive, spiritual community? From time to time such hermits or groups could even harvest medicinal plants, go into Khandbari and sell them to buy needed supplies. Living in the wilds, their feet could have become heavily callused, capable of crossing high passes and walking snowfields.

As I stare at the print, now encircled by my cupped hands, a couple of large flakes of ash fall from the edge into the depression formed by the ball of the creature's foot, ashes adjusting to pressure from my hands. The print might be very fresh, might be made just before dawn. Last night here in this shelter both a fire and a footprint were signed into the earth.

Outside the ledge there are no further signs to show where the maker of the signature went. I could stay here and hope the being returns. But the traces of fire show that it comes here only occasionally, probably just while passing through. I can stay in the Barun and look for other places, for the places where it lives. But I'm not looking for one animal. One animal cannot survive. I'm looking for a small colony. Where in the Barun is there enough space and enough privacy for a small colony? Having three times flown the Barun by helicopter, I know of no probable site down-valley. It is all jungle, with no visible caves or sanctuaries.

My best chance is to wait, let the yeti come to me. But I don't have that much time. I have only a week's food. I have an airplane ticket back to the States to Jennifer, Jesse, Tara, and Luke. I must go to Saldima and look for smoke. The rock-circled lake is the best possible hiding place. It is high and therefore cold. Food would have to be brought in to such a place, but maybe a colony could live there. Without the help of the satellite photos, we never would have discovered it. Could that lake be their sanctuary and the Kama Valley in Tibet their food source?

Two valleys separate Saldima from the upper Barun – and crossing them is not like ridge-hopping in West Virginia. I can descend the river to where its water meets the Mangrwa, then work my way up the Mangrwa to Saldima. But traveling through the Barun jungle, even just a couple of hundred yards without a trail, sometimes takes half a day. Lendoop said there was no way of getting from Makalu Jungli Hotel to here. It would be stupid for me to assume that he's wrong and try to figure out a way.

But Tashi described in fair detail a smuggler's route, a secret trail he learned of when he was doing research in the villages of the lower Ishwa and Kasuwa valleys, a trail I have seen in the Saldima Valley. Someplace out of this valley leading toward that in Saldima is that route. There is some profit to be made sneaking supplies between Nepal and China – pots and pans made in India, spices and foodstuff grown in the hot lowlands, and even water buffalo skins. On the trip back the smugglers bring high-quality manufactured goods from China – sneakers, cloth, porcelain cups, tape recorders, and detergent – and low-cost agricultural produce from Tibet – brick tea, home-woven women's aprons, dried meat and cheese, and stud bull yaks.

Crossing mountain passes in bad weather and second-guessing demand in commodities ranging from yaks to detergent, smugglers ply a complex trade. Success requires a lot more than crossing the border undetected with profitable materials. Successful smuggling is a trade of interrelationships, starting with reliable, closed-mouthed suppliers and ending with quick-moving, closed-mouthed buyers: no questions; definite payments. It is a simplified ecosystem.

Smugglers need a route that can handle this traffic with little breakage and little attention. The Himalaya is earth's highest fence, a rock and ice barrier that stops high-soaring rain clouds and is relatively easily patrolled at passes and gorges. Both rain clouds and legitimate foot traffic have long used the Arun River Gorge. The Arun flowed here long before the land was lifted out of the collision of Indian and Asian plates. The Arun, more ancient than these still-rising mountains, has carried much traffic for many centuries. Smugglers need a lesser-known way than following the Arun, and Tashi reports that one begins on the several commonly used trails of western Sankhwasabha District, far from police checkposts in central Nepal. Once the snow melts, it crosses Shipton's Pass into the uninhabited upper Barun Valley. What Tashi couldn't tell me is how the trail passes from here in the upper Barun to Saldima. That is the route I must now find.

From Saldima I know, because I have crossed it, that an easy 13,200-foot pass is all that separates Nepal from Tibet's uninhabited Kama Valley. There smugglers reportedly camp and quietly send out word of their arrival. Then the middlemen of Karta Valley come in over one of three passes, the Chog La, Cho La, and Langma La. All passes, at 16,100, 16,400, and 17,700, are difficult, and only those who know the way make it. These middlemen take the merchandise to Shegar and Tingri, where larger-volume operators move the goods on to Lhasa and even the heartland of China.

Seven centuries earlier, Marco Polo followed such a route. Today the process is much the same. The manufactured goods of India travel slowly for months toward China, passing from hand to hand, never kept long in inventory in any one place. The profit margin is small – a penny or two here, half a percentage point there. The merchandise passes through many hands. The risks are high, mostly risks of weather and trail; the risks of being caught are predictable and have been worked out. Smuggling basic life goods, sneakers and spices, is a subsistence business. Great fortunes are not made.

ınding a route out of any valley involves finding the hourglass funnel where trails come together at the low point of a ridge. Where are such passes leading north out of the Barun? One difference between now, when we are building a park, and before, when Jennifer, Bob, and I were searching for a bear, is that I now carry special tools, including a Space Shuttle photograph of this area.

I go to camp and roll the photograph out on the grass underneath the large oak. Enlarged by computer to a scale of 1:100,000, it makes planning routes and calculating distances easy. I study the image with a magnifying lens. The trail will cross at passes that in mountains with sedimentary soil are formed where feeder streams wash out the same soft stratum on two sides of a ridge. Passes drop through the points where ridges are worn especially low because of that softness.

My photograph shows two such valleys on either side of the ridge just down-valley from where I sit. Presumably, therefore, a pass exists between them. I look up and track what I have been looking at on the image. There, that gully. The slope seems less severe up the left. If it is the smugglers' route, I should find the trail once I reach the pass and be able to follow it down on the other side. Although it is probably not the easiest way, I decided to climb up high and then traverse – there will be less undergrowth. Then I can start looking for the trail.

Chapter Thirty-Three

I break camp. This morning feels like the end of a mystery novel, when the detective finally identifies his quarry, pulls on his overcoat, and heads out after it. I roll up the satellite photo, stow my gear, fill my quart-size water bottle for the trail, hoist my pack, and set out to discover what secrets surround the hidden lake above Saldima Valley.

My trip earlier in the morning to the cave and back made me get a late start, eleven o'clock. Will I find the route out and cross today to the other valley? Or will I have to bivouac below the pass? It's probably 4,000 vertical feet from here to the top and water is going to be scarce. I start bushwhacking up through rhododendron, wishing Lendoop were here with his kukri. I push hard and cover the first 2,000 feet in three hours. For half an hour I rest beside what might be the last trickle of water, forcing myself to drink all I can. At high altitudes one's body never has enough water. Three quarts can get me through eighteen hours. Inside is the most efficient place to carry the fluid I'll need. I gulp down one quart straight, then mix a second quart with Tang and force that down with a few peanuts and raisins. Half-hour breaks are great — you can lie back, look at clouds rolling by above, disengage your mind completely as time slides. After one trip gets set on the shelf of memory beside other finished trips, I remember the breaks more clearly than the hard climbs.

What's ahead? There's still no sign of any trail, but most of the forest is now well below. Despite the higher altitude, walking up here should be easier because there's less ground cover. Now I can plan my route better. I just might make the pass by five, cross, and find a campsite with water on the other side before night falls at seven. Rested, I start climbing again.

One thousand feet below the pass I encounter the smugglers' trail. This is not a game trail. The track has been made by men with pack animals. It shows a lot of use; slipping hooves have cut their scars into the hillside for decades. With each trip the cumulative cut on the earth gets deeper. The trail is better than I expected and will be easy to follow.

Unlike roads in America, where travelers expect others to take care of construction and maintenance, trails in the Himalaya are tended to by all who pass over them. Each herder as he walks behind his animals fills in potholes, moving stones to build a staircase for the next string of animals that passes this way, placing poles along the side to make animals less conscious of the drop. Even smugglers, I now find, work on their trails. This knowledge of their kindness to the road somehow renews my energy. I cover the final thousand feet to the pass quickly, my throat dry, my legs sore, but my heart happy.

The pass itself is rocky and clean, free from even cigarette butts. There are no prayer flags anywhere; so the people who control this route must be Hindus from Nepal, not Buddhists from Tibet. But two small cairns beside the trail attest to the spiritual recognition all Himalayan peoples feel who cross from one side to another. It is like going from one life into the next, an old woman once told me as we paused and talked on a top. For me, a pass is a point where energy focuses, gaining speed and force like the wind that also funnels, and then almost instantaneously opens outward on the other side. People acknowledge and celebrate this passing by lifting and placing one stone upon another.

Since our son Luke was born (we gave him the middle name of Cairn), at the top of each pass I cross I stop long enough to start another cairn. None of us really ever walks alone. Reaching this high point, I rest briefly, looking south, behind, then north, ahead, absorbing a trail that I probably never will trace again, making it part of my inner history. Too soon, it's time to leave. There's not enough daylight left for spending half an hour here. Placing my stones on top of one another, I hurry down the cut. An hour or a little more of evening light still shines. I can get down at least 3,000 feet and maybe find some water.

I look around, taking in the signs of this new valley; the soil is lighter-colored and grittier. The vegetation on this side of the pass is sparser. One more valley farther north toward the dry Tibetan Plateau, fewer clouds surmount the immense heights. After pulling the straps tight on my pack, I start running lightly down.

The key is lightness. In downhill running, each stride must flow seamlessly into the next. It takes practice, but Himalayan children know how. Downhill running Western style, from foothold to foothold, however nimbly, still destroys the knees, because it requires the body to absorb half a ton of pressure with each stride, downward and twisting torque. The knee, though, rebounds instantaneously ready to take the next hit. Delicate films of bone-end cartilage collide on each collision, bounce out again ready to absorb the next impact. Across surfaces far more complex than an automobile's shock absorber, the egg white–like synovial fluid rushes back and forth to lubricate and nourish. The forces the knee absorbs from downward running are the most extreme the body joints are asked to take. American boys routinely destroy their knees while playing Western sports. Himalayan boys learn to cascade down a slope with the smoothness of running water over rocks.

I intend to run 3,000 feet straight down, stopping every twenty minutes or so to rest. In such running the legs burn both calories and oxygen faster than the arteries can replenish them. Keeping the mind focused is a challenge, too; at this altitude the mind wants to float higher and higher into ethers of unreality. But each step down such a slope is unique, a crisis of judgment, a call for foot placement where the accuracy must be within millimeters. It is important to keep oxygen well supplied to the brain.

Momentum soon established, I rush downward with fast steps, my pack a light forty pounds and riding close on my back, tiny steps, but feet always in touch with the ground. Soon, the pass is 2,000 feet above and only a memory. Soon I will find a spot to camp tonight. I think I can smell the campfire burning. Exhilarated, I bound on. Breaking good running practice, I start to leap high. It feels like flying. I come around a turn. Standing before me and below me with mouths agape are five men with three ponies and two stud buffalo yaks. Their campfire is burning.

I can't tell who is more startled, the smugglers or me. The ponies bolt against their leads, but they have been well tied. Leaning backward to stop my descent I fall off-balance onto my seat. A Nepali villager coming down the slope might be expected, but they certainly don't expect to see a lone Westerner way back here north of the Barun.

Tired, hurting from the fall, I sit and look. My muscles are so tired; the load on my back feels impossibly heavy. I don't think I could move if I had to. But mostly I am profoundly afraid. The awareness floods over me: these men might kill me. I am alone and far from any help; it would take police ten days to reach this place. Out here on the smugglers' trail, my remains will never be found – except by omnivorous ground bears or sharp-eyed griffons.

Had I thought faster, I could have – should have – bounded through this camp and down the slope into the night, leaving the smugglers with the apparition of a pale-skinned creature bursting over their camp, then vanishing. They would then have huddled around their campfire all night stricken with the fear of returning ghosts, maybe even the yeti. As I sit on my hurt tail, I know I made a mistake, a bad mistake for a forty-three-year-old fool.

Nobody likes to be made a fool of. Nobody likes to be burst upon while settling in at night – especially people errant from the law with good cause to be nervous. As their shock ebbs, their anger visibly rises. Within seconds I'm surrounded by five angry, suspicious men. One of them who'd been splitting wood for the campfire holds his kukri, his still-unsheathed blade in his hand. My legs are drained empty of strength, my stomach wants to go sick.

"I am thirsty, some tea?" I ask in a tired voice. "I am thirsty. Some tea?"

The oldest man turns and heads to the fire. The others look at me. The two youngest are still clearly angry, perhaps less inclined toward hospitality to a traveler. All are still suspicious. The old man takes the lid off the pot and ladles tea into a much-chipped white enamel mug. He returns, holding the mug in two hands. As I say thanks, I force a smile and look each of the five in the eye.

"Here, I brought you raisins and American barley," I say. Still unable to rise, I unleash the straps of my pack. Struggling to stand I pass around a box of raisins, then a box of Grape-Nuts, and move down by the fire, to their temporary wilderness hearth. I adjust my pack and lean back against a stone to look as though I want to talk. Their meal is rice and lentils. Hoping that they'll invite me to join them, I offer peanuts and my half-full bag of m&ms. We share the meal and conversation. The evening passes and the time. Finally comes to go to sleep. Each of my companions lies down.

I lie in my sleeping bag ramrod straight on my back. Never in my life have I fallen asleep while lying on my back. I intend to lie awake all night, watching, waiting, half-expecting trouble. We are no different; all of us are careful. Each of them has gone to sleep with his kukri. It is a comforting enough thought. Tired muscles overwhelm fear, though, and I at last fall asleep.

The next morning we share hot sweet tea, the last box of Grape-Nuts, then depart in different directions. They are headed into the Barun to the ledge – they know of it, we talked about it last night. My rations are now down to two pounds of peanuts, a pound of raisins, and enough milk powder to make three quarts. If I stop for only two nights at Saldima and if I can find the trail and cover the distance from Saldima to the villages north of Shakshila in two days, I can make it to villages that sell rice and lentils. Four days and three nights – peanuts, raisins, milk powder and water – as I hike I think about the twelve combinations of these and decide that my rations should suffice.

Seven long hard hours later I walk into the pasture of Saldima. It's three o'clock. The yak herder's hut where we had our meeting still stands. The waterfall still flows from the rocky slot high above. Except for stops to drink water, I walked through the morning without rest. It is now two-thirty. I'm tired. I take out a handful of peanuts and fill my water bottle. Leaning back against my pack, chewing one peanut at a time, sipping the water slowly, I watch two ravens circling overhead. If they see food, they come. In 1971 ravens attacked food packets left lying at 27,000 feet on Everest, just 2,000 feet below the summit. Including humans, only five species on earth have been known to go so high on their own. My eyes wander to the waterfall. No smoke is rising from behind it. Was that mist, then, that we saw three years ago? Should I wait here and watch? I lean back, resting, legs tired, eyes tired.

A chill wind awakens me. My watch says five-thirty. My leg muscles are tight with fatigue, hard, ready to knot. My shoulders are convulsed in giant shivers. Nightfall is two hours away. My stomach is cramping from hunger. But I must keep going. My food can be stretched for only three more days. If I leave now for the lake, I can climb 2,000 feet and be back here tomorrow evening. After that, hiking out over the eastern ridge, I should be able to reach the villages with food in two days – as long as I can find and keep the trail. Lendoop said that herders with sheep cover the distance in three days. I have learned the value of talking about trails over tea: A map builds in the mind, the land develops enough character that it can be remembered. One never knows what one might need on a later trip. Over the centuries, before travel

Leading yaks loaded with "trade goods" across a snowfield north of Makalu

became a matter of following lines on folded paper, this is how people learned geography and found their natural resources. Sharing knowledge at way stations requires a different way of thinking, a pre-paper way of tracing our paths.

Before pulling on my pack, I take out a half-handful of peanuts to help keep my blood sugar and salt level up. For their weight, peanuts pack a lot of calories, which they release at a steady rate: first the carbohydrates, then the oils. Best of all, they don't require a stove.

Up through scrub rhododendron and thigh-high juniper, it is hard climbing. I know that driving them hard for two hours is about all my legs can do. Two hours and 2,000 feet should bring me almost to the rim of the cliff. Early tomorrow morning I should be able to look down onto the lake. That's when the smoke rises.

What will I see there? Saldima meadow is 10,000 feet. The waterfall is about 400 feet high. If the lake is level with the slot in the rock, then it must be about 10,500 feet at the lake. At this time of year all ice at that elevation should be melted. From the rim of the cliff down to the lake's surface should be a drop of about 1,500 feet. The satellite image shows the cliff encircling the lake except on the north, where a trough appears to lead up to high meadows, snowfields, and beyond that into Tibet's Kama Valley. I'll be approaching the rim from the east. To descend to the lake, look around, climb back to the rim, and return through this scrub to Saldima – tomorrow is going to be a long, hard day.

The good thing about high-altitude scrub is that finding a route is easy – the rhododendron and juniper aren't tall enough to block views and even on a steep slope there's no way to fall and roll any distance. I power my way forward through the stiff branches. My thick pants help blunt the juniper prickles.

Camp that night is under an overhanging rock. I wake before the sun. Lying there waiting, I'd like to make a fire with the dead juniper twigs at hand. It's great to lie in a sleeping bag before sunrise and look at the flames leap, to watch the fire die and the day grow. And juniper fires smell so good – Tibetans burn the branches as offerings. Making hot milk would also bring comfort to this morning. But a fire's smell would disturb the morning, and certainly consume valuable time. I'll save it for tomorrow morning on the way back home.

I leave my rock. The western sky ahead is dark, the sky behind is light. My sleeping gear are cached beneath the overhanging rock. My pack contains rope, emergency supplies, the rest of my food, and cameras. This is among the most remote of Himalayan valleys. I am very conscious of how alone I am. A small cairn is built on top of the big rock where my gear is cached. I triangulate an alignment off of peaks in the lightening eastern sky that will target me back to this spot. But the cloud from the Barun will probably rise behind me during the morning. To find this place when engulfed by a cloud, I need another plan too.

Noting that my route is on a slightly ascending traverse to the northeast across an alpine meadow, in a white-out I could get disoriented in the meadow. I'll need a big target to hit, something like a quarter-mile-wide line to intersect, not simply one boulder in the fog. The old seat-of-the-pants flying rule is not to try to hit the target, but to create a line out on a known side of the target, a recognizable line that can be intersected and then used to bring you to the target. Therefore as I start out, I hold my traverse line straight for the first quarter of a mile, making simple three-rock-high cairns every twenty-five paces.

Twenty stacks later, the line from the rock meets a gentle ridge that leads up to the rim. The ridge gives an added bonus, a line I can find and also hold closely to in a white-out. At the ridge's crest I'll make a large cairn. Then I'll have a track tying my route together all the way back to my sleeping bag. The western sky is now fully light. Chamlang stands silhouetted behind me, its north face still in cold, white shadow, its icy eastern ridge etched diamondlike in brilliant light.

Mountain skies lighten an hour before the sun itself rises, and I have been walking about that long. As I'm about to crest the ridge and near the rim to look down onto the hidden lake, the sun bursts behind me over the curvature of the earth and sends shafts of warmth onto my back. My shadow appears and leaps forward ten yards tall. Across my feet, crystals of frost sparkle on alpine grass, like fairy jewels cast with abandon across the meadow. The morning in high-altitude splendor is radiant with light and life.

At the rim the cliff falls in a straight drop to the lake 1,500 feet below – so far below that it is hard to see detail on the shore or water. From its mile-wide surface mist rises. But off to the right, to the north, smoke rises. There the circle is broken by a great ramp sloping from the meadow down to the shore of the lake. Along the sides of this ramp down by the lake are a series of overhangs in the sides of the rock as if the ramp was once covered with moving ice that scoured out deep grooves back in the rock. In a dozen places under the overhangs, stones appear to have been piled to make walls, creating rooms back underneath the overhangs. From several of these seep wisps that look like smoke.

Dropping to the ground, I dig my binoculars out of my parka. Yes, the wisps look like smoke – three are coming from three different shelters. I move sideways into some rocks to get protection from the wind and to reduce my profile on the rim. When my arms tire from holding the binoculars, I lower them and continue looking with my eyes alone, waiting for the strength to renew in my arms so I can hold the binoculars steady again. I've been climbing hard. My head is spinning. My throat is dry. My focus turns inward. Like the mist gently rising off the lake, a vision engulfs me. . . .

The most resilient among all species, the only species that can cure its individual members when sick, must now collectively learn how to attend to the needs of its planetary home. The resilience required is more than stretching capacity, finding new technologies and new organization, learning new methods to live in an increasingly marginal world. The resilience required is also that of stepping back toward our wild heritage, rediscovering lost roots, changing the momentum of living from being a journey away from intimacy with our wild past into being a new integration with wildness. Adequate wild spaces in which to live no longer exist, so it is not a process of each finding his or her fig tree to meditate under. The wildness we still have is set off as parks. We must complement the parks with symbols that connect us to our wild roots through pictures, music, clothing, myths – the building of nature into our increasingly unnatural lives. We must spend time amid the wildness that is still left. Otherwise, an unplanned and out-of-control wildness will come if we try to leave it more distantly outside. Our roots are not in civilization; they are in wildness. Civilization is that process of one group of people joining with another. The voice inside that says that the yeti is real is the voice inside that knows there is wildness in each of us.

I am startled by snowflakes sprinkling on my face. The vision burning inside suddenly changes character and melts like the snowflakes on my face. I awake convulsively, my bones rattling as though devoid of their flesh. Cold. My fire's weak inside me. While my mind turned inward, once again the cloud rose up from the Barun, up the Mangrwa, and engulfed the Saldima Valley and me with it. I am shaking. I am low on blood sugar. I am also afraid – at least two days from a fresh supply of food.

I don't know whether the smoke is still rising from the shelters below, for the cloud totally surrounds me. But it seems clear that the people (if they are people) who by choice live here privately, apart from others, want to be left alone. They may have discovered the complementary consciousness: of *yin* with *yang*, of rebirth from this life into new forms of life, balancing animation in a physical and living reality with another animation in a nonphysical reality of spirit and mind space. They may have discovered grace. Whatever their reclusive quest, let that community below pursue its quest, undisturbed.

I turn my back. By the cairns I have left I must guide my footsteps away from the lake and toward those who live back at my home. I turn my back on the frozen lake and walk into the snowstorm.

Postscript

Although in three instances the sequence or placement of anecdotes in this narrative were changed, the people, times, and occurrences themselves are all factual – with one exception. The frozen lake above Saldima is as described and was discovered as described, but it is not where the real hidden community lives; nor does this community exist anywhere in the Barun or Kama Valleys.

Notes

1. Eric Shipton, *The Mount Everest Reconnaissance Expedition 1951,* London: Hadden & Stoughton, 1952, p. 54.

2. L. A. Waddell, *Among the Himalayas,* London: Constable, 1980.

3. J. R. P. Gent, Letter to Royal Geographical Society. Complete letter is provided in Bernard Heuvelmans, *On the Track of Unknown Animals,* New York: Hill & Wang, 1958, pp. 135–6.

4. N. A. Tombazi, *Account of a Photographic Expedition to the Southern Glaciers of Kanchenjunga in the Sikkim Himalaya,* quoted in Bernard Heuvelmans, *On the Track of Unknown Animals,* New York: Hill & Wang, 1958, p. 130.

5. Ibid., p. 131.

6. Frank Smythe, quoted in Bernard Heuvelmans, *On the Track of Unknown Animals,* New York: Hill & Wang, 1958, p. 134.

7. *The World Book Encyclopedia 1961: Annual Supplement*, S. V. E. Hillary, Chicago: Field Enterprises.

8. William C. Osman Hill, "Abominable Snowmen: The Present Position," *Oryx,* Vol. VI, No. 2, August 1961, pp. 86–98.

9. Edward W. Cronin, *The Arun: A Natural History of the World's Deepest Valley,* Boston: Houghton Mifflin, 1979, p. 153.

10. Ibid., p. 167.

11. Shipton, *The Mount Everest Reconnaissance Expedition 1951,* p. 54.

12. John Napier, *Bigfoot: The Yeti and Sasquatch in Myth and Reality,* New York: E. P. Dutton, 1973, p. 141.

13. *Cryptozoology.* Interdisciplinary journal of the International Society of Cryptozoology. Vol. 6, 1987.

The author, from a camp in an ice cave at 19,000 feet, looking across the GosainKund peaks (photo by Lorenz Perincioli)

About the Author

DANIEL TAYLOR-IDE spends much of his adult life traveling in the United States, China, and Nepal, working with the United Nations, USAID, and the government of Nepal. He was knighted by the king of Nepal for his efforts in developing new approaches to conservation summarized in this text. He was also awarded an honorary professorship by the Chinese Academy of Sciences for this work. He founded the Woodlands Mountain Institute, an organization dedicated to sustainable development planning for mountain regions. Currently he is the president of a nonprofit organization, Future Generations Inc., and has a senior research appointment at Johns Hopkins University in the School of Hygiene and Public Health. He lives on Spruce Knob Mountain in West Virginia with his wife, Jennifer, and three children, Jesse, Tara, and Luke. Among his other interests, he breeds the rare bearded mountain dog, the Tibetan KyiApso, and flies home-built, high-performance aircraft.

Preserve Yeti Habitat

Through work started by the search described in this book, the homeland of the yeti is being saved. The lower Barun Valley would today be fields of tobacco and corn if early action had not been taken. Across the international border, the Qomolangma (Mt. Everest) Nature Preserve, also created as a result of this yeti search, has been functioning since 1989, protecting snow leopards, blue sheep, wild ass, and magnificent trees. In Nepal and China, this wilderness now needs your support. Please send a tax-deductible contribution or write for more details to:

Future Generations
Yeti Fund
PO Box 10
Franklin, WV 26807 USA

Designed and typeset by Thomas Christensen in Adobe Caslon with Caslon Openface display; printed by Data Reproductions on acid-free paper.